The Witness *of the* Hebrew Bible *for a* New Testament Church

Christina Bucher, David A. Leiter, and
Frank Ramirez, editors

Brethren Press·

The Witness of the Hebrew Bible for a New Testament Church

© 2010 Brethren Press

Published by Brethren Press®. Brethren Press is a trademark of the Church of the Brethren, 1451 Dundee Avenue, Elgin, Illinois 60120. Visit www.brethrenpress.com for publishing information.

Library of Congress Cataloging-in-Publication Data

The witness of the Hebrew Bible for a New Testament church / Christina Bucher, David A. Leiter, and Frank Ramirez, editors.
   p. cm.
  Festschrift for Robert W. Neff.
  Summary: "A collection of essays highlighting several important themes found in the Hebrew Bible, or Old Testament, that are relevant to a New Testament church. The essays reflect an Anabaptist and Pietist theological/historical perspective"—Provided by publisher.
  Includes bibliographical references (p.   ) and index.
  ISBN 978-0-87178-145-1 (pbk.)
  1. Bible. O.T.—Theology. 2. Church of the Brethren—Doctrines. I. Bucher, Christina. II. Leiter, David A., 1958- III. Ramirez, Frank, 1954- IV. Neff, Robert W. V. Title.

  BS1192.5.W58 2010
  230'.0411--dc22

2010016119

14 13 12 11 10   1 2 3 4 5

Printed in the United States of America

Contents

Preface

*"What does the LORD require of you but to do justice,
and to love kindness, and to walk humbly with your God?"*
—*Micah 6:8*

The purpose of this collection of essays is twofold. First, we hope the essays contained in this volume will challenge readers to consider ways in which the writings of the Old Testament contribute (or might contribute) to Christian faith and practice. Second, we dedicate this volume to a great teacher and fervent advocate of the Hebrew Scriptures, Robert W. Neff, in gratitude for his many years of service to the church. Known throughout the Church of the Brethren for his great energy, good humor, and passionate commitment to the church and its mission, Bob challenges us to take seriously the witness of the Hebrew Scriptures.

Bob has served the church in many different capacities: seminary professor, denominational executive, college president, preacher, and writer. After receiving a bachelor's degree in zoology and entomology from Penn State University in 1958, Bob went to Yale Divinity School to study church history, but under the influence of the eminent biblical scholar Brevard S. Childs, Bob decided to study the Old Testament instead. While at Yale Bob received a Two Brothers Fellowship, which funded his studies in Germany and Israel. After completing B.D. and M.A. degrees at Yale and finishing his doctoral coursework, Bob took a teaching position at Bridgewater College in Virginia. In 1965, he received a call to join the faculty at Bethany Theological Seminary, which at the time was located in Oak Brook, Illinois. For a little over a decade (1965-1977), Bob educated men and women for Christian ministry. To help his students engage deeply with the biblical texts, Bob developed learning strategies and tools, particularly biblical simulations. With his Bethany colleagues Graydon F. Snyder and Donald E. Miller, Bob published two volumes of biblical simulations, *Using Biblical Simulations I and II* (Judson Press, 1973; 1975).

Biblical scholarship in the 1960s and 70s was deeply entrenched in the methods of historical criticism. Although best known for his work in canonical criticism, Brevard S. Childs was also a form critic; and as a student of Childs, Bob's scholarship was grounded in form criticism, one of the subfields of historical criticism. Soon after joining the faculty at Bethany, Bob completed his Ph.D., writing a dissertation on "The Announcement in Old Testament Birth Stories." Bob continued to do form-critical work, publishing two articles in *Biblical Research*: "Birth and Election of Isaac in the Priestly Tradition" (1970) and "Annunciation in the Birth Narrative of Ishmael" (1972), and contributing the chapter on "Saga" to a volume on Old Testament form-critical genres, edited by George W. Coats (*Saga, Legend, Tale, Novella, Fable*. JSOT Press, 1985).

Family has also been central to Bob Neff's life. In 1959, Bob and Dorothy (Dottie) Rosewarne married. They have two children, Scott Neff and Heather Neff. In 1973, Bethany Theological Seminary granted Bob a leave to study at Cambridge University in the United Kingdom. Bob, Dottie, Scott, and Heather spent a delightful year together in Cambridge. A close-knit family, they continue to spend time together whenever they can arrange it in their busy schedules. Over the years, the church has made many demands on Bob's family life. As his former students, we express our gratitude to Bob's family for sharing him with us.

Making what was a surprise move to some people, in 1977 Bob accepted the call to become general secretary of the Church of the Brethren. As the chief executive officer of the Church of the Brethren, Bob continued to engage Brethren in the study of the Scriptures. During his term as general secretary (1977-1986), the denomination embraced Micah 6:8 as guidance for the church's mission: "What does the LORD require of you but to do justice, and to love kindness, and to walk humbly with your God?" An active ecumenist—nurtured, no doubt, by his earlier experiences in Germany, Israel, and the United Kingdom—Bob served on the

Governing Board and Executive Committee of the National Council of Churches and was a member of the Central Committee of the World Council of Churches.

In the two decades in which he served the Church of the Brethren as seminary professor and denominational executive, Bob contributed frequently to Church of the Brethren publications, including *Brethren Life and Thought, A Guide for Biblical Studies*, and *Messenger* magazine. *Brethren Life and Thought* published four articles Bob wrote relating to the Bible: "Paradigms of Peace in the Book of Genesis" (1978), "Taking Biblical Authority Seriously" (1983), "The Biblical Basis for Political Advocacy" (1987), and "The Bible, Devotion, and Authority" (1998). His exegetical work can be found in *A Guide for Biblical Studies* and, more recently, in *Messenger* and the *Gather 'Round* Sunday school curriculum. Bob has also interpreted the Bible for audiences at the Annual Conference, various district conferences, and the National Older Adult Conference of the Church of the Brethren.

After a decade as general secretary, Bob returned to the world of higher education, becoming president of Juniata College in 1986, a position he held until his retirement in 1998. Since leaving Juniata, Bob has served as a resource development executive at The Village at Morrisons Cove, a retirement community, but he devotes much of his time to study and teaching. Since 2005, he has authored and co-authored four Bible studies in the Covenant Bible Study series for Brethren Press: *Voices in the Book of Job; Country Seer, City Prophet; The Five Festal Scrolls;* and *The Chronicler.* Bob has used all of these different venues to educate pastors, church leaders, and lay persons about the importance of the church's First Testament. His clear speaking style and engaging classes have convinced many to join him in his passion. On behalf of all the contributors to this book, it is with considerable delight and pleasure that we offer this collection of essays in honor of our colleague, teacher, and friend Robert W. Neff.

Christina Bucher
David A. Leiter
Frank Ramirez

Contributors

Jeffrey A. Bach (B.A., McPherson College; M.Div., Bethany Theological Seminary; Ph.D., Duke University) is the director of the Young Center for Anabaptist and Pietist Studies and associate professor of Religious Studies at Elizabethtown College. He is an ordained minister in the Church of the Brethren. He is the author of *Voices of the Turtledoves: The Sacred World of Ephrata.*

Christopher D. Bowman (B.S., Manchester College; M.Div., Bethany Theological Seminary; D.Min., San Francisco Theological Seminary) is pastor of the Oakton Church of the Brethren in Vienna, Va. He was the 2003-2004 moderator of the Church of the Brethren. He has authored a variety of Bible study, curriculum, and devotional publications for Brethren Press.

John David Bowman (B.A., Bridgewater College; M.Div., D.Min., Bethany Theological Seminary) is a retired pastor and educator. His published works include a Covenant Bible Study on the Psalms and the hymn "Anoint Us, Lord." He has also worked as a team development coach and leadership trainer for The TEAM Approach®.

Robert C. Bowman (B.A., Manchester College; B.D., Bethany Theological Seminary) is associate professor of Religion at Manchester College and an ordained minister in the Church of the Brethren.

Christina Bucher (B.A., Elizabethtown College; M.A.Th., Bethany Theological Seminary; Ph.D., Claremont Graduate University) is the Carl W. Zeigler Professor of Religion at Elizabethtown College. She is the author of two Covenant Bible Studies (*The Prophecy* *of Amos and Hosea* and *Biblical Imagery for God*) and is currently working on a biblical commentary on the Song of Songs.

Denise D. Kettering (B.A., Ashland University; M.T.S., Emory University; Ph.D., University of Iowa) served as an archival assistant at the Brethren Historical Library and Archives, Elgin, Ill., from 2009-2010. She will be joining the faculty of Bethany Theological Seminary as assistant professor of Brethren Studies in the fall of 2010. She recently finished her dissertation, which is entitled "Pietism and Patriarchy: Spener and Women in Seventeenth-century German Pietism."

David A. Leiter (B.S., Shippensburg State College; M.Div., Bethany Theological Seminary; Ph.D., Drew University) is pastor of the Green Tree Church of the Brethren in Oaks, Pa. He has taught at New York Theological Seminary and the Ecumenical Institute of Theology in Baltimore. He is the author of *Neglected Voices: Peace in the Old Testament* and has published numerous essays and articles in Old Testament studies.

Robert W. Neff (B.S., Penn State University; B.D., M.A., Ph.D., Yale University) is associate for resource development and coordinator of chaplaincy services at The Village at Morrisons Cove in Martinsburg, Pa. He has served as professor of Old Testament Studies at Bethany Theological Seminary and as general secretary of the Church of the Brethren, and he is president emeritus at Juniata College. His published works include *Using Biblical Simulations I and II* and four Covenent Bible Studies—*Voices in the Book of Job; Country Seer, City Prophet: The Unpopular Messages of Micah and Isaiah; The Five Festal Scrolls;* and *The Chronicler.*

Frank Ramirez (B.A., La Verne College; M.Div., Bethany Theological Seminary) is pastor of the Everett Church of the Brethren in Everett, Pa. He is the author of several books, including *The Meanest Man in Patrick County, Brethren Brush with Greatness*, and *The Love Feast.* He co-authored the musicals *Angels Everywhere, A*

Simple Feast, and *The Three Visions of Israel Poulson, Sr.*, with Brethren composer Steve Engle.

Stephen Breck Reid (B.S., Manchester College; M.Div., Bethany Theological Seminary; Ph.D., Emory University) is professor of Christian Scriptures at George W. Truett Theological Seminary / Baylor University. He is the author of *Listening In: A Multicultural Reading of the Psalms* and editor of *Psalms and Practice: Worship, Virtue, and Authority.*

Eugene F. Roop (B.S., Manchester College; M.Div., Bethany Theological Seminary; Ph.D., Claremont Graduate University) is president emeritus and Wieand Professor Emeritus of Biblical Studies at Bethany Theological Seminary, and is an ordained minister in the Church of the Brethren. He is the author of many books and articles, including two volumes in the Believers Church Bible Commentary series: *Genesis* and *Ruth, Jonah, Esther.*

Graydon F. Snyder (B.A., Manchester College; M.Div., Bethany Theological Seminary; Ph.D., Princeton Theological Seminary) is former professor of Biblical Studies at Bethany Theological Seminary (until 1986) and professor emeritus of New Testament at Chicago Theological Seminary (until 1999). Among his writings are: *Ante Pacem: Archaelogical Evidence of Church Life before Constantine* and *Inculturation of the Jesus Tradition: The Impact of Jesus on Jewish and Roman Cultures.*

David M. Valeta (B.A., Geneva College; M.Div., Bethany Theological Seminary; Ph.D., University of Denver / Iliff School of Theology) is an instructor in Religious Studies at the University of Colorado, Boulder. He is the author of *Lions and Ovens and Visions: A Satirical Analysis of Daniel 1–6*, and is currently working on a study of Daniel 7–12.

Introduction

Imagine, if you will, what Christian faith and practice would look like without the Old Testament. Would we miss anything? Without the Old Testament, how well could we understand the writings of the New Testament? Would we understand the liberating power of the gospel in quite the same way without the exodus story? What kind of commitment would we have for social justice without the prophets? How would we respond to suffering and loss if we could not turn to Job and the Psalms for guidance and support? Could we fully comprehend commitment and fidelity if we lacked the stories of God's covenant with Israel?

The church affirms that its Scriptures include two major parts: a first part, which describes and reflects the covenant of God with Israel in the period before the time of Christ, and a second part, which contains early Christian proclamation of Jesus of Nazareth and reflection on God's extension of the covenant to include non-Jews. Some Christian traditions, including the Brethren, have in calling themselves "New Testament Churches" made the unspoken—and sometimes not-so-unspoken—assumption that the New Testament is not only a superior portion of the Bible, but the *only* legitimate Scripture for Christians.

The idea of a newer portion superseding an older portion may be okay in something like constitutional law. Some of us remember from our school days the way in which portions of the U.S. Constitution, such as the three-fifths clause or the original method of electing a president, are printed as if crossed out, demonstrating they are no longer valid. But nothing is crossed out when the Bible is printed, nor has any portion been repealed. Admittedly, the older story is a challenging read, but Christians benefit from the struggle to make sense of that older story within the context of their Christian faith.

In the first century, neither an "Old Testament" nor a "New Testament" existed. Evidence from the Gospels suggests that Jesus frequently cited or quoted many of the books in the collection that we now refer to as the Old Testament.[1] The New Testament writers also acknowledge many of these books as authoritative writings, although, in quoting or citing passages from these books, they reinterpret them in light of their new experience of Jesus, the Christ. Nevertheless, they view the Scriptures of the Old Testament as an authoritative source for Christian life and thought.[2] Neither Paul nor the Evangelists claim to have written authoritative Scripture. Indeed, not until the second century do we find even a suggestion that Paul's letters might be considered scriptural (see 2 Peter 3:15-16).[3] Moreover, as biblical scholar Brevard S. Childs observes, "the church did not adopt the Jewish Scriptures as merely background to the New Testament, but it made the theological claim that the Jewish Scriptures, that is, the Old or Former Testament, bore witness to Jesus Christ" (12).

As Fredrick Holmgren persuasively argues, the two testaments of Christian Scripture are "equal dialogue partners." When we study the two testaments separately, before we study them as a unified whole, we learn several things. First of all, the two testaments agree on many of the basic beliefs. Second, the New, or Second, Testament develops some of the themes, beliefs, and practices that we find in the Old, or First, Testament. Last, the older testament contains some themes that are missing or undeveloped in the newer writings (105). The essays in this volume explore themes in the

---

[1] Of the thirty-nine books that today form the Protestant Old Testament, the Gospels record that Jesus directly quotes or cites twenty-three of them. See Lee Martin McDonald, *The Biblical Canon: Its Origin, Transmission, and Authority* (Peabody, MA: Hendrickson, 2007), esp. "The Biblical Canon of Jesus," pp. 190-194.

[2] See McDonald, pp. 194-200.

[3] Although a few scholars argue for a first-century origin for 2 Peter, most scholars assume it was written in the mid- to late second century.

church's First Testament that challenge us as we seek to grow as Christians. For the most part, the essays explore themes in the First Testament that are missing or undeveloped in the Second Testament, but which are in agreement with basic Christian beliefs.

We recognize that as Christians we read through the lens of our particular faith tradition. Biblical scholar Walter Brueggemann describes the Christian reading of the Old Testament as reading "toward Jesus" (x). As members of the Church of the Brethren, we affirm that we read all Scripture with the intent of continuing the work of Jesus—peacefully, simply, and together.

What's in a Name?

For a long time Christians have been comfortable referring to the first two-thirds of their Bibles as the "Old Testament." Recently, however, biblical scholars and theologians have challenged that term. Prompted, at least in part, by a concern for Jewish–Christian relations, some biblical scholars have urged the use of different terminology. They argue that some readers today dismiss the "old," believing that "old" implies that these books are outdated and have been replaced by the New Testament. In antiquity, however, the term "old" identified something as reliable and trustworthy. Lee Martin McDonald observes, "The marvel for the church then was not that it had accepted something old but rather something new!" ("Canon of the New Testament," 542).

We get the terms "Old Testament" and "New Testament" from the Latin word *testamentum*, which means "covenant." The "old covenant" is the covenant God established with Israel before the time of Jesus and the beginning of Christianity. The "new covenant" refers to God's extension of that covenant to include non-Jews. God does not abolish the old covenant, but adds to it a new covenant. Similarly, the New Testament does not replace the Old Testament, but extends it by describing the way in which the new covenant comes about in the first century of the Common Era.[4]

---

[4] The term "Common Era" refers to the time period beginning with the year of Christ's birth. It is abbreviated CE, which is sometimes used in place of the abbreviation AD.

Some scholars propose replacing "Old" and "New" with "First" and "Second." First Testament underscores the fact that this collection was written first and leads the way to the Second, or New, Testament. Others prefer the name "Tanakh," which is the Jewish way of referring to these writings, and still others use the term "Hebrew Bible" or "Hebrew Scriptures."[5]

None of this terminology is without problems. The term "First" may lead some people to think that the First Testament has priority over the Second Testament. The term "Tanakh," the customary Jewish term, sounds strange to most Christian readers, especially those who have no knowledge of the Hebrew language. Although frequently used by biblical scholars, "Hebrew Bible" presents some problems of its own. Perhaps the most serious challenge to a Christian use of "Hebrew Bible" is that its language fails to reflect the deep connection these writings have with the church and Christian theology.

These newer designations appear primarily in academic venues and have yet to gain broader acceptance within the church. In this volume each contributor has chosen his or her preferred terminology, although we have elected to use the term "Hebrew Bible" in the book's title. In choosing the term "Hebrew Bible," we hope to elevate its significance as a testament in its own right. It is God's covenant with the Hebrew people, and it has truth and wisdom for us today—a New Testament people living as a New Testament church.

Reading the Hebrew Bible—Peacefully, Simply, Together

Contributors to this volume discover stories, instruction, poetry, and prophecy in the Hebrew Bible that help us to think meaningfully about Christian faith and practice. All the contributors have connections to the Church of the Brethren, although many of the essays do not make that affiliation explicit. In various ways, the essays

---

[5] The term "Tanakh" is an acronym created from the three Hebrew terms for the three major sections of the Jewish Scriptures: *Torah* (Instruction, or Law), *Nevi'im* (Prophets), and *Ketuvim* (Writings).

reflect Anabaptist and Pietist influences. Nevertheless, reading the Hebrew Bible as Brethren, contributors emphasize the themes of peacemaking, social justice, and the process of reading Scripture together. As Stephen Breck Reid observes in his essay, Brethren locate the authority to interpret Scripture more in the reading community than in individuals or governing bodies.

The essays by Jeffrey A. Bach and Denise D. Kettering address the historical relationship between the Church of the Brethren and the Hebrew Bible. Reid's essay approaches the theme of social justice by way of his discussion of Radical Pietist biblical interpretation. Frank Ramirez and David M. Valeta both reflect on connections between their respective Hebrew Bible texts and the Church of the Brethren. As a scholar of early Christian origins, Graydon F. Snyder looks at the way in which early Christians embraced and interpreted the story of Jonah. The remaining essays take up a theme, which they explore within the context of a Hebrew Bible text or book.

For this volume, we have chosen several important themes that will highlight the way in which the Hebrew Bible contributes to Christian faith. Our work does not pretend to be comprehensive. Rather, we seek through this volume to invite, encourage, and promote the shared reading and study of the Hebrew Bible in our churches today.

Reading toward Jesus

Common threads run throughout the essays in this volume. As Christian readers of the Scriptures, we may strive for a unified theology; however, we soon discover different voices within the Bible. Rather than harmonizing the voices, we wish to invite these differing voices into conversation with one another. As Robert C. Bowman explains and Robert W. Neff illustrates, the Scriptures are multi-layered. If we read closely, we hear not one voice, but several. We read the Scriptures out of our own personal and corporate experiences. As the essay by Snyder illustrates, early Christian interpretation in visual art of the Jonah story reflects the dangerous situation in which Christians living in the Roman Empire of the first two centuries found themselves. Research in other fields can help us make sense of biblical texts. Eugene F. Roop demonstrates this with use of conflict transformation theory, which helps us see how interpersonal conflict in the book of Genesis contributes to the transformation of characters in the narrative. All the essays convey the value of reading the Hebrew Bible within its own cultural and historical context.

In the essay "Christians Reading the Old Testament," Robert C. Bowman directly raises the question, "What should Christians do with the Old Testament?" In response, Bowman offers the following affirmations: (1) we cannot truly understand the New Testament apart from the Old Testament; (2) the two testaments form a unified whole; (3) the Bible contains multiple theological perspectives; (4) the Bible must be interpreted; and (5) each part demands its own interpretation. Affirmation five leads Bowman to observe that no single key exists that can unlock every biblical text. He cautions against violating the integrity of the Old Testament by always interpreting it in light of the New, and proposes that "the trick is to interpret . . . in such a way that the Old Testament remains the Old Testament."

Two essays focus on themes related to peace and conflict. Eugene F. Roop's essay relates the stories of Jacob in the book of Genesis to the problem of conflict. David A. Leiter takes a more comprehensive approach in his discussion of peace in the Old Testament. Focusing on the violence that can be found in the Old Testament, some Christians—even some pacifists—are led to reject the entire Old Testament as exemplifying failure. Neither Roop nor Leiter takes this approach. Both begin by identifying Old Testament texts that point us to reconciliation rather than violence, to peace rather than war.

Drawing upon the work of Mennonite sociologist John Paul Lederach, Roop relates Lederach's concept of conflict transformation to the situations of interpersonal conflict we find in the Genesis stories about Jacob. Roop cautions against overinterpreting the biblical stories to make them mesh neatly with our modern understanding of conflict transformation. Roop explores the Hebrew Bible narratives as opportunities for reflection. In a sense, the Genesis stories mirror our own struggles to transform conflict within our families and communities. They also offer glimpses of the possibilities for conflict transformation. We see both conflict and reconciliation in Jacob's life. Rather than providing techniques or strategies, the Genesis accounts inspire us to look to the future in ways that are creative, responsive, constructive, and nonviolent.

David A. Leiter's essay, "Is There Peace in the Old Testament?" answers the question in the affirmative. Drawing upon his earlier work in *Neglected Voices: Peace in the Old Testament* (Herald Press), Leiter identifies five typologies of peace in the Old Testament. He describes each of these typologies and briefly discusses texts in which each typology can be seen. Leiter recommends that rather than beginning with the problem of war and violence in the Old Testament, we should begin by studying the peace texts found throughout the Old Testament. In so doing, Christian readers may discover opportunities for growth in their understanding of God's covenant.

John David Bowman's essay, "Will We Listen? Attending to the Shema in Christian Education," affirms the continuity between the two testaments on the subject of education and faith formation. Focusing on the instruction given in Deuteronomy 6:4, Bowman proposes that for Christians "all faith essentials flow from the deep well of the Shema."[6] Turning to sources as wide-ranging as Jewish rabbis and the organizational management consultant Chip R. Bell, he demonstrates that insights come from many different directions. Nevertheless, he affirms both the basic content of the Shema and the process for learning implied by the instruction in Deuteronomy 6. Through regular engagement with Scripture and in conversation with others, we can learn from and with the Shema to affirm the unity and interconnectedness of all life, to accept our role as servants of God, and to align ourselves with nonviolent love.

Stephen Breck Reid, Frank Ramirez, and David M. Valeta identify connections between the Old Testament and the Church of

---

[6] Shema is the first word in the Hebrew text of Deuteronomy 6:4. It is the imperative (command) form of the verb "to hear."

the Brethren. Reid writes about social justice, immigration, and Brethren hermeneutics.[7] Ramirez connects the ethical instruction of Leviticus 19 with the Brethren emphasis on embodying one's faith in everyday life. Valeta connects the themes of piety, perseverance, and public responsibility to the Brethren tradition.

Reid's essay has three primary foci: (1) an exploration of the meaning of "justice" in the Tanakh; (2) a brief discussion of the way in which Radical Pietism influences a Brethren approach to Scripture; and (3) a more narrow analysis of biblical justice in relation to immigration issues. Reid rejects the antiquarian approach to Scripture that makes the Tanakh irrelevant to our lives today by emphasizing its historical and cultural differences. He also rejects approaches that would develop philosophical or moral principles based on the Bible. Rather, he views reading Scripture as an opportunity for communities of faith to engage with one another and with past communities of faith, allowing Scripture to bring alive the presence of Christ in their midst.

Ramirez draws connections between Leviticus 19, the subject of his essay, and various New Testament texts. Explaining his essay's title, Ramirez observes, "Leviticus 19, the Heart of the Holiness Code, should be called The Brethren Bible Part Too, even though it came first." Leviticus 19 speaks authoritatively to Brethren because it focuses on ethics and ethical practices: love of neighbor and resident alien, fair practices, unity within diversity. Weaving together stories from Brethren history and tradition, examples from early Christianity, and biblical analysis, Ramirez opens up this frequently overlooked chapter of Leviticus to readers interested in the way in which the two testaments are mutually supportive. For Ramirez, Leviticus 19 represents the teaching on which Jesus built his own ministry.

In "Daniel: Piety, Politics, and Perseverance," David M. Valeta explores the intersection of personal faith and public responsibilities. He observes that the themes of piety and perseverance resonate especially well with Brethren and other Anabaptists who trace

---

[7] "Hermeneutics" refers to the interpretation of written texts.

their origins to periods of persecution by other Christians in six-teenth- to eighteenth-century Europe. Valeta reads the book of Daniel as a Christian, but without explicitly appealing to New Testament texts. He concludes that the book of Daniel's message is aligned with the teachings of Jesus: "Followers of Jesus are called to be faithful advocates of an alternative reality towards politics as normal, and to persevere in their commitment to make the kingdom of God a reality in this world."

Robert W. Neff, Christopher D. Bowman, and Christina Bucher examine the contributions the Old Testament makes to our spiritual lives as Christians. Neff explores the different responses to suffering and loss that we find in the Old Testament, especially in the book of Job and the Psalms. Bowman investigates the rhetoric of the Old Testament prophets, focusing on the way in which the prophets use language to guide God's people through difficult times. Bucher discusses a theological way of reading Song of Songs[8] that can shape the way in which we think about God and our relationship to God.

In "Suffering in the Book of Job and Psalms," Robert W. Neff identifies within Scripture several distinct models of how we, as humans, respond to suffering and loss. He first describes the response of traditional piety, which is to patiently accept whatever hand is dealt us. This model can be seen in certain Psalms, in the first two chapters of Job, and in the New Testament letter of James. Without rejecting this model, Neff describes two other models: lament and complaint. The response of lament is to express one's anguish, without asking for anything to change. Lament appears in Job, in certain Psalms, and in the book of Jeremiah. To explain the difference between "lament" and "complaint," Neff observes that there are no lament departments in retail stores, only complaint departments. That is to say, the response of complaint includes a request (sometimes even a demand) that the situation be corrected. Without privileging one model over another, Neff offers these three models as authentic expressions of human loss, within which authentic faith can grow and develop.

---

[8] The book "Song of Songs" is also known as "Song of Solomon."

Christopher D. Bowman's essay, "Prophetic Rhetoric and Preaching," offers food for thought to both those who preach and those who listen to preaching. Focusing on prophetic rhetoric, Bowman urges us to get beyond the commonly held view that the Old Testament prophets serve Christianity primarily as foretellers. In doing so, he rejects the view that the Old Testament has value for Christians only in that it promises what the New Testament fulfills. Bowman observes, "There is something more than a 'predicting word' or a 'powerful word' in a 'prophetic word.'" Drawing upon the work of Walter Brueggemann, Bowman emphasizes the power of language to guide us through troubling times and to point us in a new direction that is rooted in the Divine Word.

In "Love and Desire in the Song of Songs," Christina Bucher proposes that the Song of Songs contributes to the church in two different but complementary ways. Read at one level, Song of Songs affirms human sexuality and desire. This affirmation in and of itself is significant, since the church has had an ambivalent attitude toward human sexual desire. On another level, we can read Song of Songs as the church has read the book for two thousand years as an affirmation of the love between God and God's people. Drawing upon both hymns and recent Christian theological reflection, Bucher proposes that Song of Songs supports a theology of a noncoercive God.

Graydon F. Snyder also explores the ongoing life of an Old Testament text. In "Jonah the Christian," Snyder examines the interpretation of Jonah in early Christian literature and art and concludes that "through the centuries the well-known story of Jonah went through a number of reinterpretations." He explains that writers prior to the time of the New Testament emphasize God's deliverance of Jonah from a dangerous situation. New Testament and patristic sources for the most part connect the "sign of Jonah" with the resurrection of Jesus. After examining different elements in the early Christian art of catacombs and house churches, Snyder concludes that the Jonah in Christian art of the second and third centuries represents the Christian who faces life in the alien environment of the Roman Empire.

The last two essays in the volume take a historical look at Brethren and the Old Testament. Jeffrey A. Bach examines Brethren views of the Old Testament, and Denise D. Kettering explores connections between Brethren practices and selected customs and practices found in the Old Testament.

In his article "Prefiguring Fulfillment: Brethren Approaches to the Old Testament," historian Jeffrey A. Bach provides an overview of the ways in which Brethren have read the Old Testament. From their eighteenth-century origins through the twentieth century, Brethren primarily approached the Old Testament typologically. They described the ways in which Old Testament events, individuals, and stories point ahead to Jesus of Nazareth and to the events recounted in the New Testament. Bach ends his article with a brief discussion of D. W. Kurtz, who represents the shift that occurred in the Church of the Brethren in the early to mid-twentieth century, when Brethren ministers and teachers began studying Bible and theology at major universities and divinity schools. Unlike earlier Brethren, Kurtz downplayed the importance and value of the Old Testament and challenged the unity of the testaments as forming one Scripture for the church.

Denise D. Kettering examines Brethren ordinances and relates them to Old Testament customs and practices. Although Brethren ordinances are rooted primarily in the New Testament, Kettering notes that the ordinances also have roots in the Old Testament. She draws parallels between feetwashing and Old Testament hospitality, between love feast and Passover, and between baptism and the Old Testament purification rituals. Kettering concludes that historically Brethren have had "a conflicted relationship with the Old Testament roots of their rituals."

The essays in this volume do not claim to be the final word on the subject of the Old Testament and the church. Rather, we hope to engage readers in deeper reflection upon their own understandings of the ways in which the Hebrew Bible contributes to Christian life and thought. We invite you, the readers, to engage in conversations with both the Hebrew Bible texts and the authors of the essays contained in this volume. Through these conversations, may we all grow and deepen in our understanding of Christian life and thought.

Recommended Reading

Walter Brueggemann. *An Introduction to the Old Testament: The Canon and Christian Imagination.* Louisville: Westminster John Knox, 2003.

Fredrick C. Holmgren. *The Old Testament and the Significance of Jesus.* Grand Rapids: William B. Eerdmans, 1999.

Lee Martin McDonald. *The Biblical Canon: Its Origin, Transmission, and Authority.* Peabody, MA: Hendrickson, 2007.

Christians Reading the Old Testament

Robert C. Bowman

The Problem

Christians who consider themselves New Testament people often have great difficulties with the Old Testament. What is one to do with that book—or, rather, with that part of *the* Book?

Many elements combine to make the Old Testament difficult. In the first place, parts of it are simply boring. Richard Friedman, author of *Who Wrote the Bible?* once said that if he ever got to the point where he could read the detailed instructions for building the tabernacle in Exodus without being incredibly bored, he would know that he had finally become a biblical scholar (176).

If not boring, at least great chunks of the Old Testament seem irrelevant to Christians. It seems to belong to a world that makes no sense to us. Deuteronomy 22:10 warns, "You shall not plow with an ox and a donkey yoked together." Frankly, most of us cannot remember ever being tempted to disobey this commandment. It does, perhaps, give one a sense of relief to know that there are at least some of God's commandments that we have not broken. And in that statement is part of the problem itself: in what sense should we understand the huge miscellany of laws in the Old Testament as "God's laws"?

Even more disturbing than laws that seem irrelevant are those that seem downright unethical. The Old Testament narrative seems to accept slavery, war, capital punishment, plunder, polygamy, and other elements that we find offensive. At the same time, there is strong condemnation of other actions that we no longer consider serious. Trimming the corners of the beard and wearing clothing of mixed fabrics are part and parcel of our lives even though both are prohibited in the Old Testament.

Perhaps the strongest barrier to feeling comfortable with the Old Testament is that in some places God appears far removed from the concerns of daily life, rather than the God presented by Jesus in the New Testament. When invading the Promised Land, the Israelites were instructed: "You must not let anything that breathes remain alive. You shall annihilate them—the Hittites and the Amorites, the Canaanites and the Perizzites, the Hivites and the Jebusites—just as the LORD your God has commanded" (Deut. 20:16-17). This does not sound like the God whom Jesus called Father. And the familiar story of Noah, seen from one perspective, presents us with a concept of a God who would drown all living persons except Noah and his family.

The disharmony between the two testaments was an issue among Christians early on, and it has resurfaced since the Protestant Reformation. Perhaps there is no final solution to this puzzle; however, there are certain affirmations that are helpful as one begins to explore that relationship.

Affirmation One: *The New Testament cannot be properly understood in isolation from the Old Testament.*

This affirmation stands in direct contrast to the German theologian and church historian Adolph von Harnack, who suggested nearly a century ago that to hold on to the Old Testament in the modern world was simply "the result of religious and ecclesial paralysis" (217). Harnack said this in the context of his study of Marcion, a Christian teacher and priest who, about AD 140, suggested that Christians should reject the Old Testament entirely. According to Marcion, the God portrayed in the Old Testament could not be the same as the God revealed in Jesus.

The same suggestion has surfaced in more recent times. I was once chided for my interest in the Old Testament by a respected, elder Brethren pastor who declared that there was nothing of importance whatsoever in the Old Testament. "Nothing at all!" he emphasized.

To reject the Old Testament, however, is to reject many portions of the New Testament and to place one in danger of misinterpreting the rest. In many places the New Testament declares its own dependence upon the Old Testament. When Paul insists that both the death of Jesus and his resurrection was "according to the scriptures" (1 Cor. 15:3, 5), he is suggesting that these events are only understandable against the backdrop of the Old Testament. In the familiar story of the walk to Emmaus in Luke 24, the first work of the risen Christ was to offer an interpretation of the Old Testament to his disciples. The Old Testament was the Scripture of Jesus, the disciples, and the early Christians. It was from the Old Testament that they drew their understanding of the meaning of Christ.

One not only sees the Old Testament in many direct references and indirect allusions within the New Testament, but it is also seen in what is presumed by New Testament writers on the basis of the Old Testament. Many Old Testament themes are not explicitly developed in the New Testament but still form an essential part of Christian faith. The insistence upon monotheism is a vivid example of an Old Testament theme presumed but not enlarged upon in the New Testament. The New Testament rarely mentions God as creator. For that one must turn to the Old Testament.

Some themes vitally important to our age are best seen in the Old Testament. The theme of human responsibility for the care of creation is an Old Testament idea that is presumed but rarely, if ever, mentioned in the New Testament. Social dimensions of the gospel as they relate to corporate structures are given stronger development in the Old Testament. The simple fact is that the Old Testament presents some important theological themes more clearly than the New Testament.

Today the problem of reconciling the two testaments troubles us when we try to square the Old Testament with the gospel, but the earliest Christians had the opposite problem. Their struggle involved trying to square the gospel with the Old Testament. Early Christians were grounded in the Old Testament and their problem was to find ways to fit the story of Jesus into revealed Scripture. They searched through the Old Testament trying to see ways to match the story of Jesus with Scripture (Acts 17:11). As Matthew reports the story of Jesus in his Gospel, he refers over and over again to something Jesus did with the words, "this took place to fulfill what was spoken in the prophet" (see Matt. 2:23; 8:17; 12:17).

The Old Testament, as difficult as parts of it would seem, is indispensable to our understanding of the New Testament and its themes. One cannot ignore the Old Testament without being unfaithful to the New Testament and thereby losing both.

Affirmation Two: *The Old Testament and New Testament form a unified whole.*

If the Old Testament is an essential part of Scripture, one is still left with the problem of determining its relationship to the New Testament. With the high value given to the Old Testament by the earliest Christians, one cannot be satisfied with any perspective that places the First Testament in an inferior position with regard to the New Testament. Of course, it is often easier to declare a belief in the unity of the two testaments than to perceive it.

Over the centuries there have been many popular schemes to describe the relationship between the two testaments. Some of the more familiar ones are: (1) the Old Testament is prophecy and the New Testament is fulfillment, (2) the Old Testament is law while the New Testament is grace, (3) the Old Testament describes a covenant of servitude but the New Testament a covenant of sonship. Each of these schemes, by simplifying and polarizing, tries to place the testaments on an unequal footing. The Old Testament is relegated to a second-class document. One ends up feeling that reading the Old Testament is like reading someone else's mail. Once a prophecy has been fulfilled, for example, there is no need for the prophecy itself.

Perhaps the worst of these schemes denigrating the Old Testament is one that refers to it as the record of the failure of Israel in contrast to the New Testament.

Paul may be warning about this approach when he describes the relationship of Gentile Christians to Judaism with the metaphor of an olive tree. "If some of the branches were broken off, and you, a wild olive shoot, were grafted in their place to share the rich root of the olive tree, do not boast over the branches. If you do boast, remember that is it not you that support the root, but the root that supports you" (Romans 11:17-18). While there are other interpretations of this passage, certainly one understanding of that "root" is that it stands for what we call the Old Testament. The story of the Old Testament is, in Paul's writing, the foundation underlying New Testament faith. Schemes that relegate the Old Testament to a position of inferiority would be like branches claiming to support the root.

The unity of the testaments has been the theme of many biblical theologies written in the last century. Various scholars attempted to define a particular theme running through both testaments as a unifying principle. The presence of a single theme binding the two testaments into one unit would bring together what often appears a collection of disparate elements. The themes of "salvation-history," "covenant," "the acts of God," or the "elusive presence of God" have been proposed along with others. Each of these unifying themes adds a helpful contribution for seeing the continuities between the testaments and a valuable way of thinking about the theology of Scripture. Unfortunately, no matter how helpful these proposed unifying themes are, they all leave untouched large portions of the Old Testament where these themes are not visible. What does one do with Ecclesiastes or Esther if they do not fit the proposed unifying theme?

In affirming the unity and equality of the testaments, two considerations seem important. First, granted that some portions of the Bible speak more clearly to us than others, the tension that this creates does not necessarily indicate an inevitable dichotomy between the testaments. Even New Testament persons resonate more with the Twenty-third Psalm than with the fulminations of Jude against false believers. So if there is unevenness in Scripture, it is an unevenness within the unity of the canon.

Second, portions of the Scripture, especially in the Old Testament, that seem boring or irrelevant early on often appear to be passages that are keys to interpretation later. The story of Judah and Tamar in Genesis 38 was often dismissed as an unrelated insertion into the story of Joseph until Robert Alter, in his brilliant *The Art of Biblical Narrative*, showed how the story of Judah and Tamar was tied into the story of Joseph, repeating themes that come up before and after chapter 38 (3-10).

Richard Friedman, who was mentioned earlier expressing his boredom at the tabernacle instructions in Exodus, found that those same instructions proved to be a key in his investigation into the authorship of parts of the Bible (176).

Affirmation Three: *The Bible is polyphonic and multilayered.*

Both testaments are marvelously complex and variegated. The Old Testament especially contains all types of literature and a wide variety of theological perspectives. It has a diversity of spiritual insights, some that are fully compatible with Christianity and some that are not. The material presented to us in the Bible has come from many scribes and different points of view. In addition, the manner in which the material is presented offers many layers of interpretation. The Bible means more than it says, and what it says is never obvious.

In one sense, affirming the diversity of the Bible seems like the reverse side of claiming unity for the Bible. It is the disparity of points of view in Scripture that is most troubling, especially those perceived differences between the Old Testament and the New Testament. However, we too frequently operate out of a perception of unity that demands uniformity, while the Scriptures present us with a kaleidoscope of images, voices, styles, and even occasional contradictions. A primary question is whether the multiplicity of interpretations found in Scripture represents a problem or a message.

Gabriel Josipovici puts it, "The question seems to be: how are we to retain our sense of the Bible as a single whole while doing justice to its peculiarly fragmentary and elliptical mode of narration?" (23). One might suggest that one can retain a sense of the unity of the Scriptures only when one does justice to that "fragmentary and elliptical mode of narration."

One of the achievements of the past century of biblical scholarship is the recognition of the variety of voices and perceptions in the Scriptures. New Testament scholars have learned to pay close attention to the individual voices of each Gospel writer. Old Testament scholars have learned that some portions of Scripture long thought to be a unit are actually composed of fragments of the contributions of many writers, compilers, and scribes.

It would seem that the complexity of Scripture has a purpose, and it is important for us to learn to acknowledge and respect the various voices through which the messages within Scripture come to us. Or, to put it quite bluntly, the Old Testament is not supposed to sound like the New Testament any more than John is supposed to sound like Paul.

Scripture meets us with different claims and with elusive meanings. It comes at us with the messiness of life itself. Human language, customs, problems, experiences, hopes, and fears are the warp and woof of the biblical record. And this human element in its diversity does not diminish the divine element.

Recently I read of a person surprised to find that the Bible contained the story of Lot and his daughters. This story, one of the more noxious stories in the Bible, describes the incest of daughters who got their father drunk in a cave above the valley of Sodom. As I was reading about this person's surprise, I assumed that the reader would reject the Bible for including such a story. But instead, the reader said that his surprise came from the realization that not all the persons in the Bible were plaster saints who lived perfect lives. The stories of dysfunctional families, power politics, petty revenge, and even incest reflect life as it is actually lived in the world around us. "This is a book," he said, "in which I can find my story as well!"

Affirmation Four: *The Bible requires interpretation.*

Of course the Bible requires interpretation! Even if some literalists say they want no interpretation, just the Bible itself, one cannot avoid interpreting. Many fail to realize that the very act of reading is an interpretation. It was Jonathan Swift who, years ago, parodied extreme literalists by saying that no one should use toilet paper since the Bible says, "He that is filthy, let him be filthy still" (Rev. 22:11). The point is that all language requires interpretation.

The Bible has taken great risk in delivering much of its message in narrative form. Rather than a theology about Jesus, we are given stories about Jesus and we draw our theology from those stories. Rather than a scientific description of the origins of the universe and the evolution of human beings, the Scriptures give us a story. And stories are capable of being interpreted in a myriad of ways. In fact, it is a particular characteristic of biblical narrative to demand interpretation. The Bible is reluctant to reveal the inner life of persons. The feelings and motives of characters in the New Testament and the Old Testament are left to the interpretation of the reader. Why did Naomi discourage Ruth from following her to Judea? Was Jesus laughing, scolding, or sympathizing with Peter's failure to continue walking on water? Scripture requires our engagement in the form of interpretation if we are to get past simply reading words on a page.

I'm primarily using the word "interpretation" in this section to describe how we choose to read or understand the text. I was struck by the way interpretation of the text can be a conscious decision several years ago when Bill Moyers hosted a discussion of Genesis on PBS. When the guests came to the story of Noah's flood, most of the panelists wanted to discuss the awful depiction of a God who would destroy every living creature, innocent and guilty alike. Yet one of them kept insisting that this was not a story of God's wrath; it was a story of God's rescue. And, indeed, for most of Christian history the story of the ark has functioned as the story of God's rescue; that is why the central aisle of a church building is often called a "nave" from the Latin word for ship. The church was seen as God's new ark of rescue.

To be sure, if one chooses to focus on the image of God as one who would wipe out ninety-nine percent of humanity with Noah's flood, then the story raises a host of difficult theological questions. If one chooses to focus on the image of God as one who provides rescue to the faithful in the midst of a world bent on self-destruction, then one is closer to the New Testament image of God. The place one looks to find the heart of the story can be a conscious decision.

Many problematic texts in the Old Testament can be seen in better light when one pays attention to traditional interpretations long embedded in the community of faith. In the exodus story, God's people are trapped between death by Pharaoh's army and death by drowning in the sea. According to the story, God opened a way for them to walk through the water to safety on the other side. Pharaoh's army followed them, but the waters came back and all the Egyptians were drowned. Then Moses and the Israelites, in chapter 15, sing a long hymn praising God for delivering them. "Your right hand, O LORD, glorious in power—your right hand, O LORD, shattered the enemy" (Exodus 15:6).

The destruction of Pharaoh's army is another story that troubles New Testament people, especially when they remember the instructions of Jesus to love one's enemies (Matt. 5:44). However, there is an old interpretation—a midrash—that looks at this story from a different perspective. In heaven, the midrash says, the angels were also dancing and rejoicing over the rescue of the Hebrews. Then one of the angels said, "Look! We are rejoicing, but the Creator of the Universe is crying!" They asked, "Lord, why would you weep when Israel has been delivered by your power?" And the answer was, "I am weeping for the dead Egyptians washed up on the shore—somebody's son, somebody's husband, somebody's father. The Egyptians are my children, too."

Suddenly the story of the destruction of Pharaoh's army takes on a new dimension. Surely those of us who have been rescued from certain destruction will rejoice. How could we keep from singing? But New Testament people would insist that our singing should also acknowledge the fact that all rescue comes at a cost to someone.

The destruction of the Egyptians is an example of an Old Testament text that presents an image of God that seems unworthy of the one Jesus called Father. But this old interpretative midrash on the story holds in unity both the New Testament vision and the Old Testament memory. The interpretation, while comfortable with the New Testament perspective, does not come from Christian tradition, but from Jewish tradition. The verses supporting the interpretation are drawn from Old Testament Scriptures such as Deuteronomy 23:7 where Israel is forbidden to hate Egyptians. Jewish tradition has been more respectful of traditions of interpretation, even of multiple interpretations, than has Christian tradition. Christians believe that the Holy Spirit guides the church and the risen Jesus is among us. However, we still pay scant attention to the contributions our spiritual ancestors have made to the ongoing conversation about Scripture.

The Bible calls for interpretation, and I am suggesting that it is helpful to pay more attention to two types of interpretation. First, it is helpful to make a conscious decision to interpret Scripture. Second, it is helpful to pay attention to interpretations from a wider community of faith—including those across the centuries.

Affirmation Five: *Each part of the Bible insists on its own interpretation.*

If the Bible needs interpretation, what guidelines are there for New Testament people? I was always taught to interpret the Old Testament in the light of the New Testament. But what that guideline means is not always clear.

In Acts 8, the disciple Philip met a government official from Ethiopia who was reading from Isaiah 53, "Like sheep he was led to the slaughter, and like a lamb silent before its shearer, so he does not open his mouth" (Acts 8:32). The Ethiopian was puzzled, "About whom was the prophet speaking?" Philip began with that Scripture and interpreted the story of Jesus.

Is that what it means to interpret the Old Testament in the light of the New? Is it only to find christological references throughout the Old Testament? Those passages from Isaiah being read by the Ethiopian *can* be applied to Jesus, but they do not *have* to apply to Jesus—or, perhaps, they do not *only* apply to Jesus. The suffering servant of Isaiah can also apply to Israel in exile or to the life of the church.

The history of biblical interpretation is full of exaggerated examples of christological references. Some say that the scarlet cord in the window of Rahab by which the Israelite spies were saved signified the blood of Christ. Others imagine that the outstretched arms of Moses during the battle with the Amalekites represented the cross of Christ and it was by this sign that Amalek was defeated. Rather than straining to find fanciful christological references throughout the Old Testament, a better way to interpret the Old Testament in the light of the New might be to follow an interpretation that is grounded in the key ideas of the New Testament. For example, one key New Testament idea is that the dominant characteristic of God is love. To read Jesus in the Old Testament does not only mean to find predictions of his life, allusions to his ministry, or prefiguring "types" of his divinity. It means to keep the love of God and neighbor prominent in every reading of the Old Testament.

Yet, to interpret the Old Testament in a way that makes New Testament people feel comfortable may blind us to other dimensions of the text. No one key exists or will exist that can unlock the door to every text. Even the rule of thumb for Christians to "interpret the Old Testament in the light of the New" will not unlock every door. With Jesus, new principles of Old Testament interpretation have emerged (2 Cor. 3:15*ff.*). But do these new principles emerge to replace other interpretations, or to be placed alongside them?

The problem with interpreting the Old Testament in the light of the New Testament is that sometimes it violates the integrity of the Old Testament. It is not wrong to interpret the Old Testament in the light of the New, but it may be wrong to always do so. The trick is to interpret the Old Testament in the light of the New Testament in such a way that the Old Testament remains the Old Testament. In fact, it is important to interpret Old Testament texts purely from within their own context before reaching beyond to specifically Christian interpretations. Christian interpretations of Old Testament texts may be seen as serendipitous, providing additional meanings. For example, when one reads Isaiah 7, it is clear that the primary significance of the birth of Immanuel was intended to reassure King Ahaz of God's care in the face of an international threat to his kingdom. That Matthew finds a "fulfilling" of this Scripture in the birth of Jesus is a supplementary reading that should not replace the primary significance, but only lay beside it as an added interpretation.

One of the exciting frontiers of academic biblical studies today is in the way Jewish and Christian scholars are sitting around the same table and sharing the study of the Old Testament. In this process, Christian scholars cannot help seeing Scripture from their perspective as Christians. Indeed, a Christian sees all of life from a new perspective. At the same time, Jewish scholars view the Old Testament through the lens of the Talmud and oral Torah. In the process of studying together, these two different perspectives on the Old Testament are not necessarily contradictory and are often shown to be complementary. This should not only happen in the academic world. Many Christian Bible study groups would also profit from such interfaith readings.

Walter Brueggemann, in his massive *Theology of the Old Testament*, writes, "Christians are able to say of the Old Testament, 'It is ours,' but must also say, 'It is not ours alone'" (735). The Bible belongs to the world, not just to Christians. The Old Testament, as the Hebrew Bible, has sustained the living faith of our Jewish brothers and sisters for centuries, and their insights and interpretive traditions are a valuable supplement to our own. Unfortunately, this may be asking more than many Christians are willing to grant. Why is it not possible for Christians to accept that theological interpretations other than ours can be valid alongside our own?

Unanswered Questions

In what sense are the laws in the Old Testament "God's laws"? If one accepts the laws of the Old Testament as perpetually binding on modern Christians, it would seem that one is not paying enough attention to the fact that Scripture is historically and culturally conditioned. On the other hand, to ignore the laws of the Old Testament would seem to ignore the idea of the inspiration of the Scriptures. There needs to be a way of affirming both that the laws represent *historical* revelation and historical *revelation*. In the Sermon on the Mount, Jesus warns about disobeying or relaxing even one of the laws (Matt. 5:18). Yet Jesus was criticized for relaxing the laws regarding the sabbath. The conclusion would point to the necessity of finding some balance between taking the law seriously and seeking the right interpretation of the law.

Is the "God of wrath" the same as the "God of love"? These two images of God are not strictly limited to one testament or the other. The New Testament implies that the deaths of Ananias and Sapphira were caused by God (Acts 5:1-11). And it is in the Old Testament that God says, "I am He who blots out your transgressions for my own sake, and I will not remember your sins" (Isaiah 43:25). Yet, one can't help admitting that references to the wrath of God and the punishment of sins are more prominent in the Old Testament. I believe one should be cautious before discarding images of God that do not fit one's personal notions. With the New Testament one can affirm that the dominant characteristic of God is love. But with the Old Testament one needs to admit that there is a mystery to life and not all events turn out to our liking. New Testament people can neither completely accept verses in the Old Testament that portray God as vengeful and cruel nor completely reject them. The issue of balance is elusive.

Conclusion

One cannot deny that the Old Testament presents difficulties for New Testament people. There are angularities and intractable problems what will not go away. One writer described the Old Testament as a huge, sprawling, tactless book, and yet we are convinced that God speaks to us in the arena composed of both testaments and in the interplay between them. As the Pilgrim fathers heard before they departed for the New World, there is more truth and light yet to break forth out of God's Holy Word. And the light and truth tend to break forth at the most unexpected places.

Recommended Reading

Robert Alter. *The Art of Biblical Narrative*. New York: Basic Books, 1981.

James Barr. *Old and New in Interpretation: A Study of the Two Testaments*. New York: Harper & Row, 1966.

Alice Ogden Bellis and Joel S. Kaminsky, eds. *Jews, Christians, and the Theology of the Hebrew Scriptures*. Atlanta: Society of Biblical Literature, 2000.

John Bright. *The Authority of the Old Testament*. Nashville: Abingdon Press, 1967.

Walter Brueggemann. *Theology of the Old Testament*. Minneapolis: Augsburg Fortress, 1997.

Richard Elliott Friedman. *Who Wrote the Bible?* New York: Harper Collins, 1987.

John Goldingay. *Models for Interpretation of Scripture*. Grand Rapids: William B. Eerdmans, 1995.

Adolph von Harnack. *Marcion: The Gospel of the Alien God*. Trans. John E. Steely and Lyle D. Bierma. Durham, NC: Labyrinth Press, 1924.

Gabriel Josipovici. *The Book of God: A Response to the Bible*. New Haven: Yale University Press, 1988.

Claus Westermann, ed. *Essays on Old Testament Hermeneutics*. Atlanta: John Knox Press, 1963.

Study Questions

Prepare

Look for a copy of Bill Moyers' *Genesis: A Living Conversation* (book or DVD), featuring a conversation between experts from many walks of life. Watch or read the section on Noah.

Tell your own faith story, using passages, images, and illustrations from the Old Testament.

Ask

1. What *is* the relationship of the Old Testament to the New Testament, in the author's opinion?

2. According to Bowman, a respected Brethren elder once told him there was nothing of significance in the Old Testament. How do you respond to such a statement? Why does Bowman say this is a mistake?

3. Bob Neff used to show up at conferences and campfires carrying only his Hebrew Bible, making the statement that this was all the Bible the first Christians had. What would it be like to carry only the Old Testament? Share some of the faith stories you wrote out in advance, using passages from the Hebrew Bible.

4. Bowman gives two examples of themes developed in the Old Testament but only implicit in the New Testament: monotheism, and God as creator. Can you think of others?

5. Name some negative things you have heard about the relationship between the Old and New Testament. What is your reaction to statements like this? Discuss Bowman's second affirmation, that "The Old Testament and New Testament form a unified whole."

6. How can the Bible speak with many voices yet remain unified?

7. Some Christians who claim to be literalists eat bacon and ham, and may insist that the feetwashing mandated by Jesus was only symbolic. Talk about the different levels of Bible interpretation. How do you interpret the Scriptures? What things do you

believe pertain to you and the way you live your life? What sorts of things are irrelevant?

8. Discuss the story of Noah, based on this essay and on the chapter or episode of Bill Moyers' book on Genesis.

9. Bowman writes: "Those passages from Isaiah being read by the Ethiopian *can* be applied to Jesus, but they do not *have* to apply to Jesus—or, perhaps, they do not *only* apply to Jesus." Unpack the words can, have, and only, and discuss the three levels of understanding about Old Testament interpretation, especially in light of these methods of interpretation.

10. Mine some of the "Unanswered Questions" found toward the end of the essay.

Conflict Transformation and the Jacob Saga

Eugene F. Roop

Genesis 12–50 features some of the best-known and well-loved narratives in the Old Testament. These stories do not portray the lives of our biblical ancestors as pious and peaceful. Quite the opposite, these ancestral sagas tell us about lives painfully punctuated by crisis and conflict. To be sure, their parched and rocky land often provided a match that ignited disputes between and within families. Along with the environment, cultural patterns and family structures also served as catalysts generating episodes of conflict.

The cultural importance of offspring intensified Abraham and Sarah's struggle with infertility. This provided a catalyst for conflict between husband and wife, and with others in their community. The leadership role of the firstborn inflamed conflict between the twins, Esau and Jacob. According to the narrative, their battle began in the womb and gained steam as the years went by. Each twin sought to be recognized as the most important man in the family. The arrogant-sounding words directed by the younger Joseph to his older brothers ignited conflict in that family, a conflict so destructive that it drove their father deep into depression.

These familiar biblical stories share a common characteristic. They narrate episodes of *conflict*—conflict with God, conflict within the family, and occasionally conflict with "outsiders." The compelling nature of these conflicts has prompted scholars to explore, analyze, and explain them using all available research tools: historical analysis, psychoanalytic analysis, history of religions, gender studies, anthropological studies, folktale patterns, and literary and cultural structuralism.[1]

While these analytical tools provide valuable insights into the origin of the stories and the characteristics they share with narratives from other times and places, the studies do not replace a close, careful reading of the narratives themselves. Genesis 12–50 is not a story of peace and tranquility, but features episodes of raw conflict. Some conflicts ended in reconciliation. Others were neither well-managed nor resolved.

Conflict on Our Agenda

Conflict between individuals and groups remains one of our most vexing societal problems. Before looking further at the ancestral narratives in Genesis, I will take a brief glance at some programmatic efforts from related disciplines to respond to conflict.

Religious convictions and social commitments have led many men and women to develop nonviolent strategies to settle conflict, recognizing that responding to conflict with violence seldom, if ever, reduces conflict. Instead, violence ignites rage, generating more violence when the resentful victims gather the means to strike back.

Everyday we see the damaging result of physical violence between persons within communities and in international relationships. In addition, we have become more attentive to the psychological, sexual, and discriminatory violence afflicting families, schools, businesses, neighborhoods, and ethnic groups. While some consider it wise to maintain a distinction between physical violence and the other forms of violence, all these actions seek to settle conflict by destroying or disabling another person or group.

The women and men implementing nonviolent strategies to settle conflict share common commitments and employ many of

---

[1] Among the more recent books, see those by Mignon Jacobs; Phyllis Trible; Susan Niditch; Naomi Steinberg; and Devora Steinmetz.

the same strategies. But as we might expect, we find differences in the programs.

Three familiar terms designate such programs: *conflict management*, *conflict resolution*, and more recently *conflict transformation*. I do not propose to define these programs so as to delineate the uniqueness of each. However, I do want to suggest that each term *tends* to be used in specific contexts and to feature distinctive goals and strategies.

Conflict management is frequently used in contexts where conflict develops among people working together in some capacity, such as a classroom, a congregation, or a workplace. Conflict management employs strategies that seek to enable a group to study, work or deliberate more effectively. Those working in conflict management do not ignore the wider culture's influence, nor do they ignore opportunities to resolve conflict. Nevertheless, conflict management programs often focus on the development of skills that enable individuals to function more effectively in an organization that incorporates diverse and sometimes adversarial personalities and opinions.[2]

Conflict resolution overlaps with conflict management in skills training and even in the contexts within which the term is used. However, conflict resolution focuses much of its attention on resolving serious conflict between two individuals or groups. These antagonists may or may not work together as part of the same organization. They may be husband and wife, parents and children, siblings, or members of a business work team. However, they may be neighbors, nations, or religious groups with little personal relationship to or understanding of each other. Whatever the relationship, their interests, activities, or purposes have brought them into conflict. Conflict resolution seeks to move from destructive antagonism to a negotiated agreement, mutual respect, and perhaps reconciliation. As such, the history, concerns, and purposes of the two parties play a crucial role in efforts to resolve the conflict.

---

[2] See books by R. Butchart and B. McEwan, eds.; Richard Bowdine and Donna Crawford; Speed Leas; Barbara A. Budjac Corvette; and Deborah Borisoff and David Victor.

Depending on the conflict, an effort to build a more creative future for all the parties may be an important goal of conflict resolution.[3]

Conflict Transformation

Conflict transformation has emerged as a more recent addition to language and practice as we respond to destructive conflict. Although John Paul Lederach[4] is not the only person using this term or seeking to define the task, his work has set forth a valuable and nuanced discussion of conflict transformation. While sharing much with conflict management and conflict resolution, *conflict transformation* seeks constructive change that includes and goes beyond the resolution of specific problems.[5]

As conflict develops, understandably our attention is drawn to actions that escalate the dispute. Anticipation that conflict might become dangerously destructive often prompts us to act quickly to limit the peril. Sometimes such quick action is necessary to cool off the antagonists. Be that as it may, Lederach reminds us that working toward transformation requires that we also take time to look behind, around, and beyond the immediate episode. He affirms that a "transformational approach seeks to understand the particular episode of conflict not in isolation, but as embedded in the greater pattern" (2003, 16). Rather than act too quickly to settle a conflict, Lederach insists that we step back from the episode to understand the long-simmering issues, the patterns of relationships, and the institutional and cultural structures that influence the conflict.

Effective conflict transformation requires a second step. Not only must we give attention to the issues, relationships, and structures that affect the dynamics of a specific conflict, we must also envision "the horizon toward which we journey—the building of healthy relationships and communities, locally and globally" (2003, 4).

---

[3] See books by M. Deutsch and P. Coleman, eds.; Louis Kriesberg; Linda Lantieri and Janet Patti; and Robert J. Marzano.

[4] John Paul Lederach is the professor of International Peacebuilding with the Joan B. Kroc Institute for International Peace Studies at the University of Notre Dame.

[5] The bibliography lists several books by John Paul Lederach. His focus on conflict transformation is present in each book. Our discussion here will refer to his books published in 2003 and 2005. This note refers to 2003, 4.

Only by clearly identifying the "horizon toward which we journey" can we design a response that includes *and* goes beyond solving one specific episode of conflict. As he seeks to identify some marks of healthy relationships and communities, Lederach points to the broadly shared desire to move "from violent and destructive patterns [of interaction] toward capacities which are creative, responsive, constructive and nonviolent" (2003, 70).[6]

Recognizing that conflict transformation is easier to define than to accomplish, Lederach ponders the following question: "What enables us to transcend the ingrained patterns of violence that plague the communities in which we live?" (2005, 5). The urge to settle disputes by violence or the exercise of power to destroy the adversary frequently frustrates even the most skillful mediation and carefully designed process. John Paul Lederach insists that genuine transformation depends on building and eliciting *moral imagination*.[7] Lederach defines moral imagination in connection with conflict transformation as "the capacity to imagine and generate constructive responses and initiatives that, while rooted in the day-to-day challenges of violence, transcend and ultimately break the grips of those destructive patterns and cycles" (2005, 29).

Lederach goes on to identify some of the attitudes and practices intrinsic in a moral imagination.

1. The capacity to see the web of interdependent relationships that binds us together with our enemies. For example, the quality of our grandchildren's life is directly related to the quality of life of the enemy's grandchildren.

---

[6] Lederach does not assume that no other practitioner attends to the "horizon toward which we journey." Lantieri and Patti insist that changing a student's behavior in the school is not sufficient. In their Resolving Conflict Creatively Program they seek to develop strategies that include and move beyond any single conflict toward a more peaceable school (232-8). In the opening chapter, Cloke and Goldsmith state the goal of conflict resolution in language similar to that of Lederach: "Release ourselves from these pointless unproductive cultural patterns and create organizational cultures that value openness, honesty, dialogue, collaborative negotiation, conflict resolution, and the ability to learn from our opponents." (5). See also Part 4, "Creativity and Change," in M. Deutsch and P. Coleman, *The Handbook of Conflict Resolution*.

[7] Lederach identifies his conversation with and dependence upon many others (2005, 25-29). Especially related to this essay is the work by Walter Brueggemann in *Prophetic Imagination* and *Finally Comes the Poet*.

2. The capacity to rise above dualistic polarities (either this or that) with a sustained inquisitiveness for that which lies beyond the visible possibilities.
3. The willingness to make space for a creative act to emerge.
4. The willingness to risk a step into the unknown without any guarantee (2005, 34-38).

Turning to the Biblical Narratives

Lederach insists that developing a creative response to a destructive conflict is as much an artistic venture as a cognitive enterprise. The sensitivity of an artist is just as important as the skill of a technician. For me, that invites the biblical narratives and poetry into the conversation about conflict transformation.

Technical analysis has had an impact on every aspect of our lives, including the study of biblical narratives. Such investigation has proven indispensable, yet insufficient. Many of us have come to realize that while the biblical prophets may have had much in common in their message, role, and social standing, the prophets spoke and wrote as poets. To understand poetry, we must listen with the artist's ear. Similarly, we must resist efforts to reduce the biblical narratives *only* to ethical instruction or historical information. Biblical narratives speak imaginatively and evocatively as literary art. We must read them with an artist's soul.

I do not seek or expect to find the sagas[8] in Genesis illustrating or validating our strategies for conflict management or techniques for conflict resolution.[9] For me the value of the biblical narratives lies in their capacity to evoke possibilities that lie beyond the conventional, the accepted, the customary—possibilities that might occur to one with a mature moral imagination.

The ancestral narratives in Genesis depict interaction between agonizing episodes of conflict and the emergence of God's intended,

---

[8] The term "saga" refers to a long, prose traditional narrative that has an episodic structure. The collection of stories about Abraham, Isaac, and Jacob in the book of Genesis are often referred to as saga.

[9] See the book by Gangel and Canine for a discussion that seeks some biblical validation for specific strategies.

new future—a creative, healthy, nonviolent world. As a way to enter and explore this interaction, let us briefly turn to the Jacob saga, Genesis 25:19–36:43.[10]

Jacob in Conflict

Conflict in the family of Isaac and Rebekah affects every figure in the stories, reaching beyond the immediate family to include distant relatives. As the saga has come to us, Jacob, the central figure, manages to find himself at odds with everyone, including God—except perhaps his mother, Rebekah.

This saga constitutes the story of Israel's formation. As Fretheim notes, the saga portrays Israel's past/present with self-critical realism (516). This is not a heroic drama as frequently portrayed in our movies and television programs. The leading character, Jacob, appears as flawed as any other person in the story. We expect our heroes to be without fundamental flaws. We enjoy personality quirks in our heroic figures, but not character flaws. In the Jacob saga, we discover a family where the problems go well beyond idiosyncrasies.

Jacob vs. Esau

The saga begins with Rebekah pregnant with twins. She endures a very difficult pregnancy, so painful in fact that Rebekah cries out in anguish: "Why is this happening to me?" (25:22, NIV). God does not answer Rebekah's question, but responds to her agony by placing her painful pregnancy in a much larger, equally painful drama involving two peoples.

> Two [groups] are in your womb,
>   and two peoples born of you shall be divided;
> the one shall be stronger than the other,
>   the elder shall serve the younger (25:23).[11]

---

[10] Rather than inserting footnotes throughout this discussion, I would invite the reader to look at commentaries listed in the bibliography, including mine and those by Walter Brueggemann, Terence Fretheim, Victor Hamilton, and Sibley Towner.

[11] We usually translate the Hebrew word (*goyim*) nations (NRSV). However, in this context the word more likely refers to an entity similar to an ethnic group, as indicated by the parallel word peoples (*le'ummim*). Unless otherwise noted, biblical quotations are from the New Revised Standard Version of the Bible.

From birth Jacob strives to be the favored first son: "his brother came out, with his hand gripping Esau's heel" (v. 26). We catch a glimpse of the ongoing relationship between these twins, Esau and Jacob, in a following brief, but revealing episode (vv. 29-34). As a lead-in to the episode, the narrator informs us that Jacob's obsession to be first is not the only problem in the family. Division in the family reaches to its core: "Isaac loved Esau, because he was fond of game; but Rebekah loved Jacob" (v. 28).

Esau returns from hunting famished. The narrator reinforces Esau's critical condition. Famished is not just thirsty; famished includes serious dehydration. Jacob has made some stew. Compassion and custom prepare the reader for a charitable response, but it does not come. Instead Jacob demands *quid pro quo*, "First sell me your birthright." Esau responds, "I am about to die; of what use is a birthright to me?" (vv. 31-32). Jacob gets what he wants; Esau gets what he needs. Lest we assume that the fault lies *only* with Jacob, the narrator comments, "Thus Esau despised his birthright" (v. 34*b*).

Genesis 27 reinforces Jacob's need to be the favored first and the deep division between husband and wife with an episode set near Isaac's death. Before we go there, notice that Esau also contributed to the family discord: "When Esau was forty years old, he married Judith daughter of Beeri the Hittite, and Basemath daughter of Elon the Hittite; and they made life bitter for Isaac and Rebekah" (26:34-35).

As the time came for the elderly Isaac to bestow his final blessing, Rebekah conspires with Jacob to deceive his blind father to secure for himself the preferred blessing. Infuriated, Esau threatens to kill his twin brother. Learning of this threat, Rebekah convinces her favorite son to flee to her brother's family until Esau forgets what was done to him.

Jacob vs. Laban

Jacob travels to Haran, a Semitic city on the trade route between Mesopotamia and the Mediterranean Sea. Arriving thirsty at the community's well, Jacob meets his cousin Rachel. Jacob falls in love with this woman at the well.[12] Jacob enters the house of Rachel's father, Laban. This precipitates a second major conflict in this chiasm.[13]

What begins peacefully between Jacob and Laban turns into a series of conflicts in which each man pursues his agenda at the expense of the other. Jacob loves and wants to marry Rachel immediately even though her older sister is not married. Laban insists on holding to family values as defined by the culture, namely the sisters will marry in birth order. We do not know what the sisters think. The drama concludes with Jacob married to both of Laban's daughters, Leah and Rachel (29:1-30).

Although married to both sisters, Jacob loves Rachel. This ignites the third and central conflict in the saga (29:31–30:24). God does not change Jacob's attitude, but does act in response to Leah's pain: "When the LORD saw that Leah was unloved, he opened her womb; but Rachel was barren" (29:31). God's action provides Leah a valued place in the family narrative—fertility. However, Leah's fertility and Rachel's infertility serve to intensify the conflict

---

[12] Robert Alter discusses the woman and man "meeting at the well" as a familiar betrothal scene in biblical literature (51ff.).

[13] Chiasm is a literary device used more commonly in Hebrew poetry than in narrative. In chiasm the reader is guided through a series of literary elements leading to a central focus, followed by a matching set of literary elements leading away from that center (A, B, C, D, c, b, a). In the Jacob saga we find the Jacob-Esau conflict, followed by God encountering Jacob. Then comes the Jacob-Laban conflict. That brings the reader to the central conflict, Leah-Rachel-Jacob. Moving out from that center we find the conclusion of the Jacob-Laban conflict. God again engages Jacob, followed by the conclusion of the Jacob-Esau conflict (see diagram below). While the organization of this saga is influenced by chiasm, few narratives fit rigidly into that literary form. For a more complete discussion see Roop (166). I will not discuss all the elements of this chiastic-like literary design within the Jacob saga. Instead I encourage the reader to look at the commentaries on Genesis listed in the bibliography.

    A. Jacob and Esau (Gen. 27)

       B. God and Jacob (Gen. 28)

          C. Jacob and Laban (Gen. 29:1-30)

             D. Leah-Rachel-Jacob (Gen. 29:31–30:24)

          c. Jacob and Laban (Gen. 30:25–31:55)

       b. God and Jacob (Gen. 32)

    a. Jacob and Esau (Gen. 33)

between the sisters. Anguish and anger overwhelm these sisters throughout the narrative.

Out of the agony of these two women, Israel is born—eleven brothers and a sister.[14] The names Leah designates for her sons suggest that although she never achieves her deepest desire—to be loved by her husband—she realizes some satisfaction with what she does have. In naming her first sons, we see Leah's desire for love. Reuben, her firstborn, was named "because the LORD has looked on my affliction; surely now my husband will love me" (29:32). With the birth of her third son, Judah, it appears that Leah redirects her search for satisfaction: "This time I will praise the LORD" (29:35). Nevertheless, her competition with Rachel still burns.

Although loved by her husband, Rachel wants children, a desire she angrily expresses to her husband: "Give me children, or I shall die!" (30:1). An angry Jacob blames God for Rachel's plight. Out of her desire for a family, Rachel turns first to adoption through the use of her personal servant as a surrogate. But this choice does not satisfy her longing. Indeed, it seems to intensify her competition and conflict with Leah (30:8*ff.*). As the drama draws to a close, Rachel bears a son and names him Joseph. While this provides a measure of satisfaction, Rachel yearns for more: "May the LORD add to me another son!" (v. 24).

Leah plays a minor role in the continuing conflict between Jacob and Laban, but she eventually disappears from the drama. Near the end of his own life, Jacob comments that he buried Leah in the family grave at Mamre, but nothing more is said about her (49:29-32). Rachel gives birth to a second son, but that brings no joy. As she is dying in childbirth, Rachel names this son Ben-oni, "Son of my sorrow" (35:18). Jacob renames the son Benjamin, "Son of the right hand," in effect separating the infant from his painful past.

Jacob and Laban Again

Meanwhile Jacob's conflict with Laban resumes in earnest (30:25*ff.*). Once again their interaction begins on a positive note, but soon deteriorates with each trying to best the other over

---

[14] The narrative reports the birth of the twelfth son, Benjamin, later in the story (35:16-21).

money. The conclusion finds Jacob once again fleeing the scene of a conflict (31:1*ff.*).

The Jacob-Laban conflict ends in a negotiated settlement— not a reconciliation, but an agreement to cease hostilities. They set up a stone monument to mark their agreement. On the one hand the monument bears witness to the unresolved character of their conflict. Laban, fearing Jacob's intentions, calls on God to protect his daughters: "The LORD watch between you and me, when we are absent one from the other" (31:49). At the same time the monument serves to mark their commitment to cease their "war." Laban declares, "I will not pass beyond this heap to you, and you will not pass beyond this heap and this pillar to me, for harm" (31:52). Jacob pledges his agreement.

Jacob and Esau Again

As expected in the chiastic flow of the saga, the narrative turns back to the unfinished conflict between the twin brothers, Esau and Jacob. As he leaves Laban to return to his homeland, Jacob prepares to deal with Esau, who may not have forgotten what Jacob had done to him. The messengers whom Jacob sends to his brother report, "[Esau] is coming to meet you, and four hundred men are with him!" (32:6*b*). Filled with fear, Jacob prepares for a hostile reunion with his brother.

The initial hostility Jacob encounters comes not from Esau, but from a "night visitor" as he sleeps alone before crossing the Jabbok River for the anticipated reunion. Jacob leaves that terrifying night wounded, but blessed by God (32:29-31).

For reasons not stated, Jacob abandons his original plan (32:7-8) to divide into two companies, so as to save at least part of his family. Instead he arranges his family with the servants first, followed by Leah and her children, and finally Rachel with Joseph. Jacob walks ahead of his family bowing in honor and submission (33:3). Esau runs to Jacob and embraces his brother in a tearful reunion. The narrative does not designate one brother as more gracious and forgiving than the other. Jacob honors the brother whom he betrayed. Esau addresses the one he threatened to kill as "my brother."

To a great extent the two brothers reconcile. However, we notice that the brothers go separate ways after the reunion. Initially Jacob agrees to meet his brother in Seir, albeit traveling at a slower pace: "Let my lord pass on ahead of his servant, and I will lead on slowly, . . . until I come to my lord in Seir" (33:14). However, following Esau's departure to go south, Jacob takes a different road: "Jacob journeyed on to Succoth, and built himself a house. . . . Jacob came safely to the city of Shechem" (33:17-18). The narrative reports that the twin brothers meet one more time, to bury their father (35:29).

The Larger Drama

In the narratives these three episodes of conflict originate and develop with a measure of independence, but also interdependence. All three conflicts feature Jacob in the center of each dispute. Be that as it may, the literary shape of the Jacob saga reminds us that these conflicts function together in a larger drama, a drama that extends beyond Jacob. The genealogical lists interspersed throughout Genesis 12–50 connect this saga with the previous Sarah and Abraham saga and the Joseph saga that follows. Whatever the history that brought this material together, these three ancestral sagas function together as the narrative drama moves from the primeval story to the exodus.

Besides the genealogical lists, I want to mention another thread that connects all three ancestral narratives. God's speech to Abraham in Genesis 12:1-3 provides an important thread, perhaps the most important thread that runs throughout the ancestral stories. In that speech God announces that (1) God will make this family a great people, (2) God will bless them, (3) they will have a key role in discerning those who receive blessing, and (4) through this people all the families of the earth shall receive blessing.

As Fretheim notes, this last phrase presents the aim of all the other phrases. In creation God blessed the man and the woman (Gen. 1:28). Going forward, through this family, God intends that all the families of the earth shall receive blessing. For me it is this thread that opens the door to a valuable conversation between these texts and the conflict transformation discussion of John Paul Lederach.

Blessing

Blessing acts to bestow. It is less a wish or hope, than a bestowal. Blessing bestows upon the blessed one gifts such as creativity and community, energy and wisdom, health and peace. While there may be a "not yet" character to the bestowal, blessing begins to bear fruit in the present. With the divine bestowal of blessing, Abraham and Sarah can reasonably expect that they will have children. The realization of that expectation is delayed so long that they have almost given up. But to her surprise, "Sarah conceived and bore Abraham a son" (21:2).

The bestowal of divine blessing that initiates the story in Genesis 12 threads its way throughout the ancestral sagas, surfacing in unexpected moments. As Jacob and Laban negotiate Jacob's departure, Laban said to him, "If you will allow me to say so, I have learned by divination that the LORD has blessed me because of you; name your wages, and I will give it" (Gen. 30:27*ff.*). God's blessing continues to bear fruit. We hear echoes in Joseph's comments to his brothers: "Even though you intended to do harm to me, God intended it for good, in order to preserve a numerous people, as he is doing today" (50:20).

The blessing benefits the ancestral family itself. In addition, God assigns to the family a purpose for their life—that "all the people of the earth may receive blessing." In these narratives God's blessing begins to bear fruit—sometimes with the family's help and other times, as Joseph observes, in spite of the family's actions.

The Ancestral Family and Conflict Transformation

As key to his practice of conflict transformation, Lederach points to the importance of identifying the future toward which we wish to journey. He describes that future in language that echoes biblical blessing: *creative, responsive, constructive, and nonviolent.* A vision of this future is important if we are to work in the midst of episodes of conflict toward transformation—transformation of both the antagonists and the culture—and a new way of living.

I do not intend to allegorize the ancestral sagas to make them "fit" Lederach's discussion of conflict transformation. I do find the conversation useful as I ponder the possibilities of transformation in the midst of conflict. The three episodes of conflict above conclude quite differently. Esau and Jacob moved toward reconciliation, but the narrative leaves open whether or not they were fully reconciled. Jacob and Laban managed to negotiate a cessation of hostilities, but their conflict ends with a truce, a bit short of a peace treaty. The conflict among Leah, Rachel, and Jacob was neither well managed nor resolved. Nevertheless, all three of these conflicts functioned within and toward the realization of God's blessing: creativity and community, energy and wisdom, health and peace. In the middle of the conflict, the children of Israel—the agents of God's blessing—were born.

We too find our families, communities, and countries embroiled in conflict. Some of these conflicts can be managed and others cannot; some can be resolved and others cannot. Nevertheless, those episodes in themselves do not mark the end of the story nor prevent the emergence of a new way of living. These episodes exist not solely as islands of disruption, but as part of a larger drama that points toward times and places when "all the peoples of the earth will receive blessing."

Do we see in these biblical narratives people with *moral imagination?* We find narrative moments when the central characters exhibited "the capacity to imagine and generate constructive responses that . . . break the grip of . . . destructive patterns and cycles," such as:

- Abraham's quiet walk with Isaac toward a hilltop sanctuary in the land of Moriah (Gen. 22);
- Jacob's anxious meeting with Esau: Jacob made himself vulnerable addressing Esau as "my lord"; Esau ran to Jacob embracing him as "my brother" (Gen. 32–33); and
- Joseph's tearful reunion with his brothers (Gen. 45:50).

I am reticent to assign the term *moral imagination* to describe the motivating impulse of these biblical ancestors. Lederach's proposal speaks to and out of our culture. It is grounded in our understanding of human personality and character. These ancient narratives speak from and to a very different understanding of the human personality.[15] In general I am cautious about using such specialized terms from our culture to describe the personality of biblical characters.

Instead I suggest that we recognize and internalize the imaginative and constructive responses that we find in these narratives, responses that did serve as a catalyst to transform conflict. Daily we pray for such creativity and courage as we respond to our conflicts. Lederach suggests we will find these qualities in those who have developed a mature moral imagination. That being the case, let us commit ourselves to nurture the development of these capacities.

God's blessing empowers us to act as agents of blessing in a world of conflict. The possibility of transforming this painful world from destructive patterns "toward capacities which are creative, responsive, constructive and nonviolent" both employs and exceeds our imagination and wisdom. I pray that we will foster the inquisitiveness needed to see signs of God's blessed world as it emerges. I hope we will summon the courage and imagination to respond creatively in all the conflicts we encounter, so that all people might receive God's blessing.

---

[15] A good summary of the ancient Hebraic anthropology is found in the article by Robert Divito. The book by Hans Walter Wolff provides the starting point for understanding the anthropology that informs these ancient texts.

Recommended Reading

Robert Alter. *The Art of Biblical Narrative*. New York: Basic Books, 1981.

Walter Brueggemann. *The Prophetic Imagination*. Second ed. Minneapolis: Augsburg Fortress, 2001.

Terence Fretheim. "The Book of Genesis." *The New Interpreter's Bible*. Volume 1. Nashville: Abingdon Press, 1994.

Linda Lantieri and Janet Patti. *Waging Peace in our Schools*. Boston: Beacon Press, 1996.

John Paul Lederach. *The Little Book of Conflict Transformation*. The Little Books of Justice and Peacebuilding. Intercourse, PA: Good Books, 2003.

———. *The Moral Imagination: The Art and Soul of Building Peace*. New York: Oxford University Press, 2005.

Eugene Roop. *Genesis*. Believers Church Bible Commentaries. Scottdale, PA: Herald Press, 1987.

Study Questions

Prepare

Prior to your arrival at the small group, read Genesis 25:19–36:43 (Jacob saga) in a modern English translation.

Encapsulate and retell the story of Jacob. Draw a picture, write a paragraph, or create a diagram to retell the story.

Ask

1. Roop notes that Genesis does "not portray the lives of our biblical ancestors as pious and peaceful" but as "painfully punctuated by crisis and conflict." How were you taught these Old Testament stories when you were younger? How comfortable are you with the idea of conflict among the biblical characters and their families?

2. To what extent does your family and/or congregation exhibit the same crisis and conflict as biblical characters? Are there stories told about conflict, or are these stories rarely alluded to? Can you retell some of these stories in a safe setting?

3. Roop identifies three ways of looking at the nondestructive strategies used to settle conflict. Name these three strategies and describe them. How do they differ? Which strategies do you and/or your church use?

4. What insight can you bring to the subject of peace and conflict in light of your own experience, and in terms of your understanding of the Bible? What possibilities did you discover when reading through the description of conflict transformation?

5. According to Roop, John Paul Lederach's moral imagination "is as much an artistic venture as a cognitive enterprise." Moreover, it is stated that "we must read [biblical narratives] with an artist's soul." What do you suppose this approach means? What insight can be derived from an artistic approach that would be lacking in another approach?

6. Have your impressions about the encounter between Jacob and Esau, in which Jacob demanded Esau's birthright in exchange

for a meal, changed over the years? With which character do you most identify? Who bears the blame? Can you think of conflicts within your life or the life of the congregation that mirror incidents in the life of Jacob?

7. Roop says that Jacob and Laban came to an agreement, not a reconciliation. How crucial is it for both to be achieved? In difficult situations, such as negotiations for peace in the Middle East, is an agreement more important than a reconciliation? Laban and Jacob set up a monument to their agreement. Is a monument necessary? What monuments can you think of that commemorate peace agreements?

8. Jacob runs from Esau, but eventually the two must meet in an encounter. Roop talks about a chiastic flow to the story. What is the meaning of chiasm? Is this something you recognize in life? What lessons of conflict and transformation from the story of Jacob can be applied to life, in the family, in the community, in the church?

9. Jacob's encounter with a "night visitor" seems to be a turning point in the saga. How are we "blessed" by experiences that wound us? Is it possible to see divine intervention at the moment serious events occur, or is it easier to recognize the significance of such moments afterwards?

10. Roop sets the Jacob saga in a larger context of a story about God blessing the people through one family. The point is made that "God intends that all the families of the earth shall receive blessing." Is there a place or moment of blessing that is evident in your lives? In your community? In your congregation? To what extent has moral imagination been present or lacking in your own stories of conflict?

Real Stuff
The Brethren Bible Part Too
and the Heart of the Holiness Code

Frank Ramirez

As I prepared for my first day in first grade I wondered how long it would take for us to get past the baby work and start doing the "Real Stuff." Thanks to a private kindergarten run by a stern head-mistress, I was sure that I was way ahead of the learning curve when it came to school.

I *knew* I was ready for the Real Stuff. Still, imagine my surprise when the very first morning the nuns at Holy Trinity School announced we were actually going to the laboratory! Hooray, I cheered within my heart—the Real Stuff! Not out loud, of course. No one wanted a knuckle rap on the very first day. But it was all I could do to contain my excitement. Chemistry! Beakers and bubbling solutions, measuring and pouring, wearing white gowns over our clothes. Real experiments! Spotless white porcelain everywhere. Because we were all so young I knew everything would be over-sized, but we would manage. This is what school was supposed to be all about! I would show those nuns just how well prepared I was, thanks to Merri-Moments Kindergarten School and Mrs. Orsini.

Okay, maybe I should have cleaned my ears just a little bit before I went to school, but it probably wouldn't have helped. We were not taken to the laboratory, of course, but to the *lavatory*.

Well, at least there was a lot of white porcelain everywhere, and I'd been right about everything being oversized, but this was not what I expected. We were just going to the bathroom. What heartbreak! What a disappointment!

That's been a pattern all my life. While Gnostics, both ancient and modern, try to convince us that the Real Stuff is achieved only by advancing deeper and deeper through one inner circle after another, I find that after a good laugh you recognize that things are simpler than you think. The Real Stuff tends to be obvious, practical, and easily understood. Or at least easier than what I expected.

That proved true when I began to study the topic of holiness in the Old Testament. It seemed to me that I had finally discovered the Real Stuff of the Bible. I called to mind the Kabbala, a mystical interpretation of the Hebrew Scriptures, complete with charts, graphs, and allusive symbols that mystified rather than explained. Surely the Real Stuff of the Bible would be just as difficult to decipher.

Actually, the Real Stuff, like the laboratory/lavatory confusion, turned out to be very simple. Holiness is the concern of much of the Torah, but it is primarily found in Leviticus 17–26, often referred to as the "Holiness Code." Much of it is concerned with the arcane rules surrounding temple worship, disgusting discharges of various sorts, various incorrect sexual practices, who the priests can marry, and all sorts of bathing rituals. Leviticus 19, a unit within that unit, is concerned with how to live daily life. And that turned out to be easy, direct, and obvious. As some in my profession would say, "That'll preach." And it did. My sermons throughout Lent 2009 were all based on these verses, and they turned out to be some of the most interesting messages I have delivered.

What I will call the heart of the Holiness Code, Leviticus 19, is a rather homespun chapter full of the kinds of things Brethren do naturally. It's Matthew 25 kind of stuff.

I thought of Jacob, who woke from his stone pillow in surprise, realizing that his humble bed beneath a venerable tree was "none other than the house of God, and this is the gate of heaven" (Gen. 28:17). What we've already been doing as Brethren turns out to be heaven's gate, and we've got the key.

In brief, Leviticus 19 calls on us to treat both insider and outsider fairly, to love not only our neighbor but the alien as ourselves, to use fair measures, and to celebrate and preserve the diversity present in nature but to consider all of humanity as one. Leviticus 19 suggests that when all else fails, read the directions, including the Ten Commandments. That's the Real Stuff.

It's like James 1:27—"Religion that is pure and undefiled before God, the Father, is this: to care for orphans and widows in their distress, and to keep oneself unstained by the world."

Graydon F. Snyder, former professor of New Testament at Bethany Theological Seminary, used to refer to the letter of James as the "Brethren Bible" because its catalogue of practical ethics and ethical practices based on the teachings of Jesus formed the core of Brethren belief and practice. No other New Testament book contains so many echoes of the words of Jesus outside of the four Gospels.

Leviticus 19, the heart of the Holiness Code, should be called the Brethren Bible Part Too, even though it came first. Like the letter of James it is grounded in practical ethics and ethical practices. Stuff we're already doing. It is based on the teachings of Jesus, of course; it is the teachings Jesus based his ministry on.

So, What Is Holiness?

> The LORD spoke to Moses, saying: Speak to all the congregation of the people of Israel and say to them: You shall be holy, for I the LORD your God am holy (Lev. 19:1).

Holiness (*qadosh*) is the essential quality of the God of the Old Testament. Unlike the gods of the ancient world, who could be described, depicted, sculpted, and carried about, the God of the Hebrews was unknowable, indescribable, mysterious, separate, and wholly other than the creation—neither tied to it nor controlled by it. That is part of the purpose of the story of creation that opens Genesis—it is not meant to give a timetable to creation, but to emphasize that while primeval monsters hover over the state of creation as found when our story begins, God created everything and controls everything. The gods might be controlled by chaos, the stars, or fate. In Genesis it is God who puts things in their place and pronounces them good.

As such God is indescribable. In Exodus 24:9-11 Moses leads the elders up the mountain and they see God, but the only report they bring back is about the color of the floor. Isaiah sees God on the throne of heaven, and all he can mention of the sight is that "the hem of his robe filled the temple" (Isaiah 6:1).

So how do you describe the unknowable? Perhaps by relationships developed over duration. I'm reminded of a line from The Lord of the Rings trilogy, when Frodo asks Tom Bombadil, a folksy but ancient personage, "Who are you?" and the reply comes, "Don't you know my name yet? That's the only answer. Tell me, who are you, alone, yourself, and nameless?" (Tolkien 182).

Not even the name of God is any help. The four consonants of the name of God, YHWH, possibly pronounced as Yahweh, come from the verb "to be." God is.

Still, there is a desire to know more than God's name. And there, too, the answer has to come from God. When Moses responds to the voice coming out of the burning bush, God is self-described by the relationships established in the past: "I am the God of your father, the God of Abraham, the God of Isaac, and the God of Jacob" (Exodus 3:6). If you want to talk about God beyond the name, then call to mind the deeds of God with our ancestors. Or read Leviticus 19 where we are enjoined to act like God.

For holiness is ultimately defined by the relationship we have with God and with each other. This chapter says a lot about the nature of holiness because it defines our relationship with God and with the people of God, and therefore the nature of God. Richard Elliott Friedman in his commentary on the Torah, answers the question, "What is meant here by being holy?" with "It includes most of the Ten Commandments, sacrifices, justice, caring for the poor and the infirm, treatment of women, of the elderly, food, magic, loving one's neighbor as oneself, loving an alien as oneself.

If I had to choose only one chapter out of the Torah to make known, it might well be this one" (378).

Nahum Sarna says that it is unexpected to discover that holiness includes an "emphasis on human relations: respect for parents, concern for the poor and the stranger, prompt payment of wages, justice in all dealings, and honest conduct of business. Even proper attitudes toward others are commanded" (257).

This is reminiscent of a few key verses from the letter of James, the other half of the Brethren Bible. In response to the Pauline formulation that we are saved by our faith, not by our works, James redefines faith by stating bluntly:

> What good is it, my brothers and sisters, if you say you have faith but do not have works? Can faith save you? If a brother or sister is naked and lacks daily food, and one of you says to them, "Go in peace; keep warm and eat your fill," and yet you do not supply their bodily needs, what is the good of that? So faith by itself, if it has no works, is dead. But someone will say, "You have faith and I have works." Show me your faith apart from your works, and I by my works will show you my faith (James 2:14-18).

I am reminded of the story of Rufus P. Bucher (1883-1956), a Brethren evangelist who conducted revival meetings in forty congregations scattered over thirteen states, resulting in around three thousand conversions. He was once cornered at a train depot by an earnest member of another denomination who handed him a tract and asked, "Are you saved?" Rather than base his salvation on a verbal formulation that bordered on magic, Bucher replied, "That is a good question and deserves an answer. I think, however, that I might be prejudiced in my own behalf. You'd better go down to Quarryville (Pa.) and ask George Hensel, the hardware merchant, what he thinks about it. Or you might go to the Mechanic Grove grocer or to one of my neighbors in Unicorn. While there you might ask my wife and children. I'll be ready to let their answers stand as my own" (Morse #53).

Who is Holy? Besides God, That Is

The Torah—the first five books of the Old Testament—seems to be composed of many strands woven together into a whole.[1] There is the Yahwist strand, called that because that portion uses the name of God, Yahweh (which in our translations usually appears as LORD with small caps). By contrast the Elohist strand is so-called because it uses the word for God, Elohim, instead of the name of God. There is also the strand referred to as the Deuteronomist. This consists of the final book of the Torah, and encompasses the historical books of Joshua, Judges, 1 and 2 Samuel, and 1 and 2 Kings.[2]

Leviticus 19 is found in the middle of the larger Holiness Code of Leviticus 17–26. This in turn is found in the midst of what is called the Priestly strand. This strand emphasizes the rituals that the priests of the temple were expected to follow. The Priestly strand puts special emphasis on special people who are part of the priesthood, and special places that are sanctuaries where sacrifices take place. Holiness seems to be limited to the priesthood and the holy places.

But the Holiness Code, planted in the midst of this Priestly strand, contains the extraordinary idea that holiness is not just for the priest and the temple. This is especially emphasized in Leviticus 19. All the people are to seek holiness. Jacob Milgrom, author of a three-volume commentary on Leviticus, calls this a "revolutionary idea" because holiness is "now within the reach of every Israelite provided he or she heeds the cultic prohibitions and fulfills the ethical requirements specified in this chapter" (2000, 1598).

---

[1] For an overview of recent scholarly views of the composition of the Torah (Pentateuch), see the entries on "Pentateuch," by R.W. L. Moberly, in *The New Interpreter's Dictionary of the Bible*, Vol. 4 (Nashville: Abingdon Press, 2009), and "Documentary Hypothesis," by Pauline A. Viviano, in *The New Interpreter's Dictionary of the Bible*, Vol. 2 (Nashville: Abingdon Press, 2007).

[2] The term "Deuteronomic Source" refers to the core material of the book of Deuteronomy. The term "Deuteronomistic" is often used to identify materials in the books of Joshua, Judges, 1 and 2 Samuel, and 1 and 2 Kings that show the influence of Deuteronomy. See the entries on "Deuteronomy, Book of," by S. Dean McBride, and "Deuteronomistic History," by Steven L. McKenzie, in *The New Interpreter's Dictionary of the Bible*, Vol. 2 (Nashville: Abingdon Press, 2007).

Just as there were some who have suggested over the centuries that the Sermon on the Mount is not for ordinary believers, but only for those monastic types who are called out to live separate from society, there may be those who would say that we are not expected to be holy as God is holy since we are not perfect like God.

However, this is not optional. Just as Jesus, in the Sermon on the Mount, said to his listeners, "Be perfect, therefore, as your heavenly Father is perfect" (Matt. 5:48), so Leviticus 19 states clearly that the message is to be given to all: "You shall be holy, for I the LORD your God am holy" (19:2). And fifteen times, to reinforce the necessity of following the dictates of this chapter, verses end with either "I am the LORD" or "I am the LORD your God."

Bernard J. Bamburger addressed this universality for holiness: "Its objective is not to produce a few saints, withdrawn from the world in contemplative or ascetic practices. Rather, does the Torah aim to create a holy people which displays its consecration to God's service in the normal day-to-day relations of farming, commerce, family living, and community affairs" (203).

Or, as Milgrom puts it: "Chap 19 contains fifty-two laws grouped into fifteen subjects. . . . Yet only four laws are given a rationale. None but the first is needed, however. The first rationale covers all the others: . . . 'you shall be holy' . . . 'for I YHWH your God am holy'" (2000, 1374).

By the Manner of Their Living

This whole idea of holiness is also essentially Brethren. The first believers of 1708 reacted against the religious monopoly that the state churches of Europe claimed for themselves, the idea that an apostolic succession of dubious biblical origin conferred upon their clergy a sort of magic that no one else was allowed to wield without their permission.

Instead the Brethren believed in the priesthood of all believers. They knew from the beginning that ritual and ethical behavior, right relationship with God and fair treatment of all, both in and out of the community, was an essential part of the believer's life.

The Brethren rejection of swearing oaths—"A Dunker's word is as good as his bond"—and the more modern expression of this outlook in the song, "A Full Measure Man," by Andy Murray, demonstrate that holiness is 24–7.

But over the centuries we have struggled to define and redefine what this means. Nowhere is this struggle seen more clearly than in the issues relating to the *Ordnung*, or ancient order of the Brethren. The Brethren of the nineteenth century developed a set of rules that applied to everything in daily living from garb to the order of love feast. Brethren were called to follow this order. They were to be nonconformists by voluntarily choosing with their baptism to conform with each other (see Romans 12:1).

Now because the appearance of these nineteenth-century Brethren was preserved through drawings and photographs, there is a tendency to assume their practice was followed by the first Brethren. In point of fact it is believed that while the first Brethren may have set out to be simpler than their neighbors in dress and behavior, there is no evidence that they practiced anything close to the restrictive garb rules of the nineteeth-century church. They probably wore what their neighbors wore, but without extra adornment.

Nevertheless, this frozen picture of the Brethren in their plain clothes was accepted as the norm and ideal. However, the fact that the subject came up for review again and again in Annual Meeting suggests that it was always a struggle. And from 1880-1920 the proposition that the *Ordnung* was a legalistic construct, while true nonconformity (in effect, holiness) lay in the manner of one's living, held sway.

In his book *Could the Church Have It All Wrong?* the late Brethren writer, professor, and minister Vernard Eller challenged the church on the topic of sacraments. He suggested that a study of the Old Testament reveals two separate tracks existing side by side.

On the one hand he identified the Temple track, which conforms with much of what we have identified as the Priestly strand of the Torah. According to this way of thinking there are certain rituals that can only be performed in one way, in one place, and by a limited number of people, specifically the priests. A dizzying array of laws provides the specifics for proper practice.

Eller suggested that some denominations model their practices on the Temple track, creating sacraments, or rites, that are performed in a particular way by a priesthood.

But Eller also said there was a parallel Passover track. Passover is a rite that can take place anywhere, especially in a family setting, does not require clergy, and is authentic even when it includes outsiders. Passover is a historical recreation of an event that took place in the past that places the present participants squarely in the same room where it first took place, while looking toward a future perfection of the meal.

The Passover style of worship is associated not with the temple, but with the synagogue. Worship at the synagogue would be very familiar to the old Brethren. There was singing, and there were prayers, the reading of Scripture, and an exposition based on the text. Though there might be a synagogue leader, any number of people could preach.

Likewise the Brethren love feast takes place in a meetinghouse that is more like a home instead of a cathedral. It's not what many would consider a holy place. It is the people that are holy. The meal is a historical recreation of an event that took place in the past. In effect it places the present participants in the same room as the original participants, while looking forward to the perfect fulfillment with the Lamb in the New Jerusalem. And though there is some disagreement about this point, at different times in Brethren history open communion was and is practiced, which means that the meal is authentic regardless of whether all the participants are members.

Leviticus 19, the heart of the Holiness Code, strongly states that to be holy as the Lord is holy does not require a special building, but rather, ethical behavior among all people, both those within and beyond the community of faith.

Bricks for the Building

I sometimes say my memory is like a haphazard attic—stuff is just thrown in and I can only access those things that happen to lie on top. This nineteenth chapter of Leviticus seems to be just as un-organized.

As the key chapter of this part of Leviticus it is wide-ranging and rhetorically powerful. It extends holiness to virtually all areas of life—family, calendar, worship, business, civil and criminal law, social relations, and sexuality. Most of the laws deal with what we would term *ethical behavior*—defining our relationships with other people.

This fundamental chapter begins with the Ten Commandments, but it doesn't follow them consecutively, nor in the same order as they are found in Exodus 20. They are sprinkled throughout the section.

Sometimes there is value in rearranging the familiar, because it causes us to once more give our attention to what has become too familiar, and perhaps even to see things in a different light.

The chapter begins with two seemingly unrelated commandments squeezed together in one statement: "You shall each revere your mother and father, and you shall keep my sabbaths: I am the LORD your God" (19:3). The two appear back to back in the Ten Commandments as found in Exodus 20 but in the opposite order. Between them is the border between the commandments that regulate the human relationship with God and the human relationship with humanity.

The order of mother and father within the commandment is switched in Leviticus from the order found in Exodus. This is exactly the sort of thing that invited dialogue among the ancient rabbis. One suggested the reason was simple:

> A man honors his mother more than his father because she sways him with persuasive words. Therefore in the commandment to honor (Exodus 20:22) he (God) mentions the father before the mother…. A man is more afraid of his father than his mother because he teaches him the Torah. Therefore in the commandment (Lev. 19:3), he mentions the mother before the father…. Scripture thus declares that both are equal, one is as important as the other" (quoted in Milgrom 2000, 1609).

This imperative is expanded later in the chapter with honor extended to elders—"You shall rise before the aged, and defer to the old; and you shall fear your God: I am the LORD" (19:32). A society that honors and protects the most vulnerable, those least able to care for themselves, the youngest and the oldest, is a stable society.

The next verse, "Do not turn to idols or make cast images for yourselves: I am the LORD your God," is also a portion of the Ten Commandments. The injunction against idols was a consistent prohibition throughout the Old Testament. The ark of the covenant might have featured a throne held up by cherubim, but there was no image sitting on the throne. God was not to be represented by a depiction of any sort.

One typically hears sermons about modern-day idolatry, pointing a finger at things like television, athletics, and money. While this may be an important point, the subtler danger is syncretism, which is a word that, when applied to religion, basically means eating your cake and having it too.

The problem, when it came to God's people, wasn't a matter of rejecting Yahweh for pagan gods. The kings and the people wanted the best of both worlds. They wanted to worship both Yahweh *and* the gods of the nations.

Baal, Molech, or a goddess that some worshiped as a consort to the God of Israel were anathema to the prophets, who called kings, their courts, and the common people back to the worship of a God who jealously refused to allow another to share the throne of heaven.

This may seem disconnected from our own experience, but call to mind how some people will check their horoscope just for fun, or adopt values that have their origin in nationalism or allegiance to a political party. They may adopt spiritual practices from other disciplines. For some people angelolatry provides a diversion from the demands of discipleship. It's a lot more fun to think about fresh-faced angels doing kind deeds and demanding nothing from us. Syncretism means not having to make a choice. It means checking the box, "All of the above."

Syncretism was not an option for the early Christians. By contrast first-century Jews were protected from having the Imperial Eagle displayed in Jerusalem, nor did they have to worship the emperor as a god. Christians, however, were not exempt.

During the first Christian centuries there were many people who lived in the Roman Empire who were grateful for the Pax Romana, the peace of Rome. Roman dominance over the western world had eliminated the many wars that regularly flared up between nations. The first Christians, however, would not take part in the worship of Caesar as a god, and when forced to choose between God and government they accepted arrest, torture, and death.

The Brethren struggled to identify those things that were biblical and those that were worldly, without biblical warrant. This tension, best described in Steve Longenecker's *The Brethren During the Age of World War* and Carl Bowman's *Brethren Society*, pulled Brethren back and forth as they argued whether missions, political advocacy through the Temperance Movement, the advisability of creating insurance companies, and the paid pastorate were in line with biblical order or worldly practices. These stresses contributed to the three-way split of the 1880s, but Brethren together managed to navigate their way through these treacherous shoals.

Also included is the command to keep the sabbath. The commandment in Exodus focuses on the gift of rest to all people, and Leviticus 19:30 reads: "You shall keep my sabbaths and reverence my sanctuary: I am the LORD." This seems to suggest that part of keeping the sabbath is to engage in worship, but the verse is not specifically suggesting that one is to go to church on Sunday. That is one way to keep the sabbath, but I would suggest what the writer is really doing is reminding the people that the sanctuary, the place where they meet, is holy like the sabbath is holy.

There has always been pressure to adopt a legalistic approach to keeping the sabbath. These discussions ignore what an innovation the sabbath was. The cycle of seven days is not determined by either the Lunar or Solar calendar. Neither the 29½ days of the former nor the 365 days (give or take a leap day) of the latter are divisible by seven. The seventh day is a gift from God.

So Nahum Sarna says, "The Sabbath is wholly an Israelite innovation. There is nothing analogous to it in the entire ancient Near Eastern world." He goes on to say that this seven-day cycle demonstrates "God is entirely outside of and sovereign over nature" (111).

However it is spent, the seventh day is holy. It is different, separate, from the rest of creation. It is the rest for the created. The ancients mocked the Jews (and by extension Christians) for their sabbath practice. The philosopher Seneca pointed to the practice as proof that Jews were lazy and they wasted a seventh of their lives (quoted in Augustine 203-204). Horace, Suetonius, Tacitus, and other writers of the Greek and Roman world joined in this criticism.

Continuing, Leviticus 19:11 states, "You shall not steal," like the commandment, but it goes further to make it clear that stealing encompasses a multitude of sins, adding: "You shall not deal falsely; and you shall not lie to one another." Two verses later it reads: "You shall not defraud your neighbor; you shall not steal; and you shall not keep for yourself the wages of a laborer until morning."

This whole packet of admonitions clarifies that economic justice is an essential component of holiness, and by extension, descriptive of God. Know God, no stealing. No God, know stealing.

The definition of stealing is extended to lying, which involves stealing the truth by presenting a false reality. I wonder if punditry is a form of stealing. Pundits appear on television to insist that their partisan viewpoints are always the truth and that their opponents are always wrong. A form of reality is presented that cannot be justified or sustained. In addition, advisors who give the "truths" that are wanted in the form of faulty intelligence instead of bad news that might actually be true, are also stealing from the governments they supposedly serve.

More importantly, Scripture insists that mistreating workers is stealing. Through much of history workers have had very few rights and no recourse when mistreated. Day workers could only hope to receive what was due to them. This passage affirms the rights of workers to their just pay. The struggle of workers to gain some control over their destiny, and the counterattack implicit in so-called right to work legislation which seeks to prevent workers from organizing, could be considered the logical extension of this command to pay workers faithfully and on time.

Along the same lines the end of the chapter reads: "You shall not cheat in measuring length, weight, or quantity. You shall have honest balances, honest weights, an honest ephah, and an honest hin" (19:35-36). Holiness extends into the workplace, and there is no "safe zone" where people are exempt from the truth.

Verse 36 concludes with the phrase "I am the LORD your God, who brought you out of the land of Egypt." In a certain sense the last becomes first. The first commandment is mentioned near the end of the chapter. It includes the reminder that it is God who has created the people. The story of Passover, of slaves who were found by God who heard their cry and led them out of Egypt and into freedom, must never be forgotten. "Did we in our own strength confide, our striving would be losing," reads Martin Luther's famous hymn. Never forget. Never, ever forget.

Leviticus 19:12 ("And you shall not swear falsely by my name, profaning the name of your God: I am the LORD.") parallels the commandment from Exodus 20:7—"You shall not make wrongful use of the name of the LORD your God, for the LORD will not acquit anyone who misuses his name."

So often the word profanity is confused with vulgarity. However, the word profanity really refers to profaning the name of God. In the ancient world there was a certain power associated with the use of names. It was believed that effectively using the name of a god could lead to control of a god.

Using the name of God in an oath is the wrong thing to do because it makes God a cosigner to whatever is sworn. This is a dangerous thing, illustrated by the story of the judge Jephthah, who swore to sacrifice whatever first greeted him when he returned home, if God helped lead him to a military victory. Alas, it was his daughter who greeted him. Bound by his oath, Jephthah murdered his daughter (see Judges 11).

Brethren took this very seriously. They felt especially bound to affirm rather than swear because of the words of Jesus found in

Matthew 5:33-37 and reinforced by James 5:12. This was consistent with their belief that the life of faith was for every day, and not just in certain spheres of life.

Also sometimes misunderstood is the commandment from Exodus 20:16—"You shall not bear false witness against your neighbor." This is usually interpreted as a commandment against lying, but this is not strictly true. This is why the heart of the Holiness Code includes clear language directed at lying.

In my opinion this commandment is aimed primarily at testimony in courts. A society depends on a trustworthy legal system. Without that there is no stability, no trust, no hope. The need for a fair legal system is summed up in Leviticus 19:15—"You shall not render an unjust judgment; you shall not be partial to the poor or defer to the great: with justice you shall judge your neighbor."

Some commentators pair the well-known commandment, "*You shall not murder*," with Leviticus 19:16—"You shall not go around as a slanderer among your people, and you shall not profit by the blood of your neighbor: I am the LORD."

But a better translation might be: "You shall not stand aloof by the blood of your neighbor." Milgrom explains that under the laws of the United States, you are not required to act to save another. If someone is drowning you break no law by not attempting to rescue. Biblical law, however, demands positive action to save someone in danger. You are, after all, your brother and sister's keeper.

Rules such as the Ten Commandments provide healthy boundaries for the benefit of the community. Sometimes you hear comments about how our faith consists of a bunch of "thou shalt nots" that prevent people from doing what they enjoy. These boundaries, however, make it possible for people to live in a secure manner. But at this point this study of Leviticus 19 moves away from the Decalogue and takes up a matter of case law.

Case Law

One of the lessons I remember from junior high social studies was the assertion by one of my teachers that the Constitution of the

United States provided a framework for laws, not the laws them-selves. According to that teacher, laws that masquerade as amend-ments were the least effective. He had prohibition in mind, as I remember.

Leviticus 19 is like a constitution for "right living." For the most part it avoids case law and focuses on the framework for wor-ship and ethical living. But the following passage reads like an opaque piece of legislation:

> When you offer a sacrifice of well-being to the LORD, offer it in such a way that it is acceptable on your behalf. It shall be eaten on the same day you offer it, or on the next day; and anything left over until the third day shall be consumed in fire. If it is eaten at all on the third day, it is an abomination; it will not be accept-able. All who eat it shall be subject to punishment, because they have profaned what is holy to the LORD; and any such person shall be cut off from the people (19:5-8).

At first it doesn't seem to fit in with this section's practicality. But this offering was one of the rare cases where a holy item from the world of the priests was taken from the temple into the home. In an era without refrigeration, food did not stay fresh very long. The cooked meat needed to be eaten soon or not at all. To allow a holy thing to spoil was to render it unclean.

While some might suggest this bit of case law has nothing to do with us, this section is a reminder that some things must be en-joyed now, that life must be lived now. In the desert the people were commanded to only collect enough manna for that day, with the exception of the day before the sabbath when two days worth was collected. Collecting more than what was needed led to spoilage.

In a larger sense much of life is often deferred to the future be-cause of the demands of the day. The day itself, which is a holy gift from God, is wasted or spoiled, because we put off enjoying time with the family around the dinner table, don't get around to tak-ing a trip to a local attraction, or simply tune each other out be-cause of the many worries we share.

The Brethren knew that holiness lay not in their meetinghouse, but in daily living in the holy now. Nineteenth-century Brethren practiced the home altar, a daily time of Bible reading, exhortation, and prayer, usually led by the father of the house.

Exhibit A: The Greatest Commandment

> You shall not hate in your heart anyone of your kin; you shall reprove your neighbor, or you will incur guilt yourself. You shall not take vengeance or bear a grudge against any of your people, but you shall love your neighbor as yourself: I am the LORD (19:17-18).

It is time to talk about that most famous phrase in Leviticus— "you shall love your neighbor as yourself."

The Ken Burns nine-episode documentary on the history of baseball opens a window not only on the game, but on life as well. One of my favorite scenes is where the comedian Billy Crystal recalls the arguments kids in New York had during the 1950s over who was the best center fielder in the world. Was it Duke Snider, Willie Mays, or Mickey Mantle? Crystal creates three different voices representing three different regions of the city, as well as the cogent arguments each would have brought.

The best part of the argument is that it is never going to be settled. There are fun arguments—the best player, the best movie, the best restaurant—that don't need settling. The illuminating part is the discussion. You just go on and on and on.

In a similar fashion it was popular in first-century Judea to argue about the greatest law in the Torah. A person would set forth a verse and defend it, and others would join in with their favorite verses.

In Matthew 22:33-40 Jesus is asked which law is the greatest. The answer should be interesting, but his questioners have an ulterior motive. No matter what law he picks they'll be able to find something deficient in it, something in the way it simply doesn't measure up.

But when these games turn serious it's important to note that Jesus doesn't play any game. He responds on his own terms, quoting not one, but two laws that encapsulate the whole law. The one calls upon us to be holy, or separate, as God is holy. God treats all people as worthwhile and we are ultimately called to treat all people, including the stranger in our midst, as ourselves.

Jesus answered by quoting two verses, Deuteronomy 6:1-4 and Leviticus 19:17: "'You shall love the Lord your God with all your heart, and with all your soul, and with all your mind.' This is the greatest and first commandment. And a second is like it: 'You shall love your neighbor as yourself.' On these two commandments hang all the law and the prophets" (Matt. 22:37-40).

That first part quotes from the Shema, verses that are quoted in every synagogue service. The Shema states that God is God and there is no other—and that we should teach this to all generations. And that we should love God, once again using a word that implies action as well as emotion. And the second law comes from Leviticus 19—"You shall love your neighbor as yourself."

I remember a time when as a pastor in Los Angeles I was seated around a table with a number of politicians discussing serious issues. One told me she thought such civil rights legislation is important because, "You can't legislate feelings, but you can legislate behavior." She was saying, in other words, you can't make people love each other, but you can regulate the way they act toward each other. God's command to love is both a call to action as well as feelings.

It has been more than thirty years since I studied Hebrew at Bethany Theological Seminary under fellow editor Chris Bucher. Nowadays I tell folks that when it comes to Hebrew, I feel like I decode it rather than read it. Still, my strongest memory of working with the language is that Hebrew is a concrete language where things happen. There is less abstract thinking, more solidity.

This is demonstrated in the Hebrew word (*'ahev*) translated as love. It means more than warm fuzzies. Love is compassionate deeds.

Conversely, when it comes to hate, one is neither to shelter the emotion in the heart nor to allow it to take form in action. Jesus said this in effect when he expanded on the Law by saying, "You have heard that it was said to those of ancient times, 'You shall not murder'; and 'whoever murders shall be liable to judgment.' But I say to you that if you are angry with a brother or sister, you will be liable to judgment; and if you insult a brother or sister, you will be liable to the council; and if you say, 'You fool,' you will be liable to the hell of fire" (Matt. 5:21-22).

The heart of the Holiness Code prefaces the most famous words of this chapter with this command: "You shall not take vengeance or bear a grudge against any of your people" (19:18).

Elizabethans were as good at hunting down their enemies as anyone. Theater-goers in Elizabethan England understood this prohibition. Plays like The Spanish Tragedy, The Revenger's Tragedy, and Shakespeare's Hamlet are cautionary tales about the danger of taking vengeance into one's own hands. They were especially horrified with these plays, because not only doom but damnation awaited those who sought vengeance—at least on the stage.

The apostle Paul, with an echo of Proverbs 25:21-22, suggests that replacing vengeance, which belongs to God, with good deeds is its own revenge, in a way, when he writes: "Beloved, never avenge yourselves, but leave room for the wrath of God; for it is written, 'Vengeance is mine, I will repay, says the Lord.' No, 'if your enemies are hungry, feed them; if they are thirsty, give them something to drink; for by doing this you will heap burning coals on their heads'" (Romans 12:19-20).

Milgrom states that Leviticus 19:18 demonstrates "the remedy for taking revenge and nursing a grudge is extending love" (2000, 1403). This is reminiscent of what Martin Luther King, Jr., said on more than one occasion, that the purpose of nonviolent resistance based on love is that one hoped to save the bigot in the process. When we are at our best this is the Brethren response as well.

Since the time of Martin Luther there has been a healthy tension between the place of faith and works for salvation. According to some, salvation is accomplished by a profession of faith—"Jesus

Christ is Lord." That's good as far as it goes, but it seems to suggest that faith is like magic—say the right words, get the desired results.

Most Christians believe that it's not a matter of faith *or* works, but faith that results in works, works that build faith. Peter Nead, the closest thing in the nineteenth century to a Brethren theologian, wrote, "At the final day of reckoning, every good deed shall receive an ample compensation" (168). Nor were good deeds to be limited to fellow Brethren. Earlier in his chapter "Hospitality and Alms-giving" he noted, "The children of God will not only be kind and charitable to their brethren in the Lord, but also to the children of men in general" (166).

Leviticus 19:18 is based on that assumption. Now oddly enough, in Luke's version of this story Jesus asks his questioner to take a stab at the question himself. The same two laws are quoted and Jesus compliments the man. The man, wanting to look good, proceeds to ask Jesus, "And who is my neighbor?" (Luke 10:29). Jesus responds by telling the story of the good Samaritan, implying that even an outsider like a member of that hated group counts as a neighbor.

One of the best examples of this selfless love for neighbor, good Samaritan or otherwise, can be found in the life of the martyred Elder John Kline, of Rockingham County, Virginia. Brethren were especially unpopular in the South during the Civil War because of their united stand against slavery, and their refusal to take up arms for the so-called Glorious Cause. This made them very unpopular with their neighbors, yet they grew food and fed others, including those who stole Brethren property because they did not resist.

On Saturday, April 18, 1863, Kline learned that George Sellers, a member of the Southern army, had broken his leg while attempting to escape to the North. As a deserter his life would be forfeit if he was discovered, and those who helped him might suffer a similar fate.

Nevertheless, John Kline, a doctor as well as a Brethren elder and preacher, answered a summons at 1:00 a.m., and first set and then continued to tend Sellers' broken leg, until it was finally healed and he was able to continue his journey.

Eight days after he demonstrated that a neighbor is whoever needs us, John Kline, who was eventually martyred by Confederate guerillas, spoke on this very passage, commenting, "Brethren, does not this look like the key to salvation? Does it not open the door to a view of eternal life and blessedness? Our Lord says: 'On these two commandments hang all the law and the prophets.' When anyone gives his heart to God in a love like this, I think he is in a saved state" (quoted in Funk 464).

This redefinition of neighbor as outsider might only be implicit in this passage, but in the verses examined in the next section there will be no doubt that holiness goes beyond the greatest commandment to include the sorts of ethical standards that challenge the self-serving, fence-building notions of fear-driven societies.

The One About the Aliens

> When an alien resides with you in your land, you shall not oppress the alien. The alien who resides with you shall be to you as the citizen among you; you shall love the alien as yourself, for you were aliens in the land of Egypt: I am the LORD your God (19:33-34).

> When you reap the harvest of your land, you shall not reap to the very edges of your field, or gather the gleanings of your harvest. You shall not strip your vineyard bare, or gather the fallen grapes of your vineyard; you shall leave them for the poor and the alien: I am the LORD your God (19:9-10).

These are the most radical verses in the Bible. And they are not the work of some communist writing a turgid tome in a drafty London library. This is God who is speaking.

Milgrom says it best: "This arguably, is the ethical summit not only in this chapter, but all of scripture" (2000, 1403).

You are not merely to tolerate the alien in your midst. You are not simply to allow the aliens to live among you when it's financially beneficial to you, then kick them out when there is an economic downturn. You are not to fearmonger the populace with rumors about aliens. You are to *love* the alien as yourself.

And with words that ought to strike guilt into the hearts of those Americans who have demonized aliens and who are themselves the descendants of immigrants, the people are reminded, "for you were aliens in the land of Egypt." Finally the words make it clear that there is no choice regarding this command to love— "I am the LORD your God."

The second passage quoted guarantees the poor and the alien a part in the harvest of the country. It is not a matter of feeling good because we're doing a little charity. There is, once again, no choice in the matter. The poor, the alien, the outcast, the day-laborer, those foreigners, the marginalized, all of these are entitled.

Milgrom says, "Love, meaning compassionate deeds . . . is specified as the basic essentials for life: food and clothing" (2000, 1605). As stated before, love in the Hebrew Bible signals action.

All four of my grandparents were born in Mexico. We crossed over in 1910. Our family has been here around a hundred years. Recently one political party staked its future in part, at least, on a virulent anti-immigrant stance against Hispanics that seemed a safe political bet. Illegal aliens, undocumented workers, or whatever you want to call them, don't vote. They pay taxes (really, there's an all purpose Social Security number they use when they fill out their 1040s). They pay into Social Security and Medicare without any expectation of collecting any benefits. They do the jobs that citizens won't do. However they don't vote.

But the quality of the anti-immigrant stance alarmed Hispanic citizens, many of whom do not necessarily identify or approve of the presence of illegal aliens, but felt as if many Americans were making no distinction between documented and undocumented Hispanics.

Love the alien. There is nothing like this in the ancient world. Aliens were necessary as workers and merchants, but they might or might not have rights in the country they lived in. They could often be abused with impunity. Aliens had no recourse. They don't know the rules, don't know what is fair, and if they are in a dispute with a native, who will stand up for them? But here God proclaims they are to be shown positive love. They matter. "Scripture reveals that love and holiness are intertwined" (Hartley 323).

Love.

Remember, this is a part of a speech delivered to the whole assembly. The purpose is to call the people to holy living, separate living, different living. Loving the alien is an essential part of that. Radical.

As a nation of immigrants we forget we were aliens ourselves at one time. Whether or not we came legally, we were ridiculed, abused, ignored, harassed, and marginalized. Why do we not remember this in our attitude toward the next wave of newcomers?

Of course it's not only Hispanics who are mistreated. After September 11, 2001, citizens of Arab ancestry were demonized, even those who had been residents of the United States for over a century.

These verses from Leviticus 19 are not alone in their witness.

> You shall not wrong or oppress a resident alien, for you were aliens in the land of Egypt (Exodus 22:21).

> For the Lord your God is God of gods and Lord of lords, the great God, mighty and awesome, who is not partial and takes no bribe, who executes justice for the orphan and the widow, and who loves the strangers, providing them food and clothing. You shall also love the stranger, for you were strangers in the land of Egypt (Deut. 10:17-19).

Nor is this sentiment confined to the Torah.

> So you shall divide this land among you according to the tribes of Israel. You shall allot it as an inheritance for yourselves and for the aliens who reside among you and have begotten children among you. They shall be to you as citizens of Israel; with you they shall be allotted an inheritance among the tribes of Israel. In whatever tribe aliens reside, there you shall assign them their inheritance, says the Lord God (Ezek. 47:22-23).

Again and again we are reminded that God takes the side of the orphan and widow, and loves the stranger and the alien.

The book of Ruth, perhaps written at a time when anti-foreigner feeling was strong among the people after the return of the exiles from Babylon, demonstrates the result when these verses are lived in the real world. Ruth, a member of the hated Moabite nation, is faithful to her Jewish mother-in-law Naomi after both have been widowed in Moab. Naomi, tired of being an alien herself, returns with bitterness to her homeland and Ruth follows. The law allowing the alien to glean opens the door for her to display the steadfast love (*chesed*) that is ascribed to God. This impresses one of Naomi's relatives, who marries Ruth not because she is attractive (she's a member of the hated foreign nation after all) but because of (*chesed*). And Ruth is then identified as one of the ancestors of the greatest king of all time—King David. And later, in the New Testament, she is mentioned as one of the ancestors of Jesus.

Why is it we read of Ezra and Nehemiah commanding the Judeans to divorce their foreign wives on the one hand (Ezra 10:3-17 and Neh. 10:28-31), and then in the book of Ruth we read of the importance of foreigners, especially foreign wives, in our midst? The Old Testament does not eliminate the "wrong" theology, but keeps both in dialogue. Ruth and Ezra. Holy and priestly. Brethren scholar Robert W. Neff has been developing the idea that the Hebrew Scriptures contain competing, if not actually conflicting, viewpoints. The presence of two or more viewpoints suggests that God's people were quite comfortable with a vibrant discussion among themselves and within their sacred books, and that the tension between the varying sides did not always have to be resolved.

The book of Ruth is read aloud on the Jewish feast that celebrates the giving of the Ten Commandments. The story reminds us that good things will happen when the people live according to God's laws.

Closing Thoughts: The Extraordinary Ordinary

On that day there shall be inscribed on the bells of the horses, "Holy to the LORD." And the cooking pots in the house of the LORD shall be as holy as the bowls in front of the altar; and every cooking pot in Jerusalem and Judah shall be sacred to the LORD of hosts, so that all who sacrifice may come and use them to boil the flesh of the sacrifice. And there shall no longer be traders in the house of the LORD of hosts on that day (Zech. 14:19-20).

Pots, pans, and bells. They'll all be holy someday. The heart of the Holiness Code began with the words, "You shall be holy, for I the LORD your God am holy" (19:2). Holiness was expanded from the priestly realm to all the people. While holiness will not be fully attained by humans as a result of their will alone—we are, after all, only human—we are expected to attempt it. Not only that, but the prophetic vision is that the world will be turned upside by God and ultimately everything will be holy unto the Lord. At least that's what Zechariah suggests. Leviticus 19 suggests that holiness is a part of everything we do. Zechariah, looking to the future, suggests that this is God's ultimate aim.

Speaking of a day when all the battles shall be done and won, Zechariah sees a time when the most ordinary things, cooking pots or bells on the horses, will be just as holy to the Lord as the bowls set on the altar of the temple. Brethren who value home and hearth would agree, especially when they sit down to the wonderfully ordinary sights and smells of love feast. This is the Real Stuff we spoke of earlier, the heart of the Bible, good things.

Holiness is found in those things which are homiest, the extraordinary in the ordinary. God is not ordinary, but we meet God in ordinary things. Even the kitchen implements in our houses will become holy. Good things are coming. That is why everything is important.

Especially us.

Recommended Reading

Walter C. Kaiser, Jr. "Leviticus." *The New Interpreter's Bible*. Volume 1. Nashville: Abingdon Press, 1994.

Jacob Milgrom. *Leviticus 17–22: A New Translation with Introduction and Commentary*. The Anchor Yale Bible. New Haven and London: Yale University Press, 2000.

Graydon F. Snyder and Doreen M. McFarlane. *The People are Holy: The History and Theology of Free Church Worship*. Macon: Mercer University Press, 2005.

Study Questions

Prepare

Look up the terms "holy" and "holiness" in a Bible dictionary.

Read Leviticus 19 in its entirety. Get out a copy of the Ten Commandments. Underline verses in Leviticus 19 that might correspond to one of the commandments. See Exodus 20.

Ask

1. How did you define holiness before reading this essay? On what did you base this description? How is it defined in a Bible dictionary? What is the author's definition of holiness? Do you have the same definition that you had before looking up the word and reading this essay?

2. Richard Elliott Friedman is quoted as saying, "If I had to choose only one chapter out of the Torah to make known, it might be this one." Why would he make such a statement? What struck you as important when you read through this chapter prior to the session?

3. Describe the larger context of Leviticus 19. What are the various strands of the Torah, as described by the author? Is this idea of several strands woven together to make a whole the way you have understood biblical books to be compiled?

4. To what extent do you and your congregation conform to the world at large? Does the level of conformity rise or fall when there are national crises such as 9/11? How essential is non-conformity in being a people who practice holiness?

5. Consult and compare the lists you made of verses from Leviticus 19 that correspond to the Ten Commandments.

6. What is meant by syncretism? How is it different from what we conceive of as idolatry? How was it experienced in biblical times? How is it experienced today?

7. What are your sabbath practices? How have they changed over the years? What is the appropriate way to observe this day? Have you ever thought of the sabbath as a gift from God?

8. Define your understanding of profanity. What is the author's definition? Do you find yourself using terms like "my God" and "swear to God" very often? Do you hear these in daily conversation? How, if at all, can you challenge those around you with regards to the subject of misusing the word "God"?

9. Jesus stated that a phrase from Leviticus 19:18, ". . . you shall love your neighbor as yourself," is one of the two most important commandments from the Law. This is such a familiar phrase that it can be hard to hear now. Describe ways in which loving your neighbor can be very easy? How is it hard? When is it hard to know who your neighbor might be? When has someone been a neighbor for you?

10. Leviticus 19:33-34 and 9-10 are described as the most radical verses in the Bible. To what extent are the poor "entitled" to some of what is produced? Do you think this takes place in the United States? Why is there resentment against immigrants, especially during times of trouble? Why do you think some politicians stir up anti-immigrant feelings in a nation of immigrants? The verses remind God's people that they were aliens at one time. Do you know when your ancestors, or when you, came to this country? How were they treated? Why do people, once they are settled, turn against the next wave of immigrants?

Will We Listen?
Attending to the Shema in Christian Education

John David Bowman

Perhaps I was an atypical seven-year-old, but I have a vague rec-ollection of a conversation with one of my parents. The haunting words of "Johnny, will you *listen* to me?" reverberate deep within, triggering a sense that the question was not really a question but rather a statement of exasperation tinged with demand. I seem to recall the sentence was followed by another, "Johnny, didn't you *hear* me?" I'm quite confident my parent was not concerned with the function of my auditory nerves. It was a direct reference to something I did not do. I can't recall the provoking issues aside from my assumption that I was reluctant to provide a parent's wish fulfillment. I also suspect it was a repeated offense.

"Hear, O Israel: The LORD our God, the LORD is one."[1] These are the opening words of an ancient recitation found in the He-brew Scriptures. You'll probably recall much of this familiar recita-tion taken from Deuteronomy 6. Within Judaism, the recitation repeated thrice daily is known as the Shema. The full Shema is comprised of three scriptures (Hertz 769). It is so named because the Hebrew word *shema'*, meaning "hear" or "hearken," begins the first of its three parts.

---

[1] The Hebrew has several possible translations, including "Hear, O Israel: The LORD is our God, the LORD alone" (NRSV) and "Hear, O Israel: The LORD our God is one LORD (RSV). This translation is from the NIV.

Grammatically, the Shema is not so much a request as a command. Journalist A. J. Jacobs assumed the Shema was a prayer in his *The Year of Living Biblically*. "In fact, the *Shema* . . . is considered the most important prayer in Judaism" (242). Although in its biblical context the Shema is not technically a prayer, Jacobs' sentiment accurately reflects the level of Jewish reverence felt for the commanded recitation.

Listening or hearing in its fullest sense is central to learning, isn't it? There is a considerable amount of insight we could glean from the Shema to help us reflect upon the learning process. As a matter of interest, we see in the Shema a tiny window into the practice of education among our spiritual forebears. Not only does it directly connect to historical attitudes toward Christian education, but it has implications for faith transmission today. In their *Social World of Ancient Israel, 1250-587 BCE*, Matthews and Benjamin identify education as the power to influence from generation to generation. They point out that while some schools existed, education was informal for the most part (142).

In this essay we'll consider both the content of the Shema as well as the educational technique it intimates. We will discover how both are reinforced elsewhere in the Scriptures. The text reveals the who, where, and how of an ancient educational process. After reviewing the process, we will consider the substance, the embedded core values, of its curriculum found in Deuteronomy 6:4-5. In this simple passage of Hebrew Scripture, we will approach the focal point of a faith passed from generation to generation, and we will discover theological continuity between the Hebrew and Greek Scriptures.

What Is the Starting Point?

> *And these words which I command you this day shall be upon your heart.*
> —*Deuteronomy 6:6 (RSV)*

It begins with the human heart. Right away we know this command is not meant to be taken literally. What pen would we use to scribe on the muscle beating in our chest? Would a person survive such an operation? Ridiculous? Of course. A metaphor it is, then, but for what? In the twentieth century, we tend to associate the heart with emotions. We read or hear "heart," and we image a Valentine's Day in our mind's eye. In the ancient Hebrew worldview, deep emotions were more likely to be associated with one's bowels. The heart, however, was the source of personal motivation. This carries over in our culture with such phrases as, "I don't have the heart for it," which means, "I don't have the will to take a specific action."

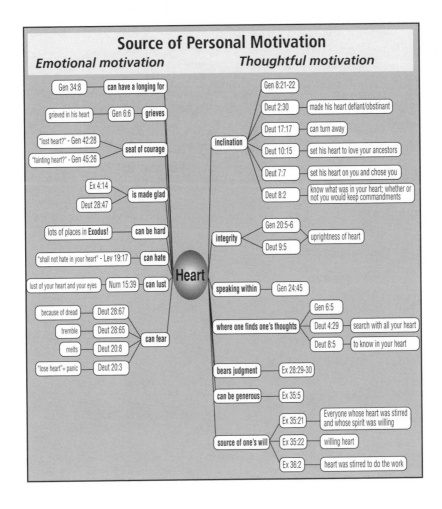

As a way of seeing this use in action, refer to the illustration on the previous page. Here you will see the various ways the Hebrew for "heart" is used in the first five books of the Hebrew Scriptures. The verses fall into two categories (emotions and thought), even as they point to that which motivates a person.[2]

The notion of placing words on one's heart was an ancient way of saying that we are to "take them to heart." In other words, it is important that we learn before we teach. Thank goodness the text does not insist that we fully understand the words we are "taking to heart"! Still, "taking to heart" implies that we hold the words as important and worthy of our reflection, devotion, and attention. Heart (Hebrew *lev* or *levav* frequently conveys the meaning of "mind" in the Bible (Fox 33).

Most people who have taught readily admit that they learn far more than they teach. This is how it should be with all educational enterprises. So, we should not be surprised to learn that the same applies to teaching the faith-laden words found in Scripture. Learning is more than memorization; it is taking things to heart, to the center of our thoughtfulness and the seat of our emotions. It is as though the Shema suggests that faithfulness in education engages our passion as well as our intellectual integrity. As one modern commentator observes, "Words that come from the heart can enter the heart" (Plaut 1374). This reminds me of my college and graduate school instructor of the Hebrew Bible, Bob Neff. One could hardly be in class and not receive both insight and a strong impression of his passion for the text and its incarnation in our lives. He passed on to me and hundreds of others both life-giving knowledge and a passion for a vibrant faith.

Who Is Responsible for Faith Education?

> *You shall teach [these words] to your children.*
> —*Deuteronomy 6:7 (RSV)*

---

[2] The illustration does not include three Torah texts using "heart" where its use as a metaphor is less easily discernible: "heart of the sea" (Exodus 15:8), "heart of the alien" (Exodus 23:9), and a reference to the "uncircumcised heart" (Lev. 26:41).

It is probably no surprise that in an agriculturally rooted culture, education took place in a family setting; the key actors of the educational process were parents and children. "Hear, my child, your father's instruction, and do not reject your mother's teaching; for they are a fair garland for your head, and pendants for your neck" (Prov. 1:8-9).[3] The woman of the household (mother) was the primary teacher. "The role of the mother as teacher was not simply a development of her physical closeness to the children," and her curriculum was not exclusively domestic (Matthews and Benjamin 26). Through the years, decades, and centuries, this parental role has been taken seriously in Jewish and Christian families.

While most Americans take the existence of Sunday school for granted, it has only been around for about 200 years. In the mid-1800s there were church leaders opposed to its existence in no small part because of a fear that it would undermine parental privilege and responsibility in the educational process. This was true among Roman Catholics, Protestant churches, and Anabaptist and Pietist groups such as the Church of the Brethren, Mennonites, and Amish.

In 1839, the Brethren official proclamation regarding whether it was right for members to take part in Sunday schools, class-meetings, and the like, stated that it was "considered most advisable to take no part in such like things" (Cover and Murray 83, Part 1). Missing from the Annual Meeting minutes are the arguments that led delegates to their final determination. Donald F. Durnbaugh, in *The Brethren Encyclopedia* article on the "Sunday School Movement," provides an important clue to their reasoning. "Opposition to the schools came not because the Scriptures were taught in them, but because it was feared that parents would consider themselves free of their responsibility to teach their own children" (1237). Brethren were not alone in expressing such caution.

In 1843, Roman Catholic Bishop Doane wrote,

I should be sorry to think of the Sunday-school as such as a permanent idea in the Church. I do not care to see it stereotyped in

---

[3] See also Proverbs 6:20 and 31:1 for other references to parental instruction.

bricks and mortar. It is the offspring of a superficial, labor-sav-
ing, self-sparing age. It has done some good, but hindered more,
and brought with it much mischief. Crowding in upon the proper
duties, making a working-day of it—a very treadmill of tasks and
teachers, of school-books and school-rooms—a dismal day of
drudgery, instead of the sweet Sabbath of the soul (Michael 196).

Should we have listened to them? One might argue that the results of Sunday school have undermined the family role in passing
on Christian faith from generation to generation. While not true
of all families, increasing numbers of people are hesitant to share
words that express their faith. What keeps them from doing so?
And now, in the last fifty years, we have seen a dramatic loss of en-
thusiasm for being part of Sunday school, which is evidenced by
diminished attendance and greater energy spent recruiting teachers. Will Sunday schools experience a renaissance? Will we, instead,
develop a new corporate delivery system for faith cultivation? Or
will parents once again take up the role assigned to them by the
Shema?

Parents teaching their children was the primary means of faith
education implied in the Shema. Of this process, an ancient Jewish sage, Hafetz Hayyin, suggested that when a child sits on a parent's lap she or he first learns to know the parent, then to love the
parent, and at length to obey (Simon and Bial 193). There is in
this image an ideal of intimacy implied by the parent/child relationship even though in the harsh reality of our world this is not
true of all families. Is it within the realm of integrity to interpret
the Shema in such a way that considers the parent/child image
metaphorical? Might it be that the intent of spiritual nurture is to
be delivered in the context of loving intimacy such as should be in
every family?

If we are willing to include the metaphoric interpretation, it
opens the door to other person-to-person faith sharing. The par-
ent/child relationship can stand for how a person relates to anyone
with whom one has intimacy and influence. Not everyone has biological offspring, but everyone has a circle of influence around

them. Everyone has "children" to teach. We may think of it best with pairings like master/apprentice, mentor/protégé, rabbi/disciple, big sister/little brother, or spiritual director/directee. At the heart of each of these, if it is to measure up to the Shema's description, we would expect that the relationship is one of integrity and warmhearted intimacy.

In his book *Managers as Mentors: Building Partnerships for Learning*, Chip Bell explores the increased emphasis upon the notion of mentors in the business community and other aspects of organizational life. A mentor, he writes, "is someone who helps us learn something that would have otherwise been learned less well, more slowly, or not at all" (5). His book amplifies the methodology we find in the Shema's commanding call for an intimate and caring culture of learning. Bell affirms that in such a setting, both the mentors and the protégés are learners. It is a testimony to the power of an intimate, caring culture of learning.

How Do We Educate?

> *You shall teach [these words] diligently . . . and shall talk of them.*
> —*Deuteronomy 6:7 (RSV)*

Ancient interpreters of the Scriptures spent a significant amount of energy paying attention to the verb in this sentence. Translated "diligently teach" by the RSV, the underlying Hebrew carries the meaning of sharpening or cutting something. It is the word used when describing the sharpening of an arrow or preparing words of judgment. The image evoked is of working with a child like a carver crafting a piece of wood. Sifri, one of the ancient rabbis, taught, "Let them have a clear, and not a confused or stammering, knowledge of the duties and teachings of their faith" (Hertz 771). It is so easy to get bogged down in all the minutiae of dogma and lose the practical significance of the words of the Shema. It is at those times when we need to cut through the layers of tradition, doctrine, and codified applications and get back to basics.

There is another image that can help modern English readers appreciate the meaning of the verb translated "teach." The underlying Hebrew can be translated "to cut in." The image comes from the kitchen. Many recipes call for the cook to "cut in" butter, meaning to incorporate the butter bit by bit. Imagining the process of education this way, the Shema invites us not to overwhelm but to proceed little by little. This appears to be the common practice of education in the ancient Hebrew world. Consider, in support of this concept, Isaiah 28:9-13. While the Isaiah passage is not about education per se, it expresses a note of sarcasm by referring to adults speaking as one might teach a child. "For it is precept upon precept, precept upon precept, line upon line, line upon line, here a little, there a little" (v. 10). As such, it intimates a role of repetition, persistence, and patience.

The combined images of the carver and of the cook provide us with a powerful picture of the educational process in the world of the Hebrew Scriptures. It is to present the cutting edge of faith with all of its core values, instructive paradoxes, and mystic insights. This is to be done patiently and persistently, little by little. One thing at a time improves retention. Even though that thing is knowingly incomplete and inadequate, the wise teacher knows that the next teaching, or the one after that, will flesh out the balancing perspective.

It is not enough to *present* our faith instruction; the Shema instructs us to *talk* about them. The words of the Shema and the concepts they present are to be the frequent focus of family conversation. It is a delicate thing, is it not? One does not want to appear to the child as though our faith is all that we can discuss, but at the same time it is essential that those we love understand just how our faith is connected with the stuff of life: cleaning toilets, changing spark plugs, eating food, listening to music, scoring an albatross, riding a bike, or playing with Legos. Education regarding our faith is a matter of helping others see the important connections of life, while triggering memory of what has been learned before.

To talk about something is to engage in conversation, questioning, and discussion. It is not the same as a lecture; it is a shared exploration into that which is to be learned together. The very concept of learning through conversation expresses a hermeneutic of community. We learn best when our own views can be sharpened, expanded, and enlightened by others.

Where Does Education Take Place?

> *Talk about them when you are at home and when you are away.*
>   —*Deuteronomy 6:7 (NRSV)*

We have learned that the educational process of the Shema is one of persistence and patience. The persistent nature is further illustrated as the scripture points out that the proper place of faith sharing for educational purpose is best made in two places—when we are at home and when we are not at home. Frankly, it makes me giggle! The Shema's subtlety here is hardly missed. We are to be teachers in every life location.

Currently, I live in the southeastern quadrant of Pennsylvania. It is not at all rare in public places to observe people giving quiet but clearly audible prayer before they eat. In my birth family we did not do such a thing. At home, holding hands around the table, we engaged in family prayer usually expressed by my father. In a public restaurant, the custom was to offer a silent prayer (or nod to God) as unobtrusively as possible. When I first observed these Pennsylvania families engaging in verbal restaurant prayers, I thought about Jesus' warning against blowing trumpets: "Do not sound a trumpet before you, as the hypocrites do in the synagogues and in the streets, so that they may be praised by others" (Matt. 6:2).

I think differently now. I've come to suspect that those who engage in such prayers are engaging in religious education for each other and for those of us who observe or overhear. It can be a gentle way of remembering that the world and all of its wonderful delights are not merely ours for the taking, but are resources provided by the One spoken of in the Shema. Such a notion needs to get out into the open, to be talked about in conjunction with the core values found in the words of the Shema.

All conversation about our faith does not have to be so devotional. If our faith is as vibrant as life, there are all kinds of ways to express that what we are doing is related to who we are as a people of God. Sometimes it is more in the way we are doing something than in the words we use as we do it. Sometimes! The Shema reminds us that merely doing the right things does not, by itself, educate. We are to talk about the connections.

When Do We Educate?

> *Talk about them . . . when you lie down and when you rise.*
> —*Deuteronomy 6:7 (NRSV)*

There's that veiled subtlety again. There are a couple of ways we might understand this text. Reclining and rising represent two states of our being. We recline in bed, chair, or sofa, and we rise to walk or stand. More in keeping with the ancients who first interpreted the Shema, rising represents the first thing we do upon waking, and reclining represents the last thing we do before sleeping. The basic point of the text is the same. The proper time for talking about the implications of the Shema is any time.

Exploring the implications of reciting the Shema upon rising, Samson Hirsch writes: "Fresh like the light of dawn that greets you, fresh like the deep breath of pure air that you draw in is the Word of God to remain for you; every day given to you just 'to-day,' every day brought home afresh to you, and its contents to bring afresh to your mind the task of your life that new day" (98). What an exciting way to think about it!

The *Mishna*,[4] in Berakoth 1.3, tells of a disagreement regarding the proper physical stance one should take when reciting the Shema. The school of Shammai taught that one must be recumbent in the evening and standing in the morning when reciting the Shema. The school of Hillel decided that any respectable position

---

[4] The *Mishna* is a law code that is one of the first written documents of Rabbinic Judaism. This particular text discusses the physical posture one should assume when reciting the Shema.

in which one happened to be was quite satisfactory. The point is not to chuckle over how picky people of faith can become about the details, but to be in awe at how important these people of faith felt it was. They took the instruction of Shema seriously. Through the years the Jews came to the practice of reciting the Shema morning, evening, and upon retiring for the night.

We are not to cultivate our faith as a side dish to the entrée of life. Teaching is important so that the words of our faith not only reaches the minds of the hearer, but exerts an influence upon our lives and thus are taken into our hearts.

What Are Some Learning and Teaching Aids?

> *Bind them as a sign on your hand, fix them as an emblem on your forehead, and write them on the doorposts of your house and on your gates.*
> —*Deuteronomy 6:8-9 (NRSV)*

Memory is critical for learning. There is a human propensity toward forgetfulness. The Shema faces this reality head-on and takes it quite seriously. Built into the instruction to teach the words of the Shema is a method of ensuring that one does not forget—creating memory joggers. Among some Orthodox and Conservative Jewish groups, these two verses are taken quite literally as evidenced by the phylacteries (*tephillin*) worn by the men and the *mezuzahs* angled on door jambs. Reform Jews understand these verses more metaphorically, much as one would understand Song of Solomon 8:6, "Set me as a seal upon your heart, as a seal upon your arm; for love is strong as death, passion fierce as the grave."

These verses are not a rabbit's foot on a chain; they're not intended to be magic charms to protect the believer. While the rationale is not explicitly stated in these two verses, subsequent verses in Deuteronomy emphatically point out the perils of forgetfulness. There is no need to stretch the imagination to grasp that the purpose of the *tephillin* and the *mezuzah* was to trigger the mind to remember the words contained within them. "[The *mezuzah*] .

. . is a solemn reminder to all who go out and in, that the . . . [household] . . . is devoted to the ideals of *Shema*" (Hertz 771).

I have placed an adapted *mezuzah* on the doorposts of my home since 1984. I can't say that it has made me a better man, but it hasn't damaged me in any way either. I can say that when I spy it on my way into the house I recall the words inside it, the Shema, and ponder whether or not the core values they express are alive within me. Usually, I end up determining that I want to be more enthusiastic about living them. I have found my *mezuzah* to be a valuable and useful tool in my spiritual growth.

Before taking up the substance of the words we are urged to take to heart, let's summarize the five elements of the method identified in the Shema:

- Take the words of the Shema to heart.
- Teach the words to those under your influence.
- Use patience and persistence in the process (bit by bit).
- Discuss and explore the meaning and implications of words.
- Create reminders helping us recall and live out the Shema.

Writing on the centrality of education in the Hebrew Scriptures, Everett Fox gives special attention to the Deuteronomistic historians' eagerness for generational transmission of the meaning and the practice of Torah.[5] "Crucial here is the concept that constant recital of key ideas and experiences, and making sure to pass them on to new generations, will insure the observance of the commandments and hence Israel's good life on the promised soil" (878).

What Are the Core Values in the Shema?

> *Hear, O Israel: The LORD is our God, the LORD alone.*
> *You shall love the LORD your God with all your heart,*
> *and with all your soul, and with all your might.*
> *—Deuteronomy 6:4-5 (NRSV)*

---

[5] The Deuteronomistic historian represented a tradition of scribes responsible for preserving one strand of the oral tradition, including most of the book of Deuteronomy, along with most of the history that follows through 1 and 2 Kings.

Turning our attention from educational methods found in the Shema, we now are free to enjoy the richness and depth of its substance. We move from *how* to teach to *what* to teach. Deuteronomy 6:4-5 contains one descriptive statement about God and one command regarding our relationship to God. People from Jewish and Christian traditions are likely to be so familiar with these words that they may not have given them full attention.

We have here one of four variations of the commandment/ covenant tradition (Exodus 20:1-17; Exodus 34; Lev. 19; and Deut. 5–6), which attempts to present readers with what is expected of those who adhere to the faith tradition (Thompson 283). The Shema stands as the epitome of these commandment/covenant traditions. As such, we find it carries over into the faith of Jesus as represented in each of the synoptic Gospels explicitly and in Fourth Gospel implicitly.

It opens with a critical faith statement. The underlying Hebrew can be translated several ways. The NRSV, in a footnote, indicates alternative translations to include: "The LORD our God is one LORD," "The LORD our God, the LORD is one," or "The LORD is our God, the LORD is one." Rather than a declaration that there is only one God, all variations point to the unity of God (YHWH, one of the terms for God in the Hebrew Scriptures). God is whole, not fragmented or incomplete.

There is a certain audaciousness displayed when anyone speaks of God. In the ancient world it was believed that to know someone's name was to have power over them. Today, we see remnants of this belief in the act of name-dropping. That ancient belief may have helped determine the scribal practice of not putting vowels into the name of God (YHWH). As readers in the twenty-first century, we no longer have a magical view of the power of names. Yet there remains a certain amount of arrogance when we presume to speak as though we have definitive knowledge of the Divine. Just what do we mean when we speak of God?

How then shall we deal with the bold assertion of the Shema? First, we must recognize that people of faith have a need to give structure to the trust they place in life. The very notion of God, or gods, expresses a human awareness that there is more to life than meets the eye. Thanks to the beautiful gift of human imagination, men and women began to speak of their awareness of this "more to life" using metaphors of familial relationships. Our meaning becomes a bit muddled by the inconsistency of the realities behind these images. Is God really like a father? For a girl or boy who only associated abuse or indifference with fathers, what meaning does that metaphor convey? Language about God easily became more muddled as concepts of magic were introduced. While a magical worldview once prevailed, we now live in a world of scientific pragmatism. Neither science nor magic is particularly helpful when it comes to understanding the realm of the spirit.

And so we come to the boldness of the Shema. To say that our God is one is not to define God, or even to argue the existence of the spiritual realm. Without definition, the Shema assumes that life comprises more than empirical reality. It is not so much an argument as an affirmation that:

- the speaker and the hearer share a relationship with the Divine (our);
- God (YHWH) is the name by which we experience the Divine;
- and God is a unified whole (one).

At the time of its writing, this was a radical faith statement in relationship both to the religion of the Canaanites and to the various traditions about God among the Israelites. Note that the text does not say, "There is only one God"; rather, all variations in translation speak of the unity of the God named YHWH (sometimes spelled with added vowels—Yahweh—and usually translated "the LORD"). As such the Shema was differentiating YHWH from less holistic understandings of God.

When the Israelites entered the Promised Land, they moved into the world of a fully established Canaanite religion; it gave its people a sense of connection with life. In the Canaanite pantheon the head God was El. The fact that Hebrew names for God often include "El" is not insignificant: Elohim, El Shaddai, and El Elyon.

The Canaanite El, whose lordship was over the moral and social dimensions of life, consorted with the female goddess Asherah, whose divinity was connected to fertility. Among their children were Hadad (god of seasonal weather and fertility) and Anat (goddess of war). In Canaanite mythology, it was true that for both generational levels, neither god nor goddess alone was sufficient for fullness of life. The biblical term Baal—meaning owner, husband, or lord—was also used to refer to various gods (Achtemeier 84). It was the term most identified with Hadad (Gray 328).

In the context of making sense of and controlling the agrarian way of life, the Canaanite pantheon held a strong attraction to the Israelites as evidenced by the frequent rise of prophets who challenged the priests of Baal. This was the immediate context of the Shema, although its value remained authentic through the subsequent centuries. It declared that the true God, YHWH, was a unified whole.

The Shema contrasted the God of Israel with the Canaanite high gods who had consorts. YHWH has no need of any consort since YHWH is complete alone; YHWH is not divided but a unity. For the modern reader, it is a reminder that life is not a matter of randomly discrete experiences. We do not live in a fragmented universe; there is an overarching unity. This is celebrated in Bob Dylan's song, *Ring Them Bells:* "Ring them bells, sweet Martha, for the poor man's son. Ring them bells so the world will know that God is one" (Cahill 156). In his book *Ancient Secrets*, Rabbi Levi Meier writes about the application of the Shema this way: "And to live that belief means bringing oneness and wholeness into the world. It means bringing people together, bringing unity and peace into the lives we touch" (208).

So the affirmation about God is, on one hand, a distinction that "your God is YHWH, alone." YHWH has no need of another to become complete. As such the worship of YHWH is an affirmation that in our relationship with YHWH we find the wholeness of life. All of life—as it is—comes from YHWH. Tragedies and joyful surprises alike are a natural consequence of the world created and sustained by God.

On the other hand, when translated differently, the Shema affirms the unity of God. As such it was a rallying cry to consolidate the many different traditions among the Israelites' practice of religion. There were multiple sanctuaries, traditions, and words for God (von Rad 63). Even the names for God held within them various understandings of the nature of God. Elohim, a plural term, was portrayed as the distant Unknowable One, while YHWH was more often portrayed in anthropomorphic[6] terms suggesting intimacy and presence. Therefore, the Shema was a call to unity within the faith.

This first sentence of the Shema bears a curiosity missed by those who read the text in English. The final letters of the first word ("Hear") and last word ("one") are enlarged. According to most of the ancient interpreters, these anomalies draw attention to the importance of the faith affirmation. The first word's ending letter was enlarged, they taught, to distinguish it from the similarly spelled Hebrew word for "perhaps." The last word's final letter was enlarged to distinguish it from a similar word meaning "another" (Plaut 1373). They did not want to risk a reading like, "Perhaps, Israel, YHWH our God, YHWH is another."

The scribes wanted to make certain that this text remained a faith statement with clarity and without reservation. Several Jewish commentaries point out that the two enlarged letters combine to form the Hebrew word 'ed which means "testimony" and "witness" (Hirsch 91). This tradition underscores the role of continuing education and conversation.

On Loving God

> *You shall love the LORD your God with all your heart,*
> *and with all your soul, and with all your might.*
> *—Deuteronomy 6:5 (NRSV)*

The Torah asks us to love three times. We are commanded twice in Leviticus to love human beings, your neighbor, and the alien as

---

[6] This refers to the attribution of human characteristics or traits to God.

yourself (19:18 and 34 respectively), and here in Deuteronomy we are directed to love God. Could it be that only after we have learned how to love each other are we able to love God? The linking of these love-commanding words has ancient roots among Hasidic Jews as well as Christians. Mark 12:29-31, with its parallels in Matthew and Luke, bears witness to how the early church, and possibly Jesus, understood these texts were linked.

If we are to accept that loving God is a core value to be taught, it would be wise of us to examine with some care what was meant by the Hebrew verb *'ahav*, translated "love." Just how, we might wonder, does a person love God? In 1963, William L. Moran revealed the startling meaning of "to love" in this context as "to be a servant" (Kugel 354-355). Moran further demonstrated that the notion of love as service was a fundamental theme in Deuteronomy. So, while pietistic ambition may cause us to yearn for a full scale deep-in-my-heart devotion to God, the scripture is actually asking us simply to be God's servants. There is nothing wrong with intimacy with God, but what is called for is servanthood and discipleship.

In what way is such love, defined as service, to be expressed? Everett Fox's translation of the text is illuminating: "Now you are to love YHWH your God with all your heart, with all your being, with all your substance!" (881).[7] Our scientific minds are aware that the only purpose of the heart is to pump blood. In the context of the Shema, ancient and modern readers alike recognize that these three aspects of humanity are intended metaphorically. Fox successfully sharpened the focus in two of the three elements, but he did not penetrate the meaning of heart (except in his translation's footnotes).

Referring back to the illustration on page 81, the human heart was associated with both cognitive and affective functions. What unified the functions associated with the heart was human will, or personal motivation. As found in the Torah, the thoughts or emotions associated with the heart were all linked in one way or another to the driving force behind a person's behavior. It becomes

---

[7] The NRSV translates the primary objective nouns respectively as "heart," "soul," and "strength."

easy to understand why the "heart" was expanded to be "heart and mind" when we find Mark giving us Jesus' version of the text (see Mark 12:29-30). Mark's Gospel was clarifying the dual dimension of one's motivations embedded in the Hebrew.

Some ancient interpreters explained the meaning of "heart" as "inclination" and recognized the dual inclinations of humanity to be for good and for ill. This dual aspect of the human will might be thought of in terms of Jungian light and shadow. Kugel quotes the midrash *Sifrei* Deuteronomy 32, "'With all your heart' means with your two inclinations, the inclination to do good and the inclination to do evil" (341). It would seem an easy thing to place one's good intentions into the service of God, but quite a challenge to do so with one's evil inclinations. It is a fascinating notion, but what does it mean to love God with one's evil inclinations? Does it mean to convert one's evil inclinations? If one does that, the inclinations are no longer evil. Does it mean to be so focused toward service in the kingdom of God that one is not immobilized by fearing one's potential ulterior or mixed motives? Answers are not easy, but the questions create a wonderful arena for introspection.

A curious interpretation emerges in Meier's *Ancient Secrets*, where he determines that loving God with both inclinations is to convert them into a unity—loving God with both our shadow and light sides—since both evil and good were created by God. Why? Curiously he writes it is because evil has a purpose! We think more deeply about the direction and purpose of our lives when we face pain and death. "Were it not for evil, how many of us would be stirred to action" (216)? Do we need evil to break the inertia of our social apathy?

To love God with all our being (Hebrew: *nefesh*) seemed to some of the ancients to be a bit redundant and so they pondered the significance of "heart and soul" or "inclination and being." The word *nefesh* can be translated as soul, appetite, breath, life-essence or self (Fox 881). Some of the ancients concluded that loving God "with all our *nefesh*" means to love God with our whole life, with our heart's last drop of blood (Hertz 770). How can we avoid understanding the call of Shema to be for anything less than placing the full essence of who we are at the unqualified disposal of God? This is radical in the deepest sense of the word.

The Shema was carefully crafted. Above we saw how its construction avoided ambiguity and uncertainty in the expression of the faith statement. Here in the subsequent command the author took equal effort to explain what is being demanded of the person of faith. YHWH is not satisfied only with one's spiritual dimensions of mental and emotional motivation, nor solely with one's inner self, but also with one's accomplishments. The third aspect of humanity's love that is called for is one's *me'od*, one's material strength. The word *me'od* can refer to physical strength, personal capacity, wealth, or substance. In essence the covenantal love called for in the Shema includes all that one is, was, and shall be.

In his commentary on the Pentateuch, Rabbi Hertz writes of the Shema, "The noblest spiritual surrender and love of God, the Rabbis held, was so to live and act toward our fellowmen as to make God and His Torah *beloved* in their eyes" (770). Another scholar and rabbi, Jacob Neusner, expresses it this way, "to love humanity is to love God in whose image human beings are made, to serve God is to serve other people, and to seek God is to seek God's face in the faces of human beings" (100).

Conclusion

For those of us in the Christian tradition, all faith essentials flow from the deep well of the Shema. Here we learn the importance of an educational process and a faith-centered curriculum.

- Serve God with devotion in ways that recognize our divine connection to others.
- Relate to God holistically and fully in service to God's creation and fellow creatures.
- Influence others within our sphere of influence with intimate caring persistence.
- Remind ourselves of our core values and calling.
- Engage our passion and our intellectual integrity with issues of our faith.

What flows from the Shema is the affirmation of the unity of life—
all creation (sacred/secular), the acceptance of our role as God's
servants, the awareness of our connection to others, and the call to
love and therefore end all homicidal violence.

Did the ancients have a more spiritual, less magical view of
God than we give them credit? Perhaps we see in the Shema the
very pattern of Scripture as a whole. The ongoing instruction is bit
by bit, line by line. The Scriptures do not shy away from paradoxes
of life nor its uncertainties. Sometimes they leave us with a bit of
a headache caused by the unresolved cognitive dissonance. We are
more likely to come to a fuller understanding by looking at the
whole rather than fixating on the parts. We will grow only as we
talk with each other about what we are learning. That is what the
Shema instructs us to do. Perhaps we are left with the need to ask
ourselves: Will we listen to what we *do* understand? Will we *truly*
listen?

Recommended Reading

Everett Fox. *The Five Books of Moses.* New York: Shocken Books, 1995.

James L. Kugel. *How to Read the Bible: A Guide to Scripture, Then and Now.* New York: Free Press, 2007.

Victor H. Matthews and Don C. Benjamin. *Social World of Ancient Israel: 1250-587 BCE.* Peabody, MA: Hendrickson, 1993.

Jacob Neusner. *Torah from Our Sages: Pirke Avot.* Chappaqua, NY: Rossel Books, 1984.

W. Gunther Plaut, ed. *The Torah: A Modern Commentary*, Revised Edition. New York: URJ Press, 2005.

Study Questions

Prepare

In what way is your faith articulated and displayed in your home, your car, or your person?

Ask

1. Read aloud Deuteronomy 6:4-9; 11:13-21; and Numbers 15:37-41. If possible, read as a group from different translations. The Shema begins, "Hear, O Israel . . . ." What does it mean to truly listen to God? What is the message of the Shema?

2. Bowman suggests that "heart" as a metaphor means something a little different in Hebrew culture than in our English-speaking culture? Define and contrast the differences.

3. Who was responsible for faith education in your life as a child? As an adult? In your family? In your church?

4. Bishop Doane is quoted as writing, "I should be sorry to think of the Sunday-school as such a permanent idea in the Church." What were his objections? How valid do you find those objections? What is the best way of transmitting the truths of the faith?

5. What sociological factors would you identify that hinder parent/child education? Did mentoring figure in your own faith development? Does mentoring figure officially or unofficially in your church's structure?

6. What kind of learner are you? Can you read something and understand it? Do you need to have something demonstrated by another for you to learn? Are you a hands-on or a book learner? Do you learn better alone or with others? In motion or seated and stationary? Are you more of a nature person or a musical person?

7. What is your morning prayer? Your evening prayer? Do you recite prayers? Compose them? Are they simply expressed without words?

8. Bowman speaks of "memory joggers" like phylacteries and mezuzahs. What memory joggers do you have in your home? Are there posters, pictures, prints, ceramics, samplers, for example, that express your faith and remind you of it? Is there anything you carry on your person that functions in the same way?

9. What is the significance and the meaning of the Shema according to the author? According to you? What does it mean to say that God is one?

10. Bowman asks, "Could it be that only after we have learned how to love each other we are able to love God?" How would you respond? What does it mean to love God with all our being (*nefesh*)?

Justice-Talk in the Tanakh (Old Testament)

Stephen Breck Reid

The contemporary convention in biblical studies is to identify the first testament of the Bible as the Hebrew Bible. This is an interesting case study in matters of power and justice. Professional societies of biblical scholars dominated by Gentiles recognized that the term "Old Testament" was a confessional category. A group of progressive Protestant biblical scholars started to use the term "Hebrew Bible" or "Hebrew Scriptures" to supplant the term Old Testament. This new language was meant to be more inclusive and acceptable to Jewish scholars in the guild. Another group of scholars maintained that the confessional language of the Old Testament was not only tradition but appropriate, if for no other reason because it was the familiar language of "regular readers."

The result from the debate is the hybridized term Hebrew Bible/Old Testament currently used in scholarly circles. However, this nod to inclusiveness overlooked the recognition that the Jewish community refers to these same books as the Tanakh. Therefore, in addition to the scholarly societies that created the designation Hebrew Bible, there remain two confessional communities that retain a more traditional title. There is the Jewish confessional community that identifies these Scriptures as the Tanakh, and the Christian confessional community that identifies these Scriptures as the Old Testament.

Names matter as we consider the theme of justice found in the Tanakh or the Old Testament or the Hebrew Bible. Each of these names represents a community, and the language of justice is comprehensible in the context of these communities. In the past scholars thought that the search for justice in the Bible could be distilled into something accessible to any enlightened person. What is wrong with typical approaches to the question of justice is a preoccupation with the dominant Western philosophical methods of analysis and interpretation. Such a designation privileges the academy-driven nomenclature of Hebrew Bible over the confessional titles Tanakh and Old Testament. While the non-confessional perspective may be able to discern justice growing out of the reading of the Scriptures, it is a mistake to assume that such discernment will overlap with the confessional understandings of the same material. For that reason I invite us to think about justice in the Jewish Tanakh and the Christian Old Testament. The operation of justice involves small language games like this performed every day in every culture.

The goal of this essay is to provoke further study of the Tanakh and the Old Testament and thereby initiate a contemporary conversation. A particularly Brethren hermeneutic—looking for the *inner* word within the *written* word, the biblical text—will guide the conversation and provide an alternative interpretive framework that's more confessional and less academic. This essay will define and describe the process of justice-talk in the Tanakh/Old Testament. It will then outline three social/cultural roles common in the biblical world—storyteller, lawgiver, and poet—that lie at the heart of this conversation (debate) on justice. The essay will then examine the issue of immigration and the sojourner as a contemporary example of justice-talk. Some applications for the church today will conclude.

Speaking the Inner Word: A Brethren Hermeneutic

When Jesus makes prophetic vocational declaration from Isaiah 61 in his sermon in Nazareth (Luke 4), he mandates it as the vocation of all his disciples. Anabaptists accent the Christian claim that in baptism we are brought into the vocation of Christ, who is prophet, priest, and king. Further, the Anabaptist emphasis on practical Christianity mandates the same prophetic vocation for every Christian. We are to proclaim God's good news—justice-talk—everywhere we go, using God's Word as our guide. Interpretation, however, is not an easy task.

One hermeneutic that might be helpful in avoiding the limitations of antiquarian or essentialist reading strategies dominant in biblical studies is the Brethren threefold use of the *inner word*.

The first use of the inner word is rooted in a theological anthropology. "The early Anabaptists were influenced by the mystics who adopted notions of the inner word. This led them to believe that children inherited not only original sin but inner light" (Brown 53). The inner word, however, was more than an expression of theological anthropology. The second form of the inner word comes from a trinitarian and christological affirmation. "The inner word is often defined as the presence of the Spirit of Christ" (Brown 105). The third and final form of the inner word is found in ecclesiology, the way the body of Christ is known in the world. Alexander Mack "insisted that the inner word needs to be checked by the outer word of the Scriptures and corporate views of the community of faith" (Brown 210).

Rather than a rationalistic modern attempt to digest a prophetic passage into a principle, this Brethren strategy allows the rhetoric of the passage to enflame the inner word read in the community. This corporate reading provides the context for the justice work of the believing community. Justice is always a gift from God (Psalm 72:1), but the ability to perceive what is just grows out of the sometimes fractious conversations of the believing community.

How you frame a question of justice sets the structure for any discussion of justice in the Tanakh. Justice is a broad conversation that touches every aspect of economic, political, and theological life of the believing community. For this reason, this essay will focus on one issue, immigration. This issue was selected because it lifts up the similarities between the biblical context and our modern-day context. And, at the same time it brings to the fore the disparity between the agrarian, traditional society type found in the Bible and the postmodern, postindustrial society type of today's readers. We will prioritize the Pietistic evocative hermeneutical approach over the Anabaptist rationalist hermeneutical approach. The Anabaptist rationalist hermeneutic typically goes back to the Bible to distill the principle that then undergirds a principle for behavior. Once one has the principle, so to speak, the Bible is no longer needed. One already has the prescription. The Pietistic evocative approach, on the contrary, returns to the text time and time again for the evocation—the emotional response—that prompts action. The differences between the biblical world and ours is significant enough that we will try not to prescribe behavior but invite the reader to be prompted anew by the biblical texts.

Justice Defined

When you describe justice in the Jewish Tanakh and Christian Old Testament you cannot paint a still-life. Justice is a conversation, an argument even. The Enlightenment-influenced sensibility to turn the Tanakh, the Christian Old Testament, into a collection of principles that may be applied to contemporary life is limiting, and the project falls short. Justice in the Tanakh is simultaneously nonpartisan, namely it cannot be possessed by one particular party, and on the other hand, it is intensely partisan as it arises out of the give-and-take of various parties. But then what is this justice?

The prophetic word of Amos describes the power of justice. Amos 5:24 proclaims, "Let justice roll down like waters, and righteousness like an ever-flowing stream." English translations consistently render the verb as a jussive, which results in the translation "let justice flow" that is based on the literary context. However, there is nothing in the grammar itself that commends such a reading. The jussive occurs when the speaker wills another entity a certain behavior, in this case "flow." Such translations understand this verse as an exhortation. I will not refute these translations, but I do want to raise a question for us to consider. Could we read this as a simple third person imperfect, "justice rolls"? Could we read this as a description of justice rather than an aspiration, exhortation, or prayer for justice?

The metaphors found in Amos 5 are creatively translated by Francis I. Andersen: "justice roll on like an ocean and equity like a perennial stream" (523). The verb "roll" as it is shaped in this passage has a reflexive as well as passive texture to it. The waters roll themselves, and they are rolled by an external force. The noun often translated "waters" can be rendered "ocean" and hence illustrates the use of the Hebrew verb stem.

Also, the careful reader notices that justice is set parallel to righteousness or equity. The combination of justice and equity occurs several times in the book of Amos (Amos 5:7, 24; 6:12). These three occurrences of the pair create a chiastic structure of Amos 5:7–6:12. This indicates that in the book of Amos and likely elsewhere, justice is part of a larger constellation that includes equity/righteousness.

The pair share basic characteristics described by the verbs in the passage, but even more so by the similes used to personify the waters/oceans and streams. In the American Southwest you have the phenomenon of a wash or arroyo, the dry bed of a stream. The Hebrew term *nakhal* has much the same meaning. Like many of the wadis in western Asia today, they have water in the wet season but hardly none in the dry season. The *nakhal* stream was a seasonal source of life-giving water. However, Amos wants to depict a distinctive type of stream, one that never runs dry no matter the season. The experience in the semiarid climate of the biblical world meant that often a stream was by definition seasonal at best and episodic at worst. Andersen uses the term "perennial." Unfortunately this rendering lacks the vibrancy of "ever-flowing" found in the NRSV.

Amos 5:24 tempers the meaning of justice. Yes, we could go with the simple indicative about justice. We could describe it as hydraulic energy. However, when this term is put in synonymous parallelism to equity with the metaphor of the stream, then the jussive reading of the verb "roll" seems the most reasonable rendering.

For today's reader knows that the hydraulic power of justice should be ongoing. Unfortunately, all too often it is episodic.

The setting of Amos 5:24 tells today's readers something about the nature of justice in the biblical period, and maybe even our own situation. The social change prompted by the prosperity of the Omride dynasty elicited the debate about the nature of justice. We have the witness of Amos, and we can but speculate on the position of Amaziah (Amos 5:7; 6:12). On the other side of prosperity, Jeremiah reflects the debate on justice amid the Babylonian onslaught (Jer. 48:47). Justice in the Tanakh and the Christian Old Testament comes out of the interplay of social roles and circumstances. The biblical texts we inherit today are the result of this interplay. Those biblical texts generate a canonical resource for today's debate on justice. Radical Pietists such as the Brethren claim that the Bible functions as an iconic manner transforming the reader. Prophetic literature finds a special place in the readings of the Pietists because of the role given this genre by the Gospels. Jesus begins his ministry with a prophetic vocation (see Luke 4).

Cultural Roles in the Tanakh

The biblical texts that the Pietistic evocative hermeneutical approach returns to are a repository of the debated conversations of the believing communities of ancient Israel. Entry into the Bible requires an understanding of the socio-religious background of the Bible in order to fully grasp the analogical parallels the Bible provides for the contemporary Anabaptist-Pietist reader. The texts that refer explicitly to justice and righteousness seem to arise from the speech of certain cultural/social roles in ancient Israel. Therefore we will outline the cultural/social roles that are at the heart of the debate about justice.

Storytellers, lawgivers, and poets shaped the cultural landscape and deliberations of the ancient Hebrews, sometimes creating harmony and other times dissonance. The storytellers dominate the early books of the Tanakh. The lawgivers' work is embedded in the narratives. Nonetheless, the plotting of the Tanakh accents the legal material as the community and personal reaction to the beneficial agency of God on their behalf.

Storytellers

The storytellers shaped the social identity through the creation of a common narrative. They provided the narrative framework to legitimize the monarch by helping "monarchs resolve crises which threatened the land and people" (Benjamin and Matthews 237).

Lawgivers

The village structure was built according to laws promulgated by the village elders. The rise of the monarchy created the royal entity of lawgiver. Even the creation of the monarchy demonstrates the following observation: "In the world of the Bible, the basis of law was not philosophy, but crisis" (Benjamin and Matthews 227). These two structures stood side by side in an uneasy juxtaposition. Villages used consensus and social constraint, and the state courts depended on police power. The monarch presided over the network of state-appointed judges to review complaints about household assessments for taxes and military service. The work of the lawgivers was embedded in the dominant narrative of the community. The larger legal units in the Tanakh are official codes.

A. Covenant Code	Exodus 20:22–23:33
B. Deuteronomic Code	Deuteronomy 12–26
C. Holiness Code	Leviticus 17–26
D. Priestly Code	Exodus 25–31; Exodus 34:29–Leviticus 16

The smaller and more famous collection known as the Ten Commandments (found in Exodus 20:1-17 and Deut. 5:6-21) also is firmly ensconced in narrative. This canonical reality embodies the theological affirmation that the law-giving task grows out of the salvation history that forged the people's identity.

Poets

Poetry as a genre spans several social institutions. It is the group that is the most complex. Some poets function as sages, others as prophets, and still others as liturgists. The reason that poetry spans several institutions is because of its inherent properties and effectiveness to provoke listeners. Hebrew poetry is intensified speech that uses rhythm, repetition and parallelism, simile and metaphor.

Sage as Poet

During the twentieth century Alan Lomax traveled the United States collecting traditional music sometimes attributed to the folk genre. Similarly, the sage in ancient Israel gathered the aphorisms from the popular wisdom of the people, adding their own poetic contributions on the nature of wisdom itself.

Prophet as Poet

The overwhelming majority of prophetic speech is presented in poetic form. The prophet uses poetic form a bit differently from the sage or the liturgist. The prophet functions as a rhetorical medium for divine speech. The language event of the prophet must grow out of the religious encounter between the prophet and God. The prophetic books sometime demonstrate the authenticity of the prophet as a poet with direct encounters with God through the visionary call narratives (Ezek. 1–3; Isaiah 6; Jer. 1; Amos 7:10-17). Divine speech through the prophets is poetic speech, rich in metaphor and simile, with a pulse and rhythm that is palpable in the Hebrew. Their words reframe the thinking of the listener through repetition and parallelism.

Priest as Liturgist

Much of the discussion of the role of the priest is preoccupied with priests as state officials who oversee sacrifices and tithes. However, the Psalms are the product of the priestly liturgists. The liturgy is easy to see in some places such as Psalm 15 and 24 where the background is clearly the entry of the pilgrim to Jerusalem. The liturgy is more obscure in some of the laments such as Psalm 88.

Group Identity and Sustainability

The world of the Jewish Tanakh and the Christian Old Testament was an agrarian, traditional society type. As a result, two issues organize the community rhetoric in general and the discussion of justice in particular. The first is *identity*. The traditional society type believed that social well-being depended on the maintenance of the cultural identity of the group. Therefore group boundaries were not very permeable. The depiction of mandated endogamy[1] in Genesis underlines the perceived importance of cultural and theological identity. The challenges that postexilic life and marriage brought to the community are outlined in Ezra–Nehemiah.

Years ago, Mennonite families sent their children to public school. As parents sent their children off to school each morning, their last words were, "Remember who you are!" The issue was one of identity. Faced with a threatening plurality, institutions emerged and persisted to maintain organizational identity. The world of the Jewish Tanakh and the Christian Old Testament was a traditional society type. For that society type relational connection was the mark of health. The relational connection had two symbiotic aspects—the relationship with God and the relationship with the family, which includes the extended family and tribe.

Relational connection is the awareness of ancestral continuity through God. One seldom if ever has a reference to ancestors apart from a reference to how they function as an intermediary or predecessor to the ongoing relationship with God. On the one hand, the text describes a community that recognizes that its God is also the God of Abraham, Isaac, and Jacob (Gen. 50:24; Exodus 3:6, 15, 16; 4:5; Deut. 9:5; 30:20). On the other hand there are points in history that should be transparent to the community. These moments provide an object lesson that God is God in the Pentateuch (Exodus 6:7; 16:12; 29:46; Deut. 29:6). This theme comes to particular prominence in the book of Ezekiel, during the social trauma of the Babylonian exile.

The second issue that pertains to the organization of community rhetoric and justice is *sustainability*. For an agrarian society type sustainability was inevitably connected to the land. The issue of land reform generated by the shift from a village economy to a

---

[1] Marriage within a specific group or clan as required by custom or law.

state economy dominates the debates of the monarchial period. Sustainability and peace overlap. Isaiah 2:2-4 and Micah 4:3*b* talk about how they shall beat their swords into plowshares and their spears into pruning hooks, but they shall sit under their own vines and fig trees, and no one will make them afraid.

> He shall judge between the nations, and shall arbitrate for many peoples; they shall beat their swords into plowshares, and their spears into pruning hooks; nation shall not lift up sword against nation, neither shall they learn war any more (Isaiah 2:4).

> He shall judge between many peoples, and shall arbitrate between strong nations far away; they shall beat their swords into plowshares, and their spears into pruning hooks; nation shall not lift up sword against nation, neither shall they learn war anymore; but they shall all sit under their own vines and under their own fig trees, and no one shall make them afraid; for the mouth of the LORD of hosts has spoken (Micah 4:3-4).

These passages speak of a time of peace. Sustainability, then, combines the economic and material aspects of the Hebrew word *shalom* (Leiter 71). The metaphor of justice as sustainability includes adequate housing, freedom from hunger and joblessness, and finally what the Declaration of Independence refers to as "domestic tranquility."

Immigration in the Tanakh

If justice in the Tanakh (Old Testament) grows out of the debate and contest of ideas, then our contemporary example of justice likewise should also be a matter of debate and contest. We will examine the justice of immigration from the role of storyteller, legislator, and poet. The narrative material points to the sojourner heritage of the Hebrews. Abram/Abraham provides the model of sojourner (Gen. 12:1-3). The early ancestors described in the book of Genesis establish the reality of the Hebrews as a people with an immigrant past. In fact, the immigrant past sets the stage for the exodus. The sojourning tradition shapes the Pentateuch. The wilderness wandering tradition reifies this past.

This passage shows the nature of migration described in the Tanakh. Even so-called voluntary migration is really forced migration. There are three types of forced migration. The story-telling tradition of the Tanakh depicts the Hebrews in each of these three over the course of history. *Derivative forced migration* occurs due to geopolitical or cartographical shifts. For instance, in antiquity when empires come into power such as the transition from the Neo-Babylonian Empire to the Persian Empire, there was a resulting derivative forced migration.

In the twentieth century a number of new states emerged as a result of derivative forced migration. When empires shifted in the twentieth century, it had a reverberating impact of creating new nation-states. The fall of the Ottoman Empire brought about the French Mandate of Syria and the British Mandate of Palestine. When the United Nations ended the British Mandate, the nations of Israel and Jordan became official nation-states. Korea became North and South Korea. The breakup of the Asian holding of the British Empire gave rise to several new nation-states such as the partition of India, Pakistan, and Bangladesh. The breakup of the Soviet Union gave rise to new nation-states such as Bosnia and Herzegovina, Croatia, Macedonia, Montenegro, Serbia, and Slovenia.

Responsive forced migration, a category sometimes mistaken for voluntary migration, comes when a person or population flees political oppression or climatological disaster such as drought or famine.

Purposive forced migration describes a type of migration instituted by a government for the purposes of furthering a hegemonic interest. The most prominent examples of this in biblical times were the resettlement of Judeans to Babylon and the resettling of exiles to Judea with the rise of the Persian Empire (Ahn 5). The story of migration is a combination of push and pulls in modernity. One might reasonably posit that antiquity had some of the same realities.

Storytellers Witness on Immigration

On one level the sojourner is us. On another level the sojourner is "other" (Spencer 104). The sojourner as us means a transgressing of boundaries as a charism. Immigration is a process of transgression, crossing borders. Transgression and border crossing go all the way back to Abram and Sarai. The call of Abram and Sarai begins with an invitation to transgress the boundaries of tradition and enter into an itinerancy of a sojourner (Gen. 12:1-3). Biblical scholar Jean-Pierre Ruiz remembers "wondering whether I was doing the right thing by leaving inner-city ministry in that Latino/a and African American community to return to Rome for a doctoral degree in biblical studies. . . . I was escaping from the daily grind of *la lucha* into the pages of the Bible" (16). Abram, Sarai, and Jean-Pierre Ruiz each in his or her own way heard God's call to transgress the boundary.

The first act of Abram and Sarai begins in 12:1-3, followed by the story of the forced migration of Abram and Sarai to Egypt (Gen. 12:12-20). "To the twenty-first century interpreters who read as and with immigrants, there is nothing unfounded at all about the fears involved in border crossings" (Ruiz 26). The vulnerability increases exponentially when one is undocumented and a woman or child. When we read these stories from the perspectives of the immigrants we see even more texture here. The sojourner described in the story is more complicated. The Hebrew sojourner is trickster instead of solid citizen. The solid citizen is a metaphor for one who corresponds to the given political and economic realities without resistance. The trickster typically is a vulnerable character who must use cunning in order to ameliorate the lack of political and economic power. In the twenty-first century, this is a stereotype that perseveres in light of this biblical trope because it invites the sojourner to be a foreigner as solid citizen without the rights of a citizen, instead of a trickster that provides a power correction. Brer Rabbit and Bugs Bunny are both trickster characters in popular North American fiction and pop culture. Abram and Sarai are co-tricksters. Ruiz and the text itself invite today's reader to empathize but not patronize the immigrant. The patronizing takes the form of depicting the immigrant as the noble "other/outsider." The sojourner who is also an ancestral forerunner was no such solid citizen, but rather a trickster.

The storyteller tradition describes three pivotal characters as self-described sojourners. Jacob is the sojourner and trickster par excellence (see Gen. 25:26-34; 27:1-45). He is a sojourner and a fugitive. Moses describes himself as a sojourner. Like Jacob, he intertwines the roles of the sojourner and the fugitive (Exodus 2:22). Elijah describes himself as a sojourner (1 Kings 17:20). He is a fugitive sojourner. However, unlike Jacob and Moses whose crimes were expressions of ambition, Elijah was a fugitive because of his obedience to God (1 Kings 19:1-3).

Sometimes sojourners were distant relations such as Ephraim, Manasseh, and Simeon, who were considered sojourners when they were in Judah (2 Chron. 15:9). The more distant relations were the Moabites. Ruth was the most prominent Moabite sojourner and refugee, a transitional figure. She is the resident alien who becomes the matriarch of King David (Ruth 1:1). Ruth is an economic refugee. She migrates to Israel as Jacob migrated to Egypt during the famine in his home country. The anti-Moabite sensibilities may be part of the background of the book of Ruth, but explicit descriptions of discrimination are never found.

During the exile the Jerusalem expatriates took on the designation sojourner (see Ezra 6:2-5; 1:4). The Chronicler also refers to the Hebrews as sojourners (1 Chron. 29:15). During the exile the Hebrews found themselves back where they began, in the role of sojourner. However, in this time period the sojourner took on a more expatriate tone. In other words, they were exiles who were sojourners of forced migration. They were not landless (Smith 41). They were deprived of their land temporarily.

The storyteller tradition describes the Hebrews as sojourners, hosts, and refugees. They were sojourners in the early stories of the ancestors, slaves, and later immigrants. They were hosts in the period of nationhood. They were refugees in the age of the Babylonian and even Persian Empires.

The Legal Parameters of Sojourners
Deuteronomy 26:5-9 stands at the intersection of legal code and

liturgy. This passage begins, "A wandering Aramean was my ancestor." The sojourner as "other" occurs often in the legal text. Moreover, the sojourner as "other" is much less transgressive than the sojourner as us. The word transgressive is from the Latin *transgressus* meaning "stepping across." When a community describes its own origins as immigrant the story describes the event as stepping out on faith, but when the writing community describes another community as immigrant or sojourner then it tends to depict that community as stepping across a moral/legal line. It all depends on perspective.

Sojourners are subject to the same laws (Exodus 12:49; Num. 15:16; Deut. 24:14). Certain laws explicitly decree that immigrant or resident alien status in no way abrogates them. The sojourner/alien must adhere to the laws of the land. Some of the legal stipulations to the Hebrews also were binding for the dissenting groups or persons. Whether it is observance of the holy days or the ritual prohibition on the drinking of blood, sojourners/aliens must comply with this stipulation in order to keep their status. Certain consistencies emerge as we look at the laws in the Holiness Code. The lawgivers of the Holiness Code and their colleagues who wrote other collections consistently mandated that some Hebrew observances were compulsory for all, such as keeping the sabbath and the prohibition against the consumption of blood.

> This shall be a statute to you forever: In the seventh month, on the tenth day of the month, you shall deny yourselves, and shall do no work, neither the citizen nor the alien who resides among you (Lev. 16:29).

> If anyone of the house of Israel or of the aliens who reside among them eats any blood, I will set my face against that person who eats blood, and will cut that person off from the people (Lev. 17:10).

> But the seventh day is a sabbath to the LORD your God; you shall not do any work—you, your son or your daughter, your male or female slave, your livestock, or the alien resident in your towns (Exodus 20:10).

> Six days you shall do your work, but on the seventh day you shall rest, so that your ox and your donkey may have relief, and your home born slave and the resident alien may be refreshed (Exodus 23:12).

The aliens/sojourners had to keep certain laws despite their religious experience. Equal legal responsibilities for these laws did not abrogate the social stratification that valued the native population. Nonetheless, some stipulations were there to protect the sojourner/resident alien.

> You shall not strip your vineyard bare, or gather the fallen grapes of your vineyard; you shall leave them for the poor and the alien: I am the LORD your God (Lev. 19:10).

> When an alien resides with you in your land, you shall not oppress the alien. The alien who resides with you shall be to you as the citizen among you; you shall love the alien as yourself, for you were aliens in the land of Egypt: I am the LORD your God (Lev. 19:33-34).

> When you reap the harvest of your land, you shall not reap to the very edges of your field, or gather the gleanings of your harvest; you shall leave them for the poor and for the alien: I am the LORD your God (Lev. 23:22).

> You shall have one law for the alien and for the citizen: for I am the LORD your God (Lev. 24:22).

> If an alien who resides with you wants to celebrate the Passover to the LORD, all his males shall be circumcised; then he may draw near to celebrate it; he shall be regarded as a native of the land. But no uncircumcised person shall eat of it; there shall be one law for the native and for the alien who resides among you (Exodus 12:48-49).

The alien/sojourner is mentioned with the other marginalized persons of ancient Israel, namely widows, orphans, and the poor [Lev. 23:22; Deut. 10:18; 24:17, 19; Jer. 7:6; 22:3; Ezek. 22:7, 29; Zech. 7:10; Psalms 94:6; 146:9] (Spencer 104).

Despite the marginal status of the alien/sojourner, sometimes they rose to economic prominence.

> If resident aliens among you prosper, and if any of your kin fall into difficulty with one of them and sell themselves to an alien, or to a branch of the alien's family, after they have sold themselves they shall have the right of redemption; one of their brothers may redeem them, or their uncle or their uncle's son may redeem them, or anyone of their family who is of their own flesh may redeem them; or if they prosper they may redeem themselves. They shall compute with the purchaser the total from the year when they sold themselves to the alien until the jubilee year (Lev. 25:47-50).

> You shall not wrong or oppress a resident alien, for you were aliens in the land of Egypt (Exodus 22:21).

> You shall not oppress a resident alien; you know the heart of an alien, for you were aliens in the land of Egypt (Exodus 23:9).

In summary, we posit that the equality under the law for the Hebrews and resident aliens redounds back to the heritage of the Hebrews as sojourners in the land of Egypt. This is made explicit in a number of passages (Exodus 23:9; Lev. 19:33-34; Deut. 10:19; 16:9-12). The alien/sojourner sometimes did well, but there were laws written to insure that the rules of hospitality did not fall away.

"While equal treatment for the sojourner is the norm, it is clear that the sojourner does not enjoy the same social status as that of the Israelite" (Spencer 104). Rather, the sojourner is referred to as one of the marginalized of the household in the Decalogue (Exodus 20:10).

Poetic Prophets and Liturgists

Sojourning takes a poetic turn in the Psalms. It comes to embody ethical orientation, whether it is sojourning with evil (Psalms 5:5; 120:5) or sojourning to the temple (Psalms 15:1; 61:5). Psalm 105 (especially vv. 12, 23) echoes the narrative tradition that locates the Hebrews as a race with sojourner origins. The storyteller tradition of the ancestors as sojourners/aliens surfaces among the poetic liturgists (Psalms 39:12 and 105:12). On one occasion the liturgists use the state of sojourning or itinerancy as a metaphor for self-estrangement (Psalms 119:19; 120:5). The prophetic poetic tradition builds on the rhetorical position of the lawgivers. The aliens/sojourners are a marginalized class that should receive protection from oppression (Jer. 22:3, 7; Ezek. 22:7, 29; Zech. 7:10; Mal. 3:5).

Conclusion

The Anabaptist rationalist hermeneutic would try to distill and reconstruct a principle to undergird public policy on immigration. Such a rationalist strategy depends on a technical "expert" as the source of biblical truth detection. A Pietistic evocative hermeneutic, however, will ask what has God put on your heart as these Scriptures resonate in the community of faith?

Here is a way one might put a Pietistic evocative approach to reading justice in the Old Testament. First, let's read the text together, in community. (The biblical texts mentioned in this article might be a good beginning place.) But before we read we need to begin with prayer. If justice is the product of contested speech, there must be a process to help contested speech, from becoming factious speech that destroys community. A prayer for openness to the Holy Spirit is likely the best ointment for this injury.

The method of listening to the text (tuning in to the *inner word*) provides a vital link in this process. The tradition of *lectio divina* might be helpful here. *Lectio divina* includes hearing the text read aloud, followed by periods of silent meditation. It slows down the process of Bible study. *Lectio divina* invites the participants to listen and be silent. The leader will ask participants to attend to images, metaphors, and feelings that they encounter in hearing God's Word. We listen in order to speak most of the time. But listening in silence has the possibility of breaking dysfunctional patterns and discovering more holistic ones.

After an appropriate time of silence, the group should "speak out of the silence," as the Society of Friends (Quakers) would say. If each participant has allowed the text to penetrate, they will have something to share if the Spirit makes it possible. This speech should be disclosive of our shared past instead of our individual positions. Preoccupation with position often sabotages dialogue. If the subject is immigration, you might speak about how your people—either your biological or religious family—got here. Share with your brothers and sisters how that shapes your hearing of the stories, laws, or prophetic passages in play during that session.

Empowered by the Holy Spirit, participants will share in verbal and nonverbal ways (such as body language), and then try as a group to summarize what has been said in a couple of short sentences. The group should take time to develop a summary that rings true for all participants.

Finally, the process should end with prayer and benediction. The closing prayer and benediction should incorporate the voices of the dissent as well as of those in agreement. I remember a Hebrew song we learned in Bob Neff's biblical Hebrew class in seminary. *Hinneh Ma Tov* is the words of Psalm 133:1: "How very good and pleasant when brothers and sisters live together in unity." The unity that gives rise to a better understanding of justice is one that knows the contested speech in its midst.

Recommended Reading

M. Daniel Carroll R. and Jacqueline E. Lapsley, eds. *Character Ethics and the Old Testament: Moral Dimensions of Scripture.* Louisville: Westminster John Knox, 2007.

Daniel L. Smith-Christopher. *Jonah, Jesus, and Other Good Coyotes: Speaking Peace to Power in the Bible.* Nashville: Abingdon Press, 2007.

David A. Leiter. *Neglected Voices: Peace in the Old Testament.* Scottdale, PA: Herald Press, 2007.

Study Questions

Prepare

Find and bring a Bible dictionary to the upcoming session. Bookmark the entry on justice.

Find newspaper or Internet articles discussing the contemporary debate surrounding immigration. Bring those with you to class.

Ask

1. What's in a name? What we call the Old Testament is the Bible for many Jews. To call it the Old Testament in relationship to a New Testament can suggest that it came first, or it can suggest that it is inferior to the other. Some prefer to call it the Hebrew Bible. Many Jews refer to the Tanakh, which includes the initial consonants of the three parts of the Hebrew Bible: *Torah* (the first five books of the Law), *Nevi'im* (the Prophetic books, including the Historical books), and the *Ketuvim*, or the Writings. Does it make a difference what you call something? Which term do you prefer?

2. Reid highlights a Brethren hermeneutic as an alternative interpretive model for us to consider in our conversation on justice. Define the three forms of the "inner light" or "inner word." How does the community of faith work together to define these concepts? Do you find this model helpful?

3. Justice may mean something quite different to one person than another. Consult your Bible dictionary for additional insight into the meaning of the biblical term. Utilizing the essay as a resource, define justice as it is found in the Bible. Define justice as you understand it.

4. Do you live in an area where rivers run all year round, or in more arid climates where rivers are seasonal? What difference does this make in terms of justice rolling, versus justice ebbing and flowing? What is your experience when it comes to the presence of justice in your community?

5. Reid lists three main cultural roles in the biblical world. What are they, and how do they function in the Bible? What roles in our society correspond to these three?

6. What is your definition of poetry? How does the author describe the three categories of poets in the Tanakh? What place does the poet have in our society? What sort of impact does the poet or poetry have in your life? Contrast this with the roles Reid outlines in his essay.

7. Reid connects sustainability to relational connections and justice. Connect the dots between these and other concepts as outlined in the section labeled "Group Identity and Sustainability." What issues are important to you, and to your church? Do any of the passages quoted in this section apply to your issues?

8. Immigration can be a controversial topic and arouses strong feelings. What opinions do members of your group share? Reid states that immigration is a major concern when it comes to justice and the Hebrew Bible. Name three different types of migration/immigration found in the Bible.

9. What images have you heard people use when they speak about immigrants, documented or undocumented? Have you ever heard the term *sojourner* used? Which biblical immigrants are described as sojourners by Reid, and how were they different from each other?

10. Read aloud in your group the passages from the Torah that apply to the treatment of aliens. Describe the rights and responsibilities of the alien or outsider? How do these compare to the treatment generally accorded aliens in our society? Are the scriptural commands applicable? Why, or why not?

Is There Peace in the Old Testament?

David A. Leiter

During the last decade or so, I have engaged numerous people in conversation regarding the topic of peace in the Old Testament. Although many people of faith acknowledge the connection between peace and the Bible, there is a strong tendency by such persons to see this connection as one that relates primarily to the New Testament, thus leaving the Old Testament out of the discussion.

In personal conversations and in teaching and seminar events, I have received three common responses when talking about peace and the Old Testament. The first response is simply a blank stare. Some people cannot see even the slightest connection between peace and the Old Testament. Using the two in the same sentence does not register to them. Either they have not read the Old Testament carefully or they have been taught and indoctrinated to believe that peace in the Old Testament does not exist. As a result, there is an inability to have even a surface conversation about the notion of peace in the Old Testament.

A second response is more inquisitive and somewhat skeptical in nature. I identify this reaction as the "Oh, really?" response. In this case at least a discussion about peace and the Old Testament begins, even if there is a sense of surprise or dumbfoundedness entering the discussion. It's as if the person I am talking with says, "Oh, really, there *is* peace in the Old Testament?" I have encountered two aspects of this response: "Oh, really negative" and "Oh, really positive." An example of the "Oh, really negative" response took place at a pastor's banquet that was held prior to a Church of the Brethren District Conference. I was writing on the topic of peace in the Old Testament at the time and a pastor and his spouse were interested in what I was doing. I explained the project to them. They were not speechless, but they expressed considerable doubt that I would have enough to say about the subject. There was a definite lack of understanding on their part regarding peace in the Old Testament.

On the other hand, the "Oh, really positive" response offers more promise. One example occurred when I was talking to a woman about the notion of peace in the Old Testament. As I made my case, she was intrigued and told me that she never would have put the two together on her own. She said, "Tell me more. There must be something there if you are writing about it." This individual did not know enough to make a solid connection between peace and the Old Testament, but the notion interested her to the point that she wanted to have a sincere conversation about it.

A third response, far more negative and resistant in nature, focuses upon the wars and violence that occur in the Old Testament. The thinking here is that because there is plenty of war and violence in the Old Testament, peace will be hard to come by. To a large extent, this response negates the existence of peace in the Old Testament. I have had people respond to me in the following way: "Well if you say so, then there must be peace in the Old Testament, but I'm sure you must really have to search quite diligently to find it." There is some acknowledgment that the notion of peace may exist somewhere in the pages of the Old Testament, but those who adhere to this response are not convinced and they often send the message that they may not want to be convinced.

If the notion of peace is prevalent throughout the Old Testament, what is behind the lack of understanding and lack of appreciation demonstrated above? As was stated in the introduction of this volume, there is a tendency by many readers of the Bible to dismiss the Old Testament altogether because of the themes of divine wrath, judgment, and war that one finds in the Old Testament. The way this normally plays out is that a God of wrath and war is associated with the Old Testament, and a God of love and peace is associated with the New Testament. Dismissal of the Old Testament on such grounds is simply not good biblical interpretation. God does not undergo a personality shift when one leaves the last book of the Old Testament, Malachi, and encounters the first book of the New Testament, Matthew. The same God exists in both testaments. The dichotomy of God in this manner is not only poor biblical interpretation but faulty logic. One does not have to look far to find passages of divine wrath in the New Testament, especially in the Gospels and the book of Revelation. At the same time, it is quite easy to locate passages that portray a God of love and peace in the Old Testament, such as Hosea 2:18-23 and Isaiah 65:17-25. Most everyone can agree that the Bible, especially the Old Testament, includes passages of divine judgment and wrath that they would rather not deal with or discuss. But it is important not to let such passages prevent students of the Bible from encountering the many significant messages of peace that emanate from the Old Testament.

When interpreters of the Bible limit their scope to seeing only a God of love and peace in the New Testament and a God of wrath and violence in the Old Testament, this view not only sets up a dichotomy of God but also a dichotomy of the two testaments. If the prevailing interpretative view is to see the Bible in this light, readers will certainly place the New Testament over and above the Old Testament. This interpretative view wedges a strong disconnect between the two testaments. By acknowledging that passages of divine wrath and violence *and* passages of love and peace exist in both testaments, biblical interpreters lessen the dichotomy between the two testaments and foster a stronger sense of continuity between the Old Testament and the New Testament.

In addition, whenever biblical interpreters dichotomize the two testaments this way, there is a strong tendency to allow the passages of war and violence in the Old Testament to supersede the passages of love and peace in the Old Testament. When this happens, more often than not, the Old Testament passages of love and peace are virtually ignored.

The purpose of this essay is to give necessary credence to the peace texts in the Old Testament, instead of ignoring them or allowing them to sit on a shelf collecting dust. In no way will there be an attempt to downplay the existence of the violent texts that occur in the Old Testament. Instead, it must be said that the existence of both violent and peace texts in the Old Testament creates a tension that may be uncomfortable for some, but a tension that must be honestly acknowledged. Once this tension is acknowledged, each set of texts can claim their proper place in the biblical canon instead of allowing one set to supersede or trump the other.

One way to give overdue attention to the theme of peace in the Old Testament is to identify significant typologies of peace in the Old Testament. The development of certain typologies of peace allows the reader to grasp particular concepts of peace, and to identify various biblical passages that address these different types of peace in a substantive manner. In *Neglected Voices: Peace in the Old Testament*, I outlined five typologies of peace that exist in the Old Testament. This essay will adopt the methodology developed in *Neglected Voices* by approaching the peace texts in the Old Testament in a thematic fashion. These five typologies, or ideologies, of peace will be discussed briefly in the pages that follow and include: (1) peace and nonviolence, (2) peace after conflict or war, (3) visions of peace, (4) mandates for peace, and (5) peace within the realm of piety and worship.

Peace and Shalom

Before we explore the various typologies of peace in the Old Testament, a brief discussion about the concept of peace is in order. Some suggest that the English word *peace* is quite limited in scope, possessing a negative focus that indicates the absence of something such as war, turmoil, or strife. This mode of thought implies that the word peace lacks a positive connotation that describes relationships and situations in the community in a fulfilling and ideal manner.

Peace, however, has a moderate range of meanings that includes both the positive and the negative. In some cases, peace indicates the absence of war and hostilities, but it also signifies harmonious relationships, security, inner contentment, serenity, and freedom from strife. This range of meanings suggests that peace involves the absence of something such as war, but it also implies positive conditions such as freedom, harmony, and tranquility.

The most common word for peace in the Old Testament is the Hebrew word *shalom*. In some instances *shalom* parallels the English word peace, but in other cases *shalom* means something very different than peace. Just as the English word peace has a range of meanings that involves quite more than the absence of war, *shalom* is even richer in the depth and breadth of its semantic range.[1] *Shalom* has an extensive amount of meanings that range from a simple greeting of an individual or a community to peace with God. The word occurs over 230 times in the Old Testament, and the various contexts in which it is used helps to determine what aspect of the variety of meanings the specific author has in mind.

It is important to note that this essay is a study of peace in the Old Testament and not a study of *shalom*. Numerous studies in recent years begin by talking about peace in the Old Testament or have the word peace in the title, but then focus primarily on the concept of *shalom*. Additionally, such studies tend to argue that *shalom* is a more exceptional word than peace because of its richness and vast range of meaning. Although it is true that the semantic range of *shalom* is much wider than that of peace, neither word is better or superior to the other. They are simply different words.

In an essay such as this, it is helpful to have working definitions of the words *peace* and *shalom*. However, the focus of this essay will be on the concept of peace and how this concept is developed in various sections and passages in the Old Testament. Therefore, I have chosen to develop the abovementioned typologies and ideologies of peace as a more comprehensive and useful

---

[1] Semantic range here simply refers to the variety of meanings that are attributed to a single word. If a word only contains one basic meaning then its semantic range is limited. On the other hand, if a word has a variety of meanings then it has a broad semantic range. This is indeed the case with *shalom*.

way of understanding and explaining peace in the Old Testament. This approach allows us to explore the connections between *shalom* and peace, instead of ignoring one over the other. It also allows us to go beyond focusing on a particular word and to strive to understand how the notion of peace plays out in various ways in the Old Testament.

Peace and Nonviolence

The Old Testament contains stories and occasions where conflict is resolved or addressed in a nonviolent manner. This does not mean that the writers who composed or preserved such passages, or the characters therein, were pacifists. Such texts do affirm, however, that in various instances individuals or ancient Israel as a whole looked to nonviolence to bring about peace in their world.

The identification of such texts as nonviolent merely suggests that alternatives to violence and war have been sought in an effort to move a particular situation forward. Peace is achieved through alternatives to war and violent acts rather than a peace that emerges as the result of violence and war. Each instance of nonviolence is different and arises out of particular circumstances. In some cases nonviolence is chosen because there is no need to resort to violence. In other instances, nonviolence is decisively and intentionally chosen over violence. In additional cases, nonviolence is chosen by an oppressed and weaker party because of its inability to overcome a foe with violence. In such cases, violence may have been chosen if it were an option but circumstances necessitate finding another solution.

Conflict was a constant part of life in ancient Israel. Israel experienced conflict with other nations, among the tribes, and even among families. In some instances, violence was the preferred method in dealing with such conflicts. On other occasions we find that peaceful acts of nonviolence resolved the conflict. The modern term *conflict resolution* has developed into a social science discipline with various theories of managing conflict. But one does not need a college degree to successfully deal with conflict. The Old Testament provides several examples of ancient Israelite culture where individuals or groups of persons embraced conflict and successfully dealt with it.

One example emerges out of Genesis 26:12-33 where Isaac has a series of conflicts with his neighbors. Each conflict pertains to the legal claim to water. Isaac redigs a well that his father had dug, and the Philistines say that the well belongs to them. Isaac lets them have it and digs another, which the local herders lay claim to. Again Isaac relents and allows them to have the well. He moves on and digs a third well. This time there is no contention. After he has an encounter with God, the Philistine officials approach Isaac to make a covenant with him. They acknowledge that God has blessed him, and they want him to promise not to harm them, just as they have done no harm to Isaac. Isaac agrees. They dine with one another, and then establish the covenant, and the Philistines depart in peace.

Isaac had several options when each conflict emerged. He could have attempted to settle the conflicts legally, since the wells in question had belonged to his father. He also could have used force to settle the conflicts. At the beginning of the passage, the narrator explicitly states that Isaac had wealth and power to the degree that the Philistines envied him. And in a speech between the Philistine officials and Isaac (vv. 26-29), Isaac's power is again underscored. Instead of resorting to violence, however, Isaac chose to resolve the conflicts in a peaceful and nonviolent manner. When one well became a problem, he did not contest it, but moved on and dug another. He did so until the conflicts ceased.

In modern terms, we might label Isaac's behavior as conflict avoidance; he did not deal directly with the dispute but simply found water elsewhere. But such behavior led to a sense of prosperity to the degree that the hostile Philistines eventually came seeking Isaac's favor (Wenham 196).

George W. Coats identifies the covenant between Isaac and the Philistines as a non-aggression pact, not an act of reconciliation (194). But Isaac's style of conflict management led to peace and nonviolence, and he reconciled himself with a group of people who ultimately become enemies of ancient Israel (Neff 44).

By responding to the Philistines nonviolently, Isaac found a way to live with them in peace.

Another example of nonviolence in the Old Testament, found in 2 Kings 6:8-23, is unusual in that it describes an unlikely situation between two countries at war. But it is out of the unusual that unexpected and transformative elements often emerge. In this story a peaceful outcome develops in creative fashion.

The story unfolds as Elisha thwarts an attack against Israel by the Arameans (that is, the Syrians). The King of Syria consults his advisors, and they identify Elisha as the culprit. The text does not say how Elisha knew about the Syrian king's planned ambushes. The text also does not say how the king's officers knew that Elisha was the one who was undermining their military schemes against Israel. In a matter of a few verses (vv. 11-14), the Syrian king accuses his officers of treason. They point the finger at Elisha, and the king accepts their answer and commands a great army to capture the Israelite prophet.

As the Syrian army approaches Elisha at Dothan, a servant informs him that the enemy is surrounding them. Elisha then calls upon God to strike the army blind. He addresses the army by saying that they are in the wrong place and, if they would simply follow him, he will take them to the one they are seeking. Elisha leads them right into Samaria and places them in the hand of the king of Israel. God then removes the blindness from the army and they see that danger awaits them. The king appears unsure of what to do next. He seeks permission from Elisha to kill the enemy. Elisha negates the request and instead commands the king to feed the army and send them on their way. The text ends by stating that the Arameans (Syrians) no longer besieged the land of Israel.

The story ends on a curious note. In the midst of a period of ancient Israelite history in which national and international conflicts are resolved through military action, a decision is made to send the enemy home instead of keeping them captive as servants or prisoners of war. T. R. Hobbs argues from a practical military standpoint and suggests that Elisha sent the Syrians home to humiliate them (78). Richard Nelson contends that Elisha used his power to control the situation by ordering a conciliatory outcome instead of a violent one (187). Walter Brueggemann states that Elisha's action brought about a sense of transformation. When Elisha delivered the Syrians, the king was prepared to kill them. But Elisha proposed that festival is better than war, and hostility at the beginning of the text was transformed into peace (13).

Although the narrator does not specifically state what Elisha's motives were in feeding the enemy and sending them away in peace, there's a clue with the last sentence of the narrative: "And the Arameans no longer came raiding into the land of Israel" (v. 23). Perhaps the Syrians came raiding no more because of the nonviolent act of Elisha and the king, or perhaps they stayed away because of God's power. If God is going to strike them blind and deliver them into the hands of the Israelites without a fight, they might as well stay away. Regardless of the practicality of the outcome, Elisha chose nonviolence when violence was a convenient and available option.

In most cases of personal, community, and global conflict, nonviolence is a viable option. Unfortunately, individuals and communities rarely consider nonviolence as an option when they are embroiled in conflict. The two examples in this section suggest that the world might be a more peaceful place if people viewed nonviolence as an alternative when dealing with all levels of conflict. Both Genesis 26 and 2 Kings 6 demonstrate that peaceful conflict resolution is in accordance with God's intentions and purposes as we strive to find ways to live together with all peoples on this earth.

A Post-violence Peace

Another typology of peace within the pages of the Old Testament is a peace that emerges after situations of violence. On numerous occasions a certain peace exists after violent deeds or acts of war. On some occasions this peace emerges when Israel is the dominant power, and in other instances when Israel is dominated by another power. This leads to two primary types of peace after violence and war: (1) when Israel is victorious, a peace in which Israel is the dominator, or (2) when Israel is defeated, a peace in which another power dominates and oppresses Israel.

When Israel Is Victorious

The Old Testament records numerous military encounters between the Israelites and their neighbors. In many of these conflicts, especially those in the books of Joshua and Judges, Israel is the victor. In some instances, the writers attribute the victory to God, and in some cases the writer explicitly states that a certain peace follows the victory. In other words, a military conflict has taken place; Israel has defeated the enemy; and peace, in some sense of the word, prevails.

The book of Judges gives accounts of the various tribes of Israel. What we find in this book is a loosely crafted literary device used to tell the story of the judges. This device takes the form of a pattern or cycle that involves idolatry, judgment, repentance, and deliverance. More specifically, the people sin against God by turning to other gods. Then God brings judgment on the people as an outside enemy oppresses them. The people cry out to God for help, and then God provides deliverance through a "judge"[2] or military leader. The land is then at rest for a time until the cycle begins again. Not every story in Judges contains all the elements of this pattern, but Judges 3:7-11 fits it perfectly.

The narrator begins the story in verse 7 by stating that the Israelites were evil in the eyes of God because they worshiped the Baals and the Asherahs, who were deities of the Canaanite pantheon. God becomes angry and allows Cushan-rishathaim, king of Aram, to oppress the Israelites. The Israelites cry out to God, and God raises up Othniel to deliver them. The text says that God's spirit came over Othniel, he judged Israel, and then he prevailed over Cushan-rishathaim. After Othniel's victory, the land experienced rest for forty years, and then Othniel died.

Of interest for our study is that there was rest in the land for forty years until the cycle of idolatry, judgment, repentance, and

---

[2] The word "judge" here refers to individuals who provided leadership to various segments of ancient Israel during the time between Joshua and David (see Judges 2:16-23).

deliverance started over again, and Ehud became the next deliverer or judge (Judges 3:12-30). Judges 3:11 is not the only place in Judges that discusses rest in the land. After the deliverances by Ehud (3:30), Deborah (5:31), and Gideon (8:28), the text states that the land rested. In Ehud's case, the land rested for eighty years; in Deborah's and Gideon's instances, the land rested for forty years. In Judges when the land is at rest, there is peace. The Israelites have repented of their idolatry, at least for the time being, and God has delivered them from oppression of an enemy. Now that they are in right relationship with God, they have the freedom to live in community by exercising their ideals of equality and justice (Hanson 45).

We have no indication that this indeed happened. We are simply told that the land rested for a time and then the movement through idolatry, judgment, repentance, and deliverance began anew. We do not know if there was internal peace among the people. All we can conclude is that there was a respite from fighting with other nations or outside forces. However vague and brief it was, peace did exist in the land. The narrator is clear about that. The narrator is also clear that this peace is not long-lasting; it fades away when the Israelites turn from God.

When Israel Is Defeated

Numerous passages in the Old Testament speak of peace after an enemy has defeated Israel. Many can be found in the prophetic literature and usually take the form of a vision. The next section will discuss such visions of peace. However, there are some passages that display the existence of peace in a practical sense that addresses the current circumstances of the people. In other words, a military conflict has taken place, Israel has been defeated, and peace in some sense of the word endures.

Jeremiah 29:1-14 consists primarily of a letter Jeremiah sent to the Judean exiles in Babylon. There were two major exilic deportations of the political and religious elite of Judah by the Babylonians. During the first deportation, in 597 BCE, King Nebuchadnezzar of Babylon took into exile the Judean king, Jehoiachin, and his leaders.

In 587 BCE, Nebuchadnezzar quelled the rebellion by King Zedekiah of Judah and deported a second group of exiles. Jeremiah addresses this letter to the first group of exiles shortly after their deportation.

The first three verses describe how the letter got to Babylon: Jeremiah sent it by way of Elasah and Gemariah as they traveled from Jerusalem to Babylon. Although Jeremiah sent the letter, the words in it are attributed to God. The instructions to the exiles are clear. They are to settle down in the land of Babylon and not look forward to returning to Judah and Jerusalem anytime soon. They are to build houses and grow their own produce. They are to marry and have families to build up their population. These are not instructions for the short term but rather for the long haul. Any plans that those in exile make should be for settling down and establishing roots, not for returning home. Apparently Jeremiah's letter was sent to rebuke other prophets, both in Jerusalem and in Babylon, who were giving hope to the people that the exile would soon end (Jer. 28:1-5; 29:8-14, 24-30). Jeremiah stood in clear opposition to those prophets as his message proclaimed a long-term stay in Babylon for the Judean exiles.

Through Jeremiah, God tells the exiles to seek the welfare and well-being of the city of Babylon. In fact, the exiles are to seek and pray for the *shalom* of Babylon, that is, its welfare or well-being. On the one hand, this makes good common sense. Since they are to live in Babylon for a long, undetermined time, praying for Babylon's *shalom* would be in their best interest. On the other hand, this is a strange notion for the exiles to swallow. They are to pray for the welfare and *shalom* of a government that oppressed them, invaded their homeland, and forced them into exile. The call to pray on behalf of Babylon, the enemy, could not have been an easy one to follow. However, this call points to the longevity of the exile itself. The instruction to settle down and to pray for Babylon leads to a sense of peace after the violent events of the exile.

Although we know little of the exact circumstances of the exilic community in Babylon, it is safe to assume that most of the exiles were not dispersed to other lands or sold as slaves. Rather, they were contained in their own communities and had some free-dom to establish a customary way of life (Clements 171). This free-dom, however artificial, constrained, and limited it may have been, allowed for some sense of peace among the exiles. The peace they experienced could not have been an ideal peace, but one that looked ahead for a future within the enemy's land and culture.

The peace of the exiles in Babylon was also limited because the events of the first deportation were still fresh. There was still ten-sion between the Babylonians and the people of Judah. Zedekiah's rebellion, the second deportation, and the destruction of Jerusalem were imminent. While the future of the exiles in Babylon was one of a settled existence and *shalom*, Jeremiah 29:16-18 sees only a fu-ture of invasion, destruction, and death for those who remained in Jerusalem and Judah (Carroll 562).

No doubt this made those living in exile anxious as they awaited the destruction of their homeland. Could the exiles in Babylon experience peace as described in 29:3-7? Perhaps, but this peace would come with considerable cost and pain. At the same time, however, God's call to pray for *shalom* indicates that peace is not always the result of a military victory. Instead of calling the ex-iles to resort to acts of revenge or hostile feelings toward the Baby-lonians, God instructs them to pray not only for their own *shalom* but also for the *shalom* of their enemies (Strecker 134). We do not know if they were able to do this. We do know that the exiles had been defeated and humiliated by the Babylonians as they were carted off to a foreign land in the first deportation. Their future and their peace were to be found "in a blend of normal existence and prayerful conformity to Babylonian life" (Carroll 556).

Visions of Peace

The Old Testament contains many visions of peace: visions that describe all nations living in peace; visions that speak of an endless and everlasting peace involving justice for everyone; visions that call for the celebration of creation; visions where people live in peace with plenty of resources on hand; and visions that speak of a new covenant through which war and violence do not exist. Such visions are replete with powerful imagery that depicts an idyllic time and a place where violence, war, and conflict over resources are a distant memory.

Many of these visions talk of a time in the future when an atmosphere of peace will exist. They are eschatological because the time in the future is not specified. The envisioned peace may lie just around the corner, or it may not arrive until the "end times" when this world as we know it comes to an end. Although many of these visions do talk of a time of peace after a time of violence and destruction, the time is unspecified, and it is not a peace that necessarily and immediately follows a time of war and violence. The distinction between the two is that the visions of peace are visions of the future, whenever that future may occur, and not descriptions of a peace that currently exists.

Many visions of peace in the Old Testament are prophetic in nature. The book of Isaiah contains more visions of peace than any other book. In addition, the books of Jeremiah, Ezekiel, and Hosea also contain such visions. Isaiah 65:17-25 will suffice as a fitting example of such a vision.

The vision begins as God announces a new creation. This creation will consist of a new heaven and a new earth, and it will bring gladness and rejoicing. The author describes this new creation by contrasting it with the current and past circumstances of Jerusalem. Israel is in transition between exile and restoration. The laments in chapters 63–64 that precede this vision suggest that there is still desolation and distress in the land. In the new era of peace outlined in the vision, however, God will rejoice in the city of Jerusalem and delight in the people. The weeping and cries of distress that permeated the city due to the Babylonian destruction will now come to an end. There will no longer be infants who die in a few days following birth, and there will no longer be people who do not live long and healthy lives.

The people will build houses and live in them, and they will grow vineyards and harvest their fruit. Gone are the times when people labor to build houses for others and do not have a place to live for themselves. Gone are the times when people plant and harvest crops only for others to eat the produce. The society envisioned in this passage is not one divided into haves and have-nots. Rather, its resources are distributed equitably among the inhabitants of the community.

The vision concludes with animal imagery similar to that found in chapter 11. Instead of predators feeding off their prey, they will eat together and coexist in peace. The wolf will no longer feed off the lamb, and the lion will eat fodder and straw like oxen. The final sentence of the vision sums up the peace described in the previous verses. People and animals will not hurt one another and there will be no destruction on God's holy mountain. The new creation will be one of long-lasting peace and nonviolence.

Isaiah 65:17-25 is a vision of an ideal community. John J. Collins argues that visions of an ideal nature such as this must be taken seriously as the depiction of a goal toward which we should strive, even if it is not attainable (449). In a similar vein, Paul Hanson suggests that this vision of the new heaven and the new earth is a vision of hope that can spur people into important and needed action. A society wanting to achieve justice and peace must create idealistic visions as well as practical programs that implement justice and peace.

Isaiah 65:17-25 is a vision that draws a fitting end to the book of Isaiah, as the final compilers of the book end it with a message of peace. Peace is one theme designed to help move the community forward from despair to hope, from desolation to restoration, from ruin to rebuilding. The message of peace occurs at various points in the book, but its presence at the end is strategic. It sets the stage for a hopeful future for the people of God—a future that will lead to a transformation from violence to peace, and from domination and injustice to liberation and justice (Leiter 2004, 250).

Mandates for Peace

The Old Testament contains various mandates for peace that issue directives or commands regarding specific behaviors or concerns within the communities of ancient Israel. Such mandates occur in legal statements, prophetic oracles, and proverbs.

Legal Mandates

Legal mandates prescribe particular actions or conduct couched in legal literary forms. Exodus 23:10-11 is an example of a legal mandate for peace. For six years the people are to work the land; they are to sow it, cultivate it, and harvest it. But in the seventh year they are to let it lie fallow. In Exodus 23:11, the primary reason the land must lie fallow is so the poor may eat. This raises obvious questions. If the purpose of the fallow year is to provide food for the poor every seven years, what are the poor supposed to eat during the other six? Will there be enough food for the poor to eat from what grows from uncultivated crops in the seventh year? What are the rest of the people supposed to do for food during the fallow year? One must recognize that the legal rule in Exodus 23:10-11 is extremely brief and is not designed to address the above questions. It simply states that the land must lie fallow every seven years so that the poor have something to eat.

Very few communities currently practice the fallow year legislation outlined in Exodus 23:10-11, and there has been considerable debate as to whether or not such legislation was widely practiced in ancient Israel. Instead of searching for a practical understanding of this legal rule, perhaps it is best to focus on the ideological meaning undergirding the fallow year. The ideological message in the fallow-year rule takes on a humanitarian concern. Apparently the authors of this legal rule were not interested in suggesting practical ways to care for the poor. Instead, they would rather present an ideological statement announcing the importance of helping those who were economically disadvantaged.

When people do not have adequate resources to live, there is pain, anguish, disease, and ultimately death. The fallow-year rule is a mandate for peace as it addresses the gap between the haves and the have-nots. It proclaims that resources for living must be available to all. When people are deprived of such resources, they lack peace and therefore so do their communities.

Today thirty thousand children will die of hunger and preventable diseases (Wallis 48). This is not peace. It is not peace for people afflicted by hunger and related diseases. It is not peace for the rest of the world. And from a theological standpoint, it is not peace for God since the children who die of hunger are God's children too. The mandate for peace in the fallow-year rule does not contain well-thought-out programs for eliminating poverty, but it does send a message of peace that is loud and clear: the poor should have food to eat.

Prophetic Mandates

Prophetic mandates normally occur in the judgment portions of prophetic literature. A typical judgment speech spells out the sins of the people or leaders in question, then predicts disaster or announces judgment. The proclaimed judgment is viewed as a foregone conclusion, something that will indeed happen because of the wrongdoings. Yet the prophetic mandate differs slightly from the typical judgment speech because the prophet calls for repentance and warns of the consequences. If the people choose repentance, judgment might be avoided. If the people do not repent, judgment will occur. Isaiah 1:16-20 serves as a prophetic mandate. Verses 16-18 contain the call to repentance, and verses 19-20 outline the consequences. Verse 19 describes what will happen if the people repent: they will enjoy the land and what it produces. Verse 20 describes what will happen if they do not repent: they will be destroyed by the sword, in this case by other nations.

The prophetic mandate is a mandate for peace because of the call to repentance. If repentance occurs, peace will be the result. Peace will exist because the people will be in a right relationship with God. They were in danger of experiencing divine judgment, but because of repentance now can have peace with God.

Proverbial Mandates

The book of Proverbs contains numerous proverbial mandates. These are found in both the longer wisdom poems in 1–9 and 30–31 and the shorter pithy sayings in 10–29. Some take the form of a short saying, which usually consists of two parallel lines. These are often in the indicative mood; the mandate is implied rather than specifically directed. Others occur as admonitions, normally written in the imperative mood and directing the reader to do or not do a particular action. A statement is often tacked on to the admonition, such as a motive clause, which serves to strengthen the admonition and give the reader reason and motivation to adhere to the admonition.

Proverbial peace mandates espouse the doctrine of retribution, which declares that the righteous are blessed with prosperity and success in life and the wicked are plagued and punished by suffering and misery. Such mandates promote those behaviors and actions that help to create a peaceful society. Typical behaviors and actions of the proverbial peace mandates include: respect of neighbor (Prov. 3:28-29; 14:21; 24:15-16); care for one's enemies (Prov. 24:17-18, 29; 25:21-22); implementation of honest scales and balances (Prov. 11:1; 16:11); care for the poor (Prov. 14:21; 22:16, 22-23; 28:3, 15; 29:14; 31:20); and controlling the tongue (Prov. 10:20, 31; 12:18-19; 17:20).

This list identifies several of the many behaviors in the book of Proverbs that lead to the well-being of society. When people emulate such behaviors, the society envisioned by the wisdom writers of Proverbs will be a society of peace. The primary message is to keep your nose clean. Put in your time. Do the right thing, and you will bring blessings and peace on yourself and your family. In a world ordered by the notion that God rewards the righteous and punishes the wicked, you will bring peace to the world if you adhere to the various mandates for peace and follow the righteous path.

The above descriptions of three types of mandates in the Old Testament show that all three are at times concerned with the notion of peace. Strikingly, the legal, prophetic, and proverbial mandates rarely contain the Hebrew term *shalom* (peace), but they deal indirectly with issues involving peace, such as equality, love of enemies, and a right relationship with God. The mandates of peace instruct and educate readers of the importance of creating a community or an environment in which peace must take precedence. Such mandates are saturated with sympathy for the disadvantaged of society. In this way they attempt to transform the plight of those in marginalized situations in an effort to lead the community as a whole to a larger sense of peace. Peace can indeed exist among the people if the ideas and notions embedded in the mandates become internalized in their thinking and behavior.

Piety and Peace

So far we have identified the notion of peace in Old Testament story and narrative, prophetic discourse, legal material, and proverbial sayings. The notion of peace is prevalent in another literary framework in the Old Testament: the Psalms. The book of Psalms is often called the prayer book or hymnbook of ancient Israel (Anderson and Bishop 10). For the most part, the Psalms reflect the piety of the people of ancient Israel. The term *piety* here will be used in a general way to refer to materials in the Old Testament that have a "worship" flavor to them. That is to say, those materials that consist of prayers, praise, laments, blessings, and benedictions reflect a sense of piety—worshipful connection—between the people of ancient Israel and God.

When we examine the liturgical and piety resources of the Old Testament, particularly in the Psalms, we find that peace is an important concept in some of them. And because of the connection between peace and worship in the Psalms, we can conclude that peace is a significant component in the piety of ancient Israel. In this sense peace and piety go together.

Not all of the Old Testament psalms follow the same format, nor do they convey the same message. In fact, there is a great deal of variety in their literary character. There are hymns of praise, which lift up the glory and greatness of God and center around God's involvement in the ancient Israelite community. There are also lament psalms, which express extreme sorrow and distress on behalf of an individual or the community as a whole. In addition to these major types are psalms of thanksgiving, psalms of trust, creation psalms, enthronement psalms (focusing on God as king), royal psalms (extolling the human king), hymns of Zion, Torah psalms, wisdom psalms, and storytelling psalms.

These literary categories help us understand the nature and character of individual psalms. When we identify those psalms that lift up the notion of peace, it helps to classify them according to their literary function within the larger genre of the psalm.

There are four major categories of psalms that connect the notions of piety and peace. Hymns of praise that lift up the notion of peace include Psalm 147 and Psalm 29. Lament psalms of peace include Psalm 85 and Psalm 120. Psalms that contain prayers of peace include Psalm 122 and Psalm 72. And a prime example of a psalm that contains a blessing of peace is Psalm 128.

On occasion, religious communities are criticized for not upholding the spiritual element in their call for peace around the world. The Old Testament psalms and many religious communities today understand that it is virtually impossible to issue a call for peace without incorporating that call in a worship context. The call for peace must involve worship of God to give its issuers a spiritual grounding, making that call effective and significant. In essence, the call for peace becomes a call to worship the Lord our God. Such a call is highly evident in the Psalter of ancient Israel.

Conclusion

This study of five typologies of peace in the Old Testament presents several implications for the church. The primary implication is, of course, that peace is central to the Old Testament. That peace is significant and widespread throughout the Old Testament has not been given adequate press in Christian communities. Not only is this true in the Christian community at large, but also in the Anabaptist tradition, which by and large holds a Marcionite view that the Old Testament is either relegated a secondary status to that of the New Testament or simply ignored altogether. This study attempts to overcome the tendency to deny the existence of peace in the Old Testament just because we find the notions of violence and the wrath of God there as well.

A second implication of this study is the hope that it may inspire others to explore peace passages in the Old Testament in addition to the ones examined here. The passages that exemplify the five typologies merely demonstrate the validity of each typology.

Perhaps this study can encourage additional, more comprehensive studies.

A third implication is the possibility of prompting further discussion on how the church may come to terms with the fact that the Old Testament contains passages of extreme violence *and* passages that are pro-peace. While many studies in recent years have explored the notion of war and violence in the Old Testament, this essay has attempted to explore peace in the Old Testament. The question that remains for further study and examination is whether or not the two concepts can be reconciled and, if so, how that is to be worked out. To put it another way, what is one to do with the existence of both concepts in the Old Testament, and how does their existence affect our faith and our understanding of God?

A fourth implication of this study is examining how peace texts in the Old Testament serve as a springboard in thinking about and creating peace in today's world. The post-violence peace passages can help us as we anticipate a time of peace after war. The nonviolent passages can send the message that we too can resort to means of nonviolence when it is very tempting to fall back on violence to resolve conflict. The visionary passages of peace can stimulate creativity, helping us envision scenarios of peace when peace seems a remote possibility. Change for the better often begins with visionary aspirations that lead to practical realities. The mandates for peace in the Old Testament can remind us that we must develop and follow certain mandates and rules to generate a long-lasting peace among the people with whom we live. And the piety and peace passages serve as a model for finding and developing liturgical materials of peace for our worship. They emphasize the fact that peace comes not only from what we do but out of our relationship with God. Out of our worship of God, peace and peacemaking can filter into our daily living.

This essay attempts to shine light on the peace passages in the Old Testament. It strongly suggests that we need not begin by looking at the concept of war and violence when addressing the concept of peace in the Old Testament. The conversation can start off with a discussion of peace. The hope is that when conversation emerges regarding the absence or presence of peace in the Old Testament, students and readers of the Bible will be able to identify various passages and address the blank stares and comments that suggest peace is nonexistent or a sidebar in the Old Testament. On the contrary, peace is a central concept in the Old Testament that gave life to the people of ancient Israel, and can give life to us today as we worship God and attempt to further God's kingdom here on earth.

Recommended Reading

Dianne Bergant. "Peace in a Universal Order." *Biblical and Theological Reflections on the Challenge of Peace*. Ed. John T. Pawlikowski and Donald Senior. Wilmington: Michael Glazier, 1984: 17-29.

Walter Brueggemann. *Peace*. Understanding Biblical Themes. St. Louis: Chalice Press, 2001. This reprint was originally published as *Living Toward a Vision: Biblical Reflection on Shalom*. Philadelphia: United Church Press, 1976.

Douglas Gwyn, et al. *A Declaration on Peace: In God's People the World's Renewal Has Begun*. Scottdale, PA: Herald Press, 1991.

David A. Leiter. *Neglected Voices: Peace in the Old Testament*. Scottdale, PA: Herald Press, 2007.

Millard C. Lind. "Perspectives on War and Peace in the Hebrew Bible." *Monotheism, Power, Justice: Collected Old Testament Essays*. Elkhart: Institute of Mennonite Studies, 1990: 171-81.

Albert Curry Winn. *Ain't Gonna Study War No More: Biblical Ambiguity and the Abolition of War*. Louisville: Westminster John Knox, 1993.

Perry B. Yoder and Willard M. Swartley, eds. *The Meaning of Peace: Biblical Studies*. Second ed. Expanded bibliography. Elkhart: Institute of Mennonite Studies, 2001.

Study Questions

Prepare

What is your definition of peace? If you have time consult a Bible dictionary or commentary to help you formulate a definition. Write out two or three sentences to describe this definition. Bring this definition with you to small group study.

Following World War II Brethren were actively involved in peacemaking through the Brethren Service Commission, the development of CROP, and the adventures of the "seagoing cowboys" who took part in Heifer International. If you have access to the four-DVD *Brethren Heritage Collection* developed by David Sollenberger, watch some of the installments, and consider bringing one to the session to share with everyone.

Ask

1. Define or describe your impression of the Old Testament. What are the three responses that Leiter says that he receives when he talks about the "notion of peace in the Old Testament"? Which of the three responses described by Leiter more fully represents your viewpoint?

2. Leiter list five typologies of peace. List and describe the differences between the five approaches. Can you think of other scriptural examples beyond the ones that are listed?

3. "Conflict was a constant part of life in ancient Israel." Can you make a similar statement about your community, your church, and your family? Compare ways in which your experience matches or contrasts with the biblical examples. Have you observed fruitful ways in which conflict is managed? How have you navigated through or around problems?

4. Leiter states, "In most cases of personal, community, and global conflict, nonviolence is a viable option." Would this be your observation? Is this option the first or last choice of people in your community or nation?

5. In the book of Judges peace is achieved after military victory. This peace is lasting, but it ultimately breaks down. Why?

Consider historical situations with which you are familiar. Why has lasting peace developed between two combatants in World War II (the United States and Germany), but did not develop after the first World War? Why do you think there were no further wars of secession in the United States after the Civil War? Would you classify the collapse of the Soviet Union and European Communism an example of peacemaking or the end result of a process of war? What conditions, in your opinion, make war unlikely in some situations, and seemingly inevitable in others?

6. How were Brethren actively involved in peacemaking efforts after World War II? If the situation allows, watch a clip or two from the *Brethren Heritage Collection*. Discuss its connection to this essay.

7. What is your vision for peace, small or great? Can peace be achieved by the individual, or only by a larger group?

8. How is a mandate for peace different than a vision for peace? The author lists three different kinds of mandates. Describe and discuss the differences.

9. What are the four major categories of peace psalms? Read examples aloud in your group. Is peace mandated or envisioned? How important is it to include psalms of peace among your worship resources?

10. Take time to share the definitions of peace you wrote before you came to group. Has your attitude toward the Old Testament and peace been challenged or changed by this essay?

Prophetic Rhetoric and Preaching

Christopher D. Bowman

*"Who in their right mind would presume to speak the
Word of God week in and week out?"*
—*Waltersdorff 12*

Displayed in the Juniata College library is a striking sculpture of
the prophet Jeremiah. The pockmarks of decay and damage found
throughout the piece are not there by accident nor have they been
artificially created. They are there because the sculptor purpose-
fully chose a damaged cherry tree, aged and filled with buckshot,
from which to hew the aged and wounded prophet Jeremiah. Describing his work, sculptor Dean Egge emphasized the importance
of paying attention to both his audience and the prophet. Once he
understood the old subject and the new recipient, the sculptor says,
"The search then began for the right log."[1]

In preaching today, this combination of listening to the original
message and knowing the new recipient is essential to finding the
right log. This essay pays attention to the rhetoric of the Hebrew

---

[1] The sculpture of Jeremiah was donated to Juniata College in 1998 by retiring president
Robert W. Neff, who said of the prophet, "I have real feeling for the story of Jeremiah,
because I felt that he, in spite of the worst kinds of turmoil, never lost direction, never
lost a sense of hope. He's sort of battered and bent, but not any less determined. Jeremiah's a symbol for me in my life." (Church of the Brethren News Services, *Newsline* May
28, 1998.)

prophets in order to gain insights that can guide the transformative task of preaching in today's Church of the Brethren.

First, we will look at the prophets to learn who they were and what they did. Second, we will identify the purpose of rhetoric and recognize how prophetic rhetoric was used. Finally, based on these insights, we will make some observations that invite prophetic preaching in our own modern-day context.

What we shall see is that biblical prophets were called to speak the timeless Word of God at a specific time. They used a variety of means to persuade their listeners to imagine and to "live toward" a life-giving, God-centered future. We will see that the prophetic voice not only called for repentance and hope but also imagined aloud an alternate world built by words. In the transformational rhetoric of these biblical prophets, Brethren preachers can find generative insights for prophetic speech of our own amid the tectonic shifts of our time.

Prophets

Male and female, young and old, before and after Jesus' ministry, prophets are an essential part of the biblical story.[2] Early in the Hebrew Scriptures Aaron and his sister Miriam are named prophets along with Moses (Exodus 7:1; 15:20). Earlier still, in a dream to a nervous King Abimelech, God identifies Abraham as a prophet (Gen. 20:7). Between the exodus and the monarchy, Deborah served as both prophet and judge (Judges 4:4). The kings of Israel were guided and challenged by prophets like Nathan, Elijah, and Elisha. King David himself is called a prophet (Acts 2:30), even though he was the recipient of more than one disapproving prophetic word (2 Samuel 12). But it was during the decline and fall of the northern and southern kingdoms that the prophetic word really flourished. All three sections of the Hebrew Bible (Torah,

---

[2] While this essay considers the prophetic voice in Hebrew Scripture, the prophetic voice is also part of the New Testament. John the Baptist and Jesus are both called prophets (Luke 1:76; 7:16; 7:26; 24:19, John 6:14; 7:40; 9:17). Prophets were active in the Christian community (for good and ill; see 1 Cor. 14:37 and Titus 1:12). The book of Revelation spends a significant amount of time warning about false prophets (Rev. 2:20; 16:13; 19:20; 20:10).

Prophets, and Writings) mention prophets, but most are found in the "Prophets," the section that reports the rise and fall of the kingdoms of Israel and Judah.

The fact that some of the Bible's historical materials (Joshua, Judges, Samuel, Kings) are in the section named "Prophets" tells us something about the ancient interpreters' understanding of history as well as their understanding of prophets. Why not, for example, name material focused on the rise and fall of the kingdoms of Israel with a title reflecting the authority and power of kings and kingdoms? Or, if the intent was to focus on the historicity of these writings, why not name the category "history" instead?

There is some value-added remembering going on here. Prophets may have served as historians, but they were not impartial or objective reporters of facts (Petersen 2). They were more like preachers than professors, interested in what happened mainly as it relates to why it happened. Historians describe history while prophets help us make spiritual sense of it. The words of the prophets present and transform historical data in a way that encourages a spiritual understanding of and personal response to that history. Prophets describe what has happened, is happening, and will happen as a collaborative story of what God has, is, and will be doing. They speak this Word in order to motivate people to join in that activity of God. Prophets help people remember something old in order to help them behold something new.

More than providing historical play-by-play, the poetic and prophetic imagination of these voices called a certain kind of future into existence. Describing these voices in *The Creative Word*, Walter Brueggemann writes, "[They are poets], not political scientists . . . not crusaders, not ethical teachers, but speakers . . . who commit linguistic acts that assault the presumed world of the king . . . who invite listening Israel to entertain new dimensions of social possibility which they had never before considered" (52).

David Petersen reminds us that "an absolute distinction between prophets and priests did not exist in ancient Israel" (5). He suggests that mixed titles of priest/prophet/historian may be similar to a pastor being called reverend/doctor/pastor. Prophets are defined by what they are called to do, not by what they are called while doing it. When the prophet in 1 Samuel 9 is called "the man of God," the people see him engage in the priestly function of the religious service (1 Samuel 9:10-12). Using a wide variety of rhetorical tools and persuasive powers, the prophet/priest/historian is called not simply to report the past, nor to embellish the past, but, standing firmly in the present, to recognize God's past-present-future activity in such a way as to call the people of God to live and work toward a God-given, God-giving future.

Prophets did not always work alone. Not only were there assistants and servants (for example, Elisha's Gehazi and Jeremiah's Baruch) but there were often sub-communities and schools of compatriots along the way that "stood in tension with the dominant community in any political economy" (Brueggemann 2001, xvi). These communities of faithfulness served as sources of support and encouragement as they attempted to proclaim and live into the future being named. Like church communities that serve as countering-cultures in the world, these prophetic communities tended the vision and carried the prophetic voice beyond the limits of an individual lifetime.

Rhetorical Studies

Much of the detail we have learned about the biblical prophets comes from the excellent work of biblical scholars. Historical criticism[3] ruled the world of biblical studies in the first half of the twentieth century, and was based on the assumption that finding the original bedrock of the Scriptures would allow us to recover the *real* Bible. And great discoveries were made. Editors and authors were identified (J, E, P, D) and theological schools were divided (Isaiah I, II, and III).

In the middle of Dr. Robert B. Coote's class on "Power, Politics, and the Making of the Bible," I could sense a growing discomfort in my hermeneutical belly. While it was impossible to

---

[3] The term "historical criticism" describes approaches to the Bible that seek to locate biblical texts within the historical contexts in which they were written or in which they were first heard or read.

argue against Coote's thesis that sociopolitical agenda was the true driving force behind the instigation of the biblical laws of temple sacrifice (Coote and Coote, chapters 4–10), I got the distinct impression that we were no longer talking about the same biblical text. By dissecting the Bible one is left with something less than the sum of its parts. James Kugel points out, "Modern scholars' explanations have proven very persuasive—and that is just the problem, since, in approaching the text in the way they have, they seemed to have stripped the Bible of much of its special status" (667).

With due respect and thanks to the academic prowess of the historical-critical method of biblical studies to find, describe, and unpack the intriguing puzzles[4] in the biblical text, historical-critical studies feel more like autopsies than conversations. And as is the case in an autopsy, when finished the body is no longer recognizable as anything more than a sum of its parts.

A significant and encouraging change is taking place, however, in biblical studies. As the prominence of historical criticism begins to fade, new tools are gaining importance. One of these is rhetorical criticism.

The birth of rhetorical criticism could arguably be dated to the 1968 Society of Biblical Literature presidential address by James Muilenburg, who named the field, defined parameters, and inspired its direction. The school found its adolescent angst in the 1987 presidential address of Elisabeth Schüssler Fiorenza who "proposed that attention to rhetorical rather than scientific categories of scholarship would raise ethical-political issues as constitutive of the interpretive process" (Brueggemann 2006, 263). The field continued to mature as Phyllis Trible's *God and the Rhetoric of Sexuality* helped us talk about the power of talking. Paul Ricoeur's work on imagination and meaning-making and Walter Brueggemann's emphasis on the "generative, constitutive power of imagination" brought about significant new views of the way biblical scholarship meets faithful meaning-making.

---

[4] In my studies I have begun to use the word "puzzle" as a more satisfying and less devaluing word to identify the various "contradictions" and "inconsistencies" within the biblical text that have challenged biblical scholars for thousands of years.

The shift was almost palpable from the Society of Biblical Literature conference floor during the presidential address of Walter Brueggemann in 1990. As a young pastor and would-be biblical scholar, I listened with interest as Brueggemann chastised biblical scholars for withholding their scholarship from the religious community. "The spillover of the text into present social reality is not an 'add-on' for relevance, but it is a scholarly responsibility," he said. "The text should have a hearing as a serious voice on its own terms," he argued. And it was the responsibility of biblical scholars to bring their expertise to the discussions now being held in the church and synagogue. The scholarly community can no longer hide behind the illusion of objectivity and neutrality. "Such 'objective' and 'neutral' readings are themselves political acts in the service of entrenched and 'safe' interpretation" (Brueggemann 2006, 265).

Brueggemann urged the scholars into an active participation in the emerging interpretation, saying, "it is possible that the text will be permitted freedom for its own fresh say. That, it seems to me, is a major interpretive issue among us. The possibility of a fresh reading requires attentiveness to the politics of rhetoric, to the strange, relentless power of these words to subvert and astonish" (Brueggemann 2006, 266).

"How Brethren," I thought to myself. This goes to show that there is a sea change afoot not just due to postmodernity, not simply in the new internetwork structure of communication and knowledge, and not just in the church, but even in the way we study and interpret the Bible. The Church of the Brethren today stands within a whirlwind of change that may be greater than what we experienced moving to the "new world" in the 1720s or the divisive disintegration of the 1880s or the "-ism" challenges of the late 1900s (feminism, activism, conservatism, liberalism, literalism).

Yet in the same way that the new approach to biblical studies has grown from and yet chastened the prior, historical-critical approach, this time of significant challenge and change may, in fact, provide the very tools and vision for the reintegration of what is being made new. Likewise, the church may find that the experience of disintegration and loss is, in fact, the environment for reintegration of the new. This call to theology as an active "Word" is a gift that could keep the academic world and the church "from being turned in upon itself, preoccupied with greater and greater intensity on issues that matter less and less" (Brueggemann 2000, 119). This is, after all, the message carried in the rhetoric of the prophet in the biblical times of disorienting, disintegrating change.

Prophetic Rhetoric

To understand rhetoric (without going into technical details or listing rhetorical devices from *acroama* to *zeugma*) we can begin with Aristotle's definition: rhetoric is "an ability, in each particular case, to see the available means of persuasion" (Koptak 26). We can narrow this definition, in our case, by adding that *biblical* rhetoric is persuasion "toward" something and not simply persuasion for the sake of persuasion itself. The prophets' rhetorical devices were used to persuade and motivate the recipient toward God. For purposes of our discussion, we will look at five accents in the prophetic voice: (1) future-voice, (2) counter-voice, (3) confessional-voice, (4) poetic-voice, and (5) personal-voice.

To fully describe the concept of "prophet" in the Hebrew Scriptures is beyond the scope of this paper. There are different words used to describe the role or title of the prophets—prophet, seer, diviner, man of God—and the scholarly community has not reached consensus on their exact usage and interplay (Petersen 4). Furthermore, within the biblical text itself we are told that the titles changed over time (1 Samuel 9:9) and the ancient title of *ro'eh* (seer) was replaced by the title *navi'* (prophet). And while accuracy in foreseeing was a test of prophetic authenticity (Deut. 18:22), other forecasters (magi, mediums, wizards) could predict the future, interpret dreams, and perform miracles but were not called prophets (see 1 Samuel 28:7). Just because someone could predict the future did not make them a prophet. Divination, in fact, often carried a negative connotation (see Deut. 18:10, 14; Jer. 14:14; Ezek. 13:6, 23). In describing the prophetic future-voice, "foreseeing" is significant but not sufficient. There is something more than a "predicting word" or a "powerful word" in a "prophetic word."

The *future-voice* of the biblical prophets expressed insight into the future in a more powerful way than fortune-telling, forecasting, or divination; it went beyond the limits of timing. Unfortunately, when we focus our attention on the predictive capabilities of the prophets by either dismissing or demanding predictive accuracy, we undermine the *kairotic* power of their words to merge the past, present, and future into a "living Word" of God. Basing our interpretations on the timing of the Word of God limits our ability to see that Word of God as timeless. When we demand (or deny) the predictive power of prophetic literature we consign biblical prophecy to the same category as weather forecasts, horoscopes, and fortune-tellers (albeit with extra "god language") and we fail to see that there is something more important than forecasting here. Rather than using prophecy to schedule the apocalypse, the future-voice of the prophet calls us to recognize and reenter the timeless stream of the divine purpose (or plan) today.

Our view of the second rhetorical tool, the prophetic *countervoice*, is often similarly shortsighted. Popular perception often limits the counter-voice to confrontation, as when we divide preaching between pastoral (comforting) and prophetic (confronting) and thus limit our understanding of prophetic preaching to confrontation (anti-*something*). Not only does this false dichotomy minimize the less confrontational aspects of some prophetic counter-speech (see Isaiah 40:1), the confrontational model is simply not reproducible in our current context.

This is not to say that the prophetic voice was non-confrontational. Quite the opposite is true. The voice of the prophet is always a counter-voice to the powers-of-this-world, often speaking in a confrontational way. The prophetic voice challenges the powers of the empire, and in the harshest terms calls people (and nations) to repent. Prophets were especially confrontational on issues of social justice and moral integrity in the face of power and wealth. As Klaus Koch writes, "Anyone who opens a prophetic book stumbles on passionate social criticism on almost every page" (190).

It is important to note, however, that the context that allowed the confrontational counter-voice of the biblical prophets to be effective "over and against" the king does not exist today. In fact, the attempt to "speak truth to power" today using the confrontational language of the Old Testament model of prophet-confronting-king results in ineffective posturing at best and outright dismissal as irrelevant at worst. Chaining oneself to the gates of the Pentagon or an abortion clinic may be commendable for several reasons, but it is not prophetic (in the biblical sense of the word), especially in our current cultural context. Recognizing this new reality, Walter Brueggemann suggests that the new prophetic counter-voice "must be more cunning and more nuanced and perhaps more ironic [than before] . . . . What is now required is that a relatively powerless prophetic voice must find imaginative ways that are rooted in the text but that freely and daringly move from the text toward concrete circumstances" (Brueggemann 2001, xii).

The prophetic counter-voice is more than confrontation. It is persuasion toward a counter-reality more faithful than the current one. By moving beyond the confrontational model, the creative counter-voice helps us recognize the ultimate bankruptcy of the empire both to enslave and to save. The prophetic counter-voice tells us not simply that the old "known world" is corrupt and coming to an end, nor simply that God is bringing a "new world" into being, but that the disruption of the old is intentional and the disclosure of the new is discernable and that this new counter-reality is a different way of living. When the current world's impotence is recognized, the disruption of the old is realized, and the disclosure of the new is discerned, the counter-voice has been heard.

A third rhetorical tool of the biblical prophets is the use of the *confessional-voice*. By this I mean the honest recognition of sin and the accompanying call to repent and turn back to God. Things don't just fall apart in the biblical world. They are disrupted by God in response to our covenant-breaking. And things don't just progressively improve; they are made new by God in response to repentance and redemption. Lest our demythologizing and source-critical hermeneutics make us too comfortable with the text, we would do well to attend more carefully to the caustic speech of the prophets about the effect of sin. Some powerful repentance is in order before "the new" can be received.

Unfortunately, we suffer from comments like those by religious celebrities who attributed the attacks of 9/11 to America's sins (Harris C03). The national offenses listed by these religious authorities, however, read not like the sins condemned by the biblical prophets but rather the agenda of a political party. There is plenty of sin to condemn in our nation, most of which can be found listed in the confessional-voice of the biblical prophets. Subordinating the prophetic voice to the power of the state (or a particular party within it) has destroyed the integrity of that voice today.

Thankfully, manipulative, politicized god-talk (from the left and the right), what we might call "false prophetic voices," is meeting growing resistance. The desire to return integrity to speech is emerging across disciplines.[5] We are recognizing the importance of resisting false speech of "ideological persuasion" which "controls through the willful, manipulative use of speech . . . that deceives, beguiles, and conjures reality in dishonest ways" (2007, 1116).

A creative way is needed to recapture the authority of the confessional-voice in modern life. Some wings of the church resist talking about "sins" or "sinners" at all. Others seem to enjoy such talk (particularly in regard to others). Clearly, we need to hear a proclaiming and reclaiming word about sin. As with other terms, pop culture has changed the power of language traditionally used by the church and turned the word "sin" into a political and colloquial toy rather than a theological confession. ("Whore" is a term of endearment among some teenagers, and the youth-group jury is still out on whether being "wicked" is good or bad.)

A fourth tool of the prophet is the *poetic-voice*. The poet creates "true fictions" or re-framed realities or structured songs or storied parables that seek to broaden our imagination (Ricoeur 1997, 64-65). Thus Ezekiel speaks of the valley of dry bones reassembling— an image even camp-kids can sing about. Jonah gives us a

---

[5] See Walter Brueggemann's review of James Boyd White's *Living Speech: Resisting the Empire of Force* in the *Michigan Law Review*, (2007, 1115-1132).

bothersome example of being bothered by grace. And a pock-marked Jeremiah carries the visible signs of the cost of his call. By using symbol and metaphor, the poetic-voice harnesses the generative power of imagination because symbols, by their very nature, provide a "surplus of meaning." Since "symbols give rise to an endless exegesis," the innovative meaning of the biblical text extends beyond our capability to exhaust it (Ricoeur 57).

In a way similar to the teaching style of Jesus, the poetic-voice provides stories, metaphors, and illustrations that invite self-reflection and recognition. They give space for the "aha" moment. They make straight new highways of understanding that broaden access to the underlying truth. This voice stirs the imagination and sponsors new insights. As Brueggemann suggests:

> One consequence of this new awareness is that biblical texts, in particular prophetic texts, could be seen as poetic scenarios of alternative social reality. The canonical text . . . might also serve to nurture and fund obedience that is not necessarily confrontational but that simply acts out of a differently perceived, differently practiced world (imagination/obedience). Thus a focus on rhetoric as generative imagination has permitted prophetic texts to be heard and reuttered as offers of reality counter to dominant reality (2001, x-xi).

Finally, along with the message brought by the biblical prophets we also hear about the prophets themselves—what I've chosen to call the *personal-voice*. Prophets are people. We hear prophets speak to the people about God's anger as they also speak to God (and anyone who will listen) about their own anger. The laments of Jeremiah about his personal suffering at the hands of his family, friends, and country show the cost of his calling (Jer. 20:14-18).[6]

While reading the prophets, we learn more than expected about the prophets themselves. We discover that the "person" of the prophet was part of the message. Their frustrations, foibles, and families could all be brought to the service of persuasion. Take for example Hosea's decision, while proclaiming Israel's unfaithfulness,

---

[6] See Robert W. Neff article, "Suffering in the Book of Job and Psalms," in this volume.

to marry a prostitute and name his children with attention-getting names such as "not mine" (Hosea 1:9), or Jeremiah's decision, while preaching hope within a hopeless situation, to buy property soon to be overrun by invading armies and bury the deed for future recovery (Jer. 32), or Isaiah's walking barefoot and naked for three years while preaching about being stripped bare by God (Isaiah 20:3). With extravagant behavior in support of their calling, the prophets were personally part of their message. It was an effective rhetorical tool.

Writing about eccentricities of past Bible professors at Bethany Theological Seminary, Robert Bowman described the antics of one Old Testament professor who would enthusiastically stand on his chair holding his Bible in one hand and throw chalk at students who were not showing sufficient excitement about the class (54-55). As with the personal-voice of the prophets, students may better remember the message of the day as they remember the messenger.

Using these, and many other rhetorical tools, the biblical prophets cajoled, convicted, and convinced God's people to live toward the divine kingdom's principles and preferences. They pointed to this divine alternative to the empire *du jour* in a time of catastrophic disintegration and disorientation. They gave people courage to imagine God's emerging future and to bring it to life in their living. They countered the dominant worldview with a kind of visionary awareness of a different way of living as they called for repair of their broken covenant with God. They found new and creative ways to sponsor meaning-giving imagination and change-making self-recognition. And they did this with all the tools at their disposal, even their own lives. Their rhetoric evoked and sponsored a new world grown from the seeds deeply planted in the fertile soil of their past. They were prophets. We could use voices like these right now.

Preaching

Brethren take seriously the transformative power of the Word of God, both as it was written and as it is preached. As stewards of the timeless message being born anew in every time, we strive to be faithful both to the actual text and to the underlying, sometimes hidden meaning —both "the words" and "the Word" (Gardner 7-14; Neuman-Lee 33-45). We believe that "the word of God is living and active" (Heb. 4:12), and so each new generation is encouraged to set aside creeds (real and imagined) in favor of discovering anew the eternal Word of God within the biblical words of God.

Writing about the 1979 Annual Conference paper, *Biblical Inspiration and Authority of the Church of the Brethren*, then General Secretary Robert W. Neff observed, "the authority of the Bible, then, does not lie in what we can say about it but in what we discover in it" (15). So our preaching rests on the authority of Scripture's recognizable, rediscoverable Word.

The prophetic voices of Scripture can help us find our voice today. As the Word participates in its own unfolding and since we expect a living Word in our Scriptures, Bible study for Brethren is a conversation and not an autopsy. In conversation with this Living Word, we hear the prophetic word and learn how we might, as Brueggemann says, "nurture, nourish, and evoke a consciousness and perception alternative to . . . the dominant culture around us," not only in response to a specific crisis, but in the week-to-week challenge of keeping this divine vision from being co-opted and domesticated by the power of the culture which surrounds us (2001, 3).

How might the rhetorical tools used by the prophets during the disintegration of Israel be used today to invite, encourage, inspire, and guide our own prophetic, imaginative preaching in the disintegrating church? "For what is now required is that a relatively powerless prophetic voice must find imaginative ways that are rooted in the text but that freely and daringly move from the text toward concrete circumstance" (Brueggemann 2001, xii). We hope to inspire creativity and persuasiveness not for their own sake but for the sake of and rooted deeply in the kingdom of God. Prophetic preaching (as is true for all acts of ministry) can stir up, shape, and reform the emerging "way of living" in response to the past-present-future voice of God.

The future-voice and the counter-voice may provide an important balance to each other. Both remind us that where we are now is not where we long to be (chronologically nor sociologically), yet they work at that truth from two different directions. The future-voice provides an energizing invocation: "Do not remember the former things or consider the things of old" (Isaiah 43:18). "Behold! God is making all things new," we say with hope-filled hearts.

To which the counter-voice provides a more critical word: "Remember the former things of old; for I am God, and there is no other declaring the end from the beginning and from ancient times things not yet done, saying, 'My purpose shall stand, and I will fulfill my intention'" (Isaiah 46:9-10). The counter-voice reminds us that the new world is necessary because the life we had been given has been co-opted by the powers around us and away from the original covenant of God. There are things we simply "are not," and doing a better job at what we are already doing is not enough to bridge that gap. The counter-voice is critical of the current reality because it knows of our ultimate inability to reform or redesign ourselves into what first God intended.

The critical counter-voice and the energizing future-voice hold each other in faithful tension. Between these two we find the invitation to confession. Whether it be simple humility or honest contrition, in choosing the log from which to carve this word, the prophetic preacher might be wise to use "we" more than "you" and to avoid "them" and "they" in the litany. The confessional-voice helps us recognize that "all we like sheep have gone astray" (Isaiah 53:6).

Although we speak (above) of future-voice, counter-voice, and confessional-voice in a sort of future, past, and present way, there are past-present-future aspects to all three voices. As did the prophets, we may find it helpful to understand the voice of God in the blending of time so that there is a kind of retrieving-attending-anticipating (past-present-future) in what we say.

A recurring call in the conversation about the church in the postmodern world is the call for creativity. The poetic-voice and the personal-voice can help us speak to this. These give permission to find new and creative words with which to speak in our new reality. We can share our lives and our limits in ways that show the Word is real in us. We can find new words to speak because the Word has already been given.

Some of the patterns of church life and church vocabulary no longer function as effectively as they have in the past. Some of our most cherished traditions have lost their ability to motivate and engage the newer generation of Christians. Some might suggest that we simply need to work harder to make the new generation adopt the traditional patterns and vocabularies of the church. And this would, in fact, assist in resisting the acculturation of the church to the surrounding empire. However, we may simply be acculturating to another idolatrous culture: our tradition. We need not abandon our tradition, but if we are no longer able to say theologically why we do the things we do, then we need to stop doing them, recalibrate the old words, or find new words.

We need not abandon our traditions, but we do need to reignite the fire in which they were forged. We need to renew their generative prophetic speech through a creative and imaginative voice today. Walter Brueggemann writes that "the church has no business more pressing than the reappropriation of its memory in its full power and authenticity" (2001, 2). The poetic-voice and personal-voice of the prophet attempt to do this. They renew the original Word by renegotiating the way we speak it in each new generation. They reappropriate the words-that-were in order to faithfully cast a vision of the world-that-will-be and call people toward that world.

The voice of the prophet is faithful when it persuades its hearer to live, act, and build toward the "new thing which God is doing" not by abandoning the past but by helping us recognize the disintegrating work God is doing in order that we might recognize and participate in the reintegrating work to be done.

Prophetic preaching of this sort is persuasive speech that moves people not simply to agree or appreciate the words, but to do them. In Ezekiel, God complains, "My people come and sit down before you to hear the things you have to say, but they do not do them. Their mouths may speak sweetly, but their minds are only on money. You—you are for them like a singer of love songs, with a beautiful voice and skilled at playing. They hear what you say, but they do not do it" (Ezek. 33:31-32). These observations are a prophetic preacher's worst nightmare.

Isaiah also speaks of the prophetic voice, saying, "the Lord GOD has given me the tongue of a teacher, that I may know how to sustain the weary with a word" (Isaiah 50:4). Yet that sustaining word is more than a spiritual antidepressant or painkiller used to help tolerate the empire surrounding us. It is a word which sustains us in our calling to live into, work toward, and do the new thing which God is birthing among us.

Preaching is genuinely prophetic when it provides a sacred space in which a transformational decision can be made between competing kingdoms or worldviews, and where those weary in the kingdom-building life can be sustained. This is a *kairos* moment both for the rhetor (public speaker) and for the listener. It cannot be created, but it can be invited. This *kairos* moment is an ancient rhetorical concept from before the time of Socrates when "*kairos* referred to the principle and power by which the opportune moment calls forth an intuitive, appropriate response." (Jost and Hyde xv).

This is the sacred space, some would argue, where rhetoric, poetics, and hermeneutics overlap in human discourse. To quote Paul Ricoeur,

> Rhetoric remains the art of arguing with a view to persuading an audience that one opinion is preferable to its rival. Poetics remains the art of constructing plots with a view to broadening the individual and collective imaginary. Hermeneutics remains the art of interpreting texts within a context distinct from that of the author and from that of the texts' original audience with a view to discovering new dimensions to reality. Arguing, fashioning,

redescribing: such are the three major operations whose respective totalizing aims . . . condemns them to complementarity
(1997, 71).

The prophetic preacher thrives in that space where persuading,
fashioning, and redescribing conspire to inspire a new direction
and decision in life.

Conclusion

"The time may be ripe in the church for serious consideration of
prophecy as a crucial element in ministry," writes Walter Brueggemann. "The prophets understood the possibility of change as linked
to emotional extremities of life. . . . Most of all, they understood
the distinctive power of language . . . to speak in ways that evoke
newness 'fresh from the word'" (Brueggemann 2001, xxiii).

The prophetic voice was present as the voice countering official power throughout most of biblical history. It provided a different way of understanding what was going on throughout biblical
history, yet immediately before, during, and after the Babylonian
exile the prophetic voice becomes *the* essential voice of understanding. When the world of the past is crumbling and the world
of the future has not yet arrived, the prophetic voice (with what
Walter Brueggemann calls "prophet imagination") is most needed.
David Petersen calls prophets "boundary figures" and notes that
some moments in history have a greater need for prophecy than do
others (6). The fall of the Hebrew kingdoms and the disruptive reality of the Babylonian exile were just such times. Some argue con-
vincingly that the church today stands at another such time.

As I have shown elsewhere, developmental psychology teaches
us that times of crisis and loss provide the cognitive dissonance
necessary for transformational change. In these times the disintegration we lament is part of the transforming "new thing" God is
doing (C. Bowman 92-93; 124-131). As did their spiritual ancestors, prophetic voices from our pulpits will help us recognize the
blessing within our lament and call us toward the timeless Word of
God unfolding anew in our time.

Recommended Reading

Prophets, Rhetoric, and Hermeneutics

Walter Brueggemann. *Hopeful Imagination: Prophetic Voices in Exile.* Minneapolis: Augsburg Fortress, 1985.

———. *The Prophetic Imagination.* Second ed. Minneapolis: Augsburg Fortress, 2001.

Walter Jost and Michael J. Hyde. *Rhetoric and Hermeneutics in Our Time: A Reader.* New Haven: Yale University Press, 1997.

James L. Kugel. *How to Read the Bible: A Guide to Scripture, Then and Now.* New York: Free Press, 2007.

David L. Petersen. "Introduction to Prophetic Literature." *The New Interpreter's Bible.* Volume 6. Nashville: Abingdon Press, 1994.

Paul Ricoeur. "Rhetoric—Poetics—Hermeneutics." *Rhetoric and Hermeneutics in Our Time: A Reader.* Ed. Walter Jost and Michael J. Hyde. New Haven: Yale University Press, 1997: 60-72.

Phyllis Trible. "Exegesis for Storytellers and Other Strangers." *Journal of Biblical Literature* 114 (1995): 3-19.

———. *Rhetorical Criticism: Context, Method, and the Book of Jonah.* Philadelphia: Fortress Press, 1994.

Homiletics

Walter Brueggemann. *Finally Comes the Poet: Daring Speech for Proclamation.* Fortress Press, Minneapolis, 1989.

Thomas H. Troeger. *Imagining A Sermon.* Nashville: Abingdon Press, 1990.

———. *Preaching While the Church Is Under Reconstruction: The Visionary Role of Preachers in a Fragmented World.* Nashville: Abingdon Press, 1999.

Study Questions

Prepare

What is the most significant or most memorable sermon you've ever heard? Was it a regular worship service at your home congregation, a revival service, or a district or Annual Conference meeting? How old were you? What do you remember best about it? Write out a paragraph about the sermon as you remember it.

Ask

1. Chris Bowman writes about a sculptor who needed to find the right log for his subject, the prophet Jeremiah. If someone were to make a sculpture of you, what sort of log would be required? How does this image pertain to the sort of person you are, and what sort of sermon is best suited for you?

2. What is meant by the prophetic voice? Describe the relationship between prophecy and foretelling the future? What books makeup the prophetic writings of the Old Testament? How does Bowman describe the prophetic nature of biblical histories?

3. Bowman writes "Prophets help people *remember* something old in order to help them behold something new." How does this statement resonate with you? How does this remembering help us make sense of history, especially faith history?

4. Brethren educator Martin Grove Brumbaugh (1862-1930) was governor of Pennsylvania, president of Juniata College, and education minister of Puerto Rico, among many other things. He wrote a progressive history of Brethren in Colonial America, claiming we were the first to invent Sunday schools, operate a denominational press, and be blessed with a highly educated clergy, none of which, according to historian Donald F. Durnbaugh, happened to be true. Nevertheless, this history may have inspired Brethren to take an active part in founding Heifer Project, CROP, Church World Service, and through the Brethren Service Commission set an example emulated by secular authorities. Can Brumbaugh's history be considered

prophetic? How important are facts in coming to an understanding of who we are?

5. C. S. Lewis once said that if you dissect a frog you might learn something about what it is made of, but you won't have a frog anymore. Bowman makes some pointed remarks about the historical-critical method of some studies that "feel more like autopsies than conversations." Contrast *historical criticism* with *rhetorical criticism*. What is the place of each? Which do you find more helpful?

6. Bowman quotes the Klaus Koch statement: "Anyone who opens a prophetic book stumbles on passionate social criticism on almost every page." How does social criticism fit into the popular image of the prophet? Name some people you might consider social critics who are also prophets? Is it easier to credit prophets when they share our political or national affiliation? Do we automatically dismiss prophets from another political background?

7. Define sin, confession, and forgiveness. Are these a part of your regular preaching experience? Share the written descriptions of the most memorable sermon you've ever heard that you prepared before the session. Is there a pattern to the paragraphs read? Are sin, confession, and forgiveness a part of these sermons?

8. What is the understanding of *rhetoric* in this essay? When have you heard, used, experienced the elements of rhetoric in your life? Have you ever been persuaded to a new point of view through a sermon? Is our culture at large open to hearing persuasive preaching?

9. Bowman suggests that traditional church patterns and vocabulary may no longer be effective. What works in your church? What does not? How do we cater to a number of competing interests when it comes to worship practices in our congregations?

10. Is the prophetic voice needed now? Is it possible for Brethren to be prophetic beyond Brethren circles? What does Bowman suggest in this regard?

Jonah the Christian

Graydon F. Snyder

If you attend a worship service at any Christian church anywhere in the world, there's a good chance you'll see a cross displayed somewhere in a prominent place. Many probably assume the same was true for the first Christians. They might be surprised to discover, however, that the cross does not appear in Christian artwork for around four hundred years. And, they might be surprised to find out that the Jonah story appears far more frequently in early Christian art than the cross.

So, why was the story of Jonah so important? In early Christian catacomb art no other picture appears as often as that of Jonah. Since no writing reflects what early Christians believed, we accept the art as an indication of what the average believer saw in the story of Jonah. We speak of this as the understanding of *local* people. For the most part it showed the Christian Jonah absorbed by a pagan society, but then regurgitated into a redeemed Christian existence. In contrast, early writers (referred to as *translocal*) went in another direction. New Testament writers saw Jonah as a sign of the passion of Jesus. Later, early church fathers, also translocal, primarily wrote of God saving the swallowed Jonah. Once Christianity became the accepted religion, there was no need for the local understanding.

The book of Jonah, one of the most popular books in the Hebrew Scriptures, tells the story of a reluctant prophet who tried to escape God's call to go to Nineveh and to "speak out" against it. As is well-known, Jonah took a ship in the opposite direction. Because of a storm sent by God, the sailors eventually cast him overboard into the sea, where he was swallowed by a fish. After the fish spit up Jonah on dry land, Jonah went to Nineveh to do God's bidding. To his amazement and anger the people of Nineveh quickly repented. There was nothing for Jonah to do, so in his distress he rested and God sent a gourd plant to shield him from the sun. The Hebrew prophet apparently could not handle the fact that his God was concerned about the Gentiles of Nineveh.[1]

Through the centuries the well-known story of Jonah underwent a number of reinterpretations. Prior to the formation of the New Testament, most documents stressed God's deliverance of Jonah from a serious predicament. In 3 Maccabees, written in the first century BCE, the old priest Eleazar prays on behalf of a group of Jews facing martyrdom. In his prayer, he recalls God's rescue of their ancestors, including God's rescue of Jonah from the belly of a sea monster:

> When Jonah was pining away unpitied in the belly of the monster of the deep, you, Father, restored him uninjured to all his household (3 Maccabees 6:8).[2]

In *The Lives of the Prophets*, also written during the first Christian century, we are told that the repentant Jonah came from the district of Kariathmos near the Greek city of Azotus. After "he had been cast forth by the sea monster" he went to live among the Gentiles rather than the Jews: "So I shall remove my reproach, for I spoke falsely in prophesying against the great city of Nineveh."[3]

De Jona, a Jewish homily from about the time of Jesus, now preserved in Greek, speaks of Jonah and the Ninevites as being

---

[1] The book of Jonah does not explain why Jonah is angered by God's behavior. It may stem from the fact that Nineveh was the capital of ancient Assyria, and the Assyrian Empire ended the independent political existence of the northern kingdom of Israel in the eighth century BCE.

[2] James H. Charlesworth, ed., *The Old Testament Pseudepigrapha*, Vol. 2 (New York: Doubleday, 1985), 526.

[3] Charlesworth, 392-393.

healed by God despite their sin of disobedience. Josephus, the first-century Jewish historian, on the other hand describes the Jonah story in a way that is very similar to the story as preserved in the Bible (*Jewish Antiquities*, 9:205-214). Except for inclusion in various lists of Hebrew heroes (for example, "A Prayer of Invocation," in *The Apostolic Constitutions* 7.37.1-5) the primary first-century references to Jonah occur in the synoptic Gospels, under the rubric "sign of Jonah." There are five such narratives: Mark 8:11-13; QS 32 (127) [Luke 11:16, 29-32; Matt. 12:38-42]; Matthew 12:15-50; 16:1-4; Luke 11:14-36.[4]

The Sign of Jonah

The primary textual sources for the synoptic Gospels are the Gospel of Mark, which was the first Gospel written according to many scholars, and the "Sayings Gospel," often referred to as *Quelle* or Q. We do not know if Q had ever been a written source, but the theory behind its existence is compelling. We define Q as those sayings held, apart from Mark, in common in Matthew and Luke. There are some exceptions, but the parallels are significantly close. We will look at each of the five narratives, including Q.

> The Pharisees came and began to argue with him, asking him for a sign from heaven, to test him. And he sighed deeply in his spirit and said, "Why does this generation ask for a sign? Truly I tell you, no sign will be given to this generation." And he left them, and getting into the boat again, he went across to the other side (Mark 8:11-13).

Mark 8:11-13 has the elements of the later "sign of Jonah" texts but lacks an actual reference to Jonah himself. There is an initial conflict with the Pharisees, a request from them for a sign from heaven, and the refusal of an aggravated Jesus to give a sign. Since Jonah has not been mentioned explicitly, some readers assume this

---

[4] QS 32 refers to saying 32 in the Q source, which is the hypothetical source of the parallel sayings in Luke and Matthew. The letter "Q" is from the German word *Quelle*, which means "source." The Q hypothesis attempts to explain the origin of the sayings that Matthew and Luke have in common, but which do not appear in Mark (or John).

story should not be considered one of the Jonah "sign" narratives. Others assume Mark eliminated the Jonah reference (seen in contemporaneous Q) because it distracted from Jesus' debate with the Pharisees, who wanted a divine sign, not a human/historical sign. Actually, there was no clear connection between the sign of Jonah and the overall message of Mark. Assuming the Jonah tradition involved the rising of Jonah from the belly of the sea monster, symbolically representing the resurrection, any correlation with Jesus in Mark would have been complex. In Mark, Jesus spoke of the suffering Son of Man (8:31; 9:31; 10:33). Even though Mark mentioned Jesus would rise in three days, actually the Gospel of Mark ended (based on the short ending at 16:8) without bodily resurrection, without a subsequent appearance to the disciples, and without an ascension. If the sign of Jonah will be the risen Son of Man to this generation, then no correlation exists for Mark.

The Pharisees wanted a sign from heaven. According to some scholars, prior to the writing of Mark and perhaps about the same time as Q, a "Signs Gospel" existed.[5] Biblical scholars believe it was incorporated into the Gospel of John at a later date. In contrast to Q, the Signs Gospel (SQ) contained no sayings—only miracle stories. Like Q there is no written evidence of the Signs Gospel, so these two early textual bodies circulated in oral form early on and are known to us today only as we extract them from Luke/Matthew and John. There are seven works of Jesus that are considered signs in the Gospel of John: turning water into wine at the wedding of Cana (2:1-11); healing an official's son (4:46b-54); healing the crippled man by the pool of Bethzatha (5:2-9); feeding the five thousand and walking on water (6:1-25); healing the man born blind (9:1-8); raising Lazarus from the dead (11:1-45); and causing the great catch of fish (21:1-14). As seen in John 2:11, the signs served as a manifestation of Jesus' relationship to God, not a description of his miraculous power: "Jesus did this, the first of his signs, in

---

[5] Unlike the synoptic Gospels, the Fourth Gospel refers to Jesus' miracles as "signs" (Greek: *semeia*). Some scholars have hypothesized the existence of a document that contained accounts of Jesus' signs. This document is considered a source in the composition of the Fourth Gospel. Scholars use the siglum "SQ" to refer to this hypothetical source (SQ stands for *Semeia Quelle*, "signs source").

Cana of Galilee, and revealed his glory; and his disciples believed in him." Throughout the New Testament a sign (Greek: *semeion*) signaled for Jews a divine presence: "For Jews demand signs and Greeks desire wisdom, but we proclaim Christ crucified, a stumbling block to Jews and foolishness to Gentiles" (1 Cor. 1:22-23). In the Mark narrative the Pharisees wanted such a sign, but, as we have seen, Jesus would not make one available.

In Q Jesus offered a sign different from what the Jews wanted. In this account of the conflict, Jesus offered a historical sign—the sign of Jonah—correlated with the Son of Man:

> Some said to him, "Teacher, we wish to see a sign from you."
>
> He answered them, "A wicked generation looks for a sign, but no sign will be shown to it, except the sign of Jonah."
>
> "For as Jonah became a sign to the Ninevites, so will the son of man be to this generation."
>
> "The queen of the south (Queen of Sheba) will arise at the judgment and condemn this generation. For she came from the ends of the earth to hear the wisdom of Solomon, and look, something greater than Solomon is here."
>
> "The men of Nineveh will arise at the judgment and condemn this generation. For they repented at the preaching of Jonah, and look, something greater than Jonah is here." (QS32, *The sign of Jonah* [Luke 11:16, 29-32])[6]

It is difficult to define the sign of Jonah, but in this early narrative the sign connects the preaching of Jonah to Nineveh with the preaching of Jesus to the Jews. Unfortunately, the preaching of Jonah had never been called a sign prior to the Q narrative.

In the conflict with the scribes and the Pharisees, Matthew keeps the reference to the preaching of Jonah, but alters the sign reference. In contrast to the Markan account Matthew stresses the three days and nights in the belly of the sea monster, which corresponds with Jesus' three days and three nights in the earth. In 12:38-42 Jesus

---

[6] Burton L. Mack, *The Lost Gospel: The Book of Q & Christian Origins* (San Francisco: Harper-Collins, 1993), 91-92.

replies to the sign request by noting they can understand weather signs, but not the sign of Jonah:

> Then some of the scribes and Pharisees said to him, "Teacher, we wish to see a sign from you." But he answered them, "An evil and adulterous generation asks for a sign, but no sign will be given to it except the sign of the prophet Jonah. For just as Jonah was three days and three nights in the belly of the sea monster, so for three days and three nights the Son of Man will be in the heart of the earth. The people of Nineveh will rise up at the judgment with this generation and condemn it, because they repented at the proclamation of Jonah, and see, something greater than Jonah is here! The queen of the South will rise up at the judgment with this generation and condemn it, because she came from the ends of the earth to listen to the wisdom of Solomon, and see, something greater than Solomon is here! (Matt. 12:38-42).

Unlike Mark and Luke, Matthew has a second reference to the sign of Jonah. Jesus responds to the request for a sign with the cynical response that the Pharisees and Sadducees wouldn't know the truth if they saw it. In this second passage there is no mention of the three days and three nights:

> The Pharisees and Sadducees came, and to test Jesus they asked him to show them a sign from heaven. He answered them, "When it is evening, you say, 'It will be fair weather, for the sky is red.' And in the morning, 'It will be stormy today, for the sky is red and threatening.' You know how to interpret the appearance of the sky, but you cannot interpret the signs of the times. An evil and adulterous generation asks for a sign, but no sign will be given to it except the sign of Jonah." Then he left them and went away (Matt. 16:1-4).

As with the preaching sign, there is confusion in the text. Jonah in the sea monster for three days and three nights marks the death and resurrection of Jesus. The actual resurrection event, however, occurred over Friday and Saturday night. That is three days and two nights. Matthew could not have made a calendrical error, could he? The sign of Jonah apparently was so crucial it even re-defined the death and resurrection of Jesus!

The Lukan context does not include a conflict with the scribes or Pharisees. We have only a large crowd pushing for healing miracles. In response Jesus says the only sign for them, in contrast to miracle healing, will be the sign of Jonah as it appears with the Son of Man (essentially the Q narrative):

> When the crowds were increasing, he began to say, "This generation is an evil generation; it asks for a sign, but no sign will be given to it except the sign of Jonah. For just as Jonah became a sign to the people of Nineveh, so the Son of Man will be to this generation. The queen of the South will rise at the judgment with the people of this generation and condemn them, because she came from the ends of the earth to listen to the wisdom of Solomon, and see, something greater than Solomon is here! The people of Nineveh will rise up at the judgment with this generation and condemn it, because they repented at the proclamation of Jonah, and see, something greater than Jonah is here! (Luke 11:29-32).

Jonah in Early Christian Writings

Following the formation of the New Testament, the Jonah story did appear from time to time in the writings of the early church fathers. For the most part these translocal references, all written by the translocal community of leaders and intellectuals, reflected some aspect of the sign of Jonah in the Gospel narratives.

1. Clement 7:7

Clement of Rome, writing to settle some quarrels among the Christians in Corinth, references the mercy of God in the Jonah story. He notes that "Jonah foretold destruction (*katastrophen*, Jonah 3:4) to the men of Nineveh; but when they repented they received forgiveness of their sins."

2. Acts of Paul 3:29

This author uses the Jonah story to stress the resurrection of Christ: "You know that Jonah the son of Amathios, when he would not preach in Nineveh (but fled) was swallowed by a whale, and after three days and three nights God heard Jonah's prayer out of deepest hell, and no part of him was corrupted, not even a hair or an eyelid. How much more, O ye of little faith, will he raise up you who have believed in Christ Jesus, as he himself rose up."[7]

3. Justin Martyr
In his *Dialogue with Trypho*, the early Christian apologist uses the Jonah story in his discussion with the Jewish scholar, Trypho. Using Matthew's Jonah narrative he argues that Jesus anticipated his crucifixion and resurrection (*Dialogue* 107).

4. Irenaeus
Irenaeus mentions the Jonah story several times in his *Against Heresies* (3:19, 2-20.1, 5:1-2, 5.31-1-2). He uses the story of Jonah in the belly of the sea monster to indicate that all humans have been swallowed by the *kētos* (sea monster) and will finally be re-gurgitated—that is, resurrected by God.

5. Clement of Alexandria
In *Quis Div. Salv.* (*The Rich Man's Salvation*), Clement, much like Irenaeus, uses the Jonah story to tell his readers that inside the belly of the whale there is time for repentance and redemption (41).

6. Tertullian
In his *Resurrection of the Flesh*, Tertullian uses the Jonah story as proof that God does indeed resurrect the dead no matter how they died (chapters 32 and 58).

7. Origen
In his *On Prayer*, Origen argues for the efficacy of prayer just as Jonah was saved after praying in the belly of the whale (14.4 and 13.4). In his commentary on Matthew 16:1-4 he says, "The sign of Jonah going out after three days from the whale's belly was indicative

---

[7] Wilhelm Schneemelcher, ed. *New Testament Apocrypha, Vol. 2: Writings Relating to the Apostles Apocalypses and Related Subjects* (Louisville: Westminster John Knox, rev. ed., 2003), 256.

of the resurrection of our Saviour, rising after three days and nights from the dead."

8. Apostolic Constitutions
The author argues that the Jonah story, along with that of Daniel and the lions and the three young men in the fiery furnace, prove God's pledge to resurrect us (5.7).

9. Methodius
In his allegorical writing entitled *On the History of Jonah*, Methodius compares the casting of Jonah into the sea to the falling of the first man, Adam. He also speaks of the release from the whale as a prototype of resurrection—not only of Christ but of all humanity (chapters 1–2).

As we turn to early Christian art, we will see how Jonah pictures were used to encourage believers involved in a society that did not accept them. The post-New Testament writers, on the other hand, dealt more with the theological implication of the Jonah narrative. In fact, Jonah was referred to more often than any other minor prophet. The most frequent use was the christological reference to the passion and resurrection of Christ (e.g., Justin Martyr). The experience of Jonah was also used as a witness to the resurrection of individual believers (e.g., Tertullian). Other writers used Jonah to call for repentance (e.g., 1 Clement), or to depend on God's mercy (e.g., Tertullian), or to anticipate the conversion of pagans (e.g., Clement of Alexandria).

Jonah in Art

While Jonah was mentioned from time to time by early Christian writers, that is, translocal types, biblical stories like Jonah also appeared in early Christian art, primarily in catacombs but also in homes and house churches. This art reflected the life of the local Christians, not the theology of patristic writers.

The story of Jonah far outnumbers any other artistic portrayal found in early Christian art. In my research I have discovered forty-two so far in catacombs and on sarcophagi, with the number

of all other biblical portrayals much less. Most scholars assume the
Jonah story is resurrection art because of its frequent use in catacombs and its connection with Jesus' resurrection in the New Testament. And there are good reasons for that understanding. As we
have seen, Matthew, Luke, and perhaps Q use the story to reference the resurrection of Jesus. The Jonah pictures we have found
do occur only in tomb ornamentation. After regurgitation by the
sea monster, Jonah appears to enjoy a resurrection rest under a
bush. However, by the time Christian art appeared (after 180 CE),
there were other uses of the Jonah story, such as God answering
prayer, or Jonah as a Christian person entering the non-Christian
world (signified by the whale's belly) just as the prophet Jonah had
entered the non-Jewish world of Nineveh. So we are not limited to
the obvious symbol of resurrection. Furthermore, the art contains
elements that will not resonate easily with the resurrection motif.
The average Christian living in the third century would have read
a different story in these symbols.

I will consider five elements in the artistic story of Jonah, and
show why the "local" or popular interpretation would have differed from that of the translocal writers. The elements found in
early Christian art include: (1) Jonah as orante, (2) Jonah in a boat,
(3) Jonah and the sea monster, (4) Jonah and the moon goddess,
and (5) Jonah under the bush with lambs.

There are two basic reasons why early Christian art depicting
the story of Jonah does not match what we find in the New Testament and the early church fathers. First, no piece of early Christian
art actually reflects the Bible. Christian art first appears about 180
CE, well before the time when biblical narrative art would have
been understood as historical. Historical biblical art first occurred
well after Constantine (for example, the mosaics of Ravenna, Italy
that date from the fifth and sixth centuries CE). Prior to that time
all Christian art is symbolic.

Secondly, most early Christian artistic representations borrowed from Greco-Roman imagery. Very little Jewish art existed at
that time (except Dura-Europas), and no Christian art earlier than
180 CE has ever been discovered. So while artisans may have been

instructed to portray a biblical scene, they would have done it with non-Christian imagery. Christians who saw the pictures may have recognized the biblical story, but they would have understood it in terms of the Greco-Roman symbols and figures they already knew. That means the message of early Christian art must be analyzed from the Greco-Roman point of view.

Figure 1. *Jonah story; Vatican #119 (Sarc #44)*

1. Jonah as Orante

Despite the uncertainty of the famous depiction of the Jonah story found in figure 1, most early Christian Jonah figures were drawn as *orantes*—figures with arms lifted up.[8] Orantes came from the Roman world, where they stood for piety. As such they appeared on coins as well as statues and drawings. Most figures in scenes taken from the Hebrew Scriptures could be seen as orantes: Noah in the ark, Daniel in the lions' den, three young men in the fiery furnace, Daniel and Susanna. The orante figures were "saved" from threatening situations (for example: lions, fire, false accusation). Though the Roman orante was female, that did not hinder artists from portraying male figures as female persons saved in the midst of difficult circumstances. Jonah was no exception. The Jonah depicted in art was a symbol of an early Christian who entered the dangerous non-Christian world.

---

[8] The term "orant" (or "orante") comes from the Latin word *orans*, which means "praying." In visual art, the term "orant" refers to a figure who stands with arms outstretched sideways (or bent at the elbow) with hands at shoulder level and palms facing forward.

Figure 2. *Jonah in a boat*; *Santa Maria Antiqua sarcophagus in Rome*

Figure 3. *Jonah, the orante, diving from a boat (Roman catacomb)*

2. Jonah in a Boat

Boats in a burial situation often symbolized the carrying of the deceased to the other world. Early Christians did not consider such a symbol necessary. The family of the deceased was buried nearby in the catacomb or a sepulcher. The living and the deceased ate together and worshiped together (St. Sebastian in Rome). The boat in the Roman world also served to carry people in the murky waters of culture (for example, Platonists). In that sense the orante Jonah sails in a boat that keeps him safe from a pagan culture loaded with demonic elements.

Figure 4. *Roman boat*

3. Jonah and the Sea Monster

Life could not exist without water, so it serves as a symbol of well-being. However, the sea presents serious problems. A ship out on the sea could be caught in a storm that resulted in the drowning of the sailors. Or the boat could lose direction because of wind or excessive waves. As a result, Roman ships stayed close to the land. When carrying merchandise to the west, Romans stopped at Corinth to unload and reload on the south side of the isthmus (later served by a canal). The possibility of attacks by sea monsters added to the fear of the sea. Such fears existed throughout ancient culture (seen in Job 41:1-11 and the stories of Hercules in Greek mythology).

Figure 5. *Hercules and a sea monster*

For some, including Jews, the sea and sea monster symbolize a demonic culture, opposed to the dominant civilization. When Jonah jumped into the mouth of the sea monster (*kētos*) he was simply doing what was necessary for every Christian. Though a saved (safe?) person, he had to leave the security of the faith community and dive (or be cast) into the watery chaos of everyday life, a culture that was alien to Christians. At the end of this process God graced him by drawing him out of the belly of the *kētos*, out of life in the cultural chaos. God did not return him to the boat, his initial safe experience. Instead, Jonah "lands" under a protective bush where he rests.

It is difficult to define this moment of God's grace. Did Jonah, the Christian, consistently jump into the chaotic culture until the time of his death? Or, does the expulsion from the belly of the *kētos* mark the end of Christian Jonah's worldly life? In that case the final scene may reflect the believer's death, and the Jonah story does belong primarily in the Christian catacombs. Nevertheless, the resting figure may not have represented a dead figure.

4. Selene, and Endymion as Jonah

The early Christian artisans often used Endymion as the model for Jonah at rest. Endymion was the primary companion of Selene, the Greek moon goddess and sister of Helios the sun god. Artists depicted her as a beautiful woman with a veil billowing over her head. She had several lovers, but mythologically the most prominent was a human, Endymion. While the myths differ, Endymion likely was a shepherd or "astronomer" who lived in Olympia (hence the attachment to the moon goddess). Selene asked Zeus to permit the handsome Endymion to lie in perpetual sleep. Zeus granted the request. Selene made frequent love with him, and they had fifty

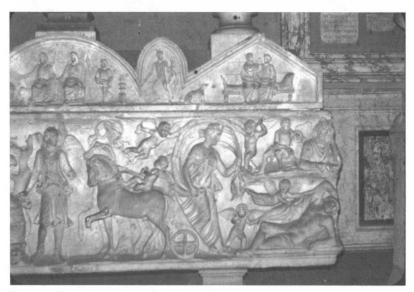

Figure 6. *Endymion resting before Selene (Roman sarcophagus)*

daughters. Endymion rested in a specific manner: usually nude, with right leg crossed over the left and right arm at rest on his head. In the non-Christian portrayals Selene often stood close by. The figure of Endymion consistently offered the model for Jonah at rest. Despite many interpretations otherwise, one must suppose that early Christians saw in Endymion/Jonah a person who rested after laboring in the aquatic world of chaos and sea monster.

5. The Lambs

On a very hot day the biblical prophet Jonah rested under a bush sent by God (Jonah 4:6-8). In early Christian art Jonah rests under a bush sometimes with lambs in it. Lambs in pre-Constantinian Christian art represented the members of the faith community. Only after Constantine did lambs reference the twelve apostles.[9] We therefore can assume that Jonah was resting in the context of his local church.

Figure 7. *Jonah under the bush and lambs (Santa Maria Antiqua, Rome)*

---

[9] "Pre-Constantinian" refers to art before the time of Constantine and the Edict of Milan in 313, which proclaimed the toleration of Christians in the Roman Empire.

Conclusion

If, in Christian art, the Jonah cycle had primarily symbolized the death and resurrection of second- and third-century Christians, then the three-fold art narrative would have continued even to this day. It did not. Symbols and art pictures that did not survive the formation of the Roman Christian church (about 313 CE) were ones that symbolized conflict between the new Christians and Roman culture. For example, the anchor, which is a symbol of divine security in the inimical water of Roman culture, disappeared after the fourth century. Or, before the establishment of Christianity as the official state religion, Jesus appeared as a seminude helper and healer. The boy Jesus assisted those who were under oppression. After 313 CE, Jesus disappeared as a helper and reappeared as a philosopher or even as a ruler. Very popular portrayals of the Jonah story came to an end. They had referenced the Christian life in an alien environment, not a theological truth such as resurrection. The biblical Jonah refused to speak as a prophet to a non-Jewish people. He was shocked and even pained to discover these Gentiles in Nineveh had been converted. In a somewhat similar pattern, the Jonah of early Christian art was depicted as a Christian compelled to enter the non-Christian society in which he lived. Nevertheless, God redeemed Jonah out of the mouth of the kētos.

Following the demise of the medieval church and the subsequent formation of many smaller faith communities, the book of Jonah took on more significance. As the earliest Jonah art indicated, we also are forced to live in societies that no longer take seriously the close community of the first Christians. So, now, as with Jonah, we can have faith that God will "snatch us from the belly" of social chaos and place us "under the bush" with the redeemed. As we trust in Christ who rose after three days and three nights, so, after three days and nights, we too will rise with him in his redeemed body. We, then, shall have a new life, as Jonah has shown.

Recommended Reading

Simon Chow. *The Sign of Jonah Reconsidered: A Study of Its Meaning in the Gospel Traditions.* Stockholm: Almqvist & Wiksell, 1995.

Richard A. Edwards. *The Sign of Jonah in the Theology of the Evangelists and Q.* Naperville, IL: Alec Allenson Inc., 1971.

Graydon F. Snyder. *Ante Pacem: Archaeological Evidence of Church Life before Constantine.* Revised ed. Macon, GA: Mercer University Press, 2003.

Study Questions

Prepare

Draw your own picture of the story of Jonah, using whatever medium you choose. Make sure those items you consider most important are central.

Read the book of Jonah, highlighting those passages that seem most significant to you.

Ask

1. Describe the worship center in your church? How often is it changed? How prominent is the cross? What other symbols are used?

2. Retell the story of Jonah, using the artwork you prepared prior to this session. What was the most important thing about the story when you were a child? What about now?

3. Snyder describes the story of Jonah in its original Hebrew setting. What was important about the story then? Name some of the ways early Christian non-biblical writers interpreted the story of Jonah. Contrast the two perspectives.

4. Some biblical commentators have deduced oral collections of sayings and stories that circulated before the written Gospels. Sometimes these are referred to as Q and the Signs Gospel. How are these defined in the article? How is Jonah used in these sources?

5. Snyder suggests that in one Gospel Jonah's preaching is considered a sign, but in another Jonah's time in the fish prefigures the death and resurrection of Jesus. What is the difference between these two interpretations? How would you use the story of Jonah as a sign?

6. Snyder uses the terms *local* and *translocal* to describe two different communities. The first consists of people in the local church. The second term refers to "official" writings by recognized authorities. There is a necessary tension between the two, two thousand years ago as well as today. If the early church fathers

quoted in the article are the translocal community, what different ways do they interpret the story of Jonah?

7. In the section "Jonah in Art," Snyder describes the way Jonah was used by the local Christian community. This is deduced not from writings, but from the artwork people chose, in the same way that hymns used in worship say more about what local people believe than scholarly articles that represent the translocal. Name different ways Jonah appear in these local settings.

8. The fourth-century emperor Constantine legalized Christianity and made it the official faith of the Roman Empire. There is a marked contrast between the Christian faiths that existed before and after Constantine. What is a basic difference about Christian art before and after the legalization of Christianity?

9. Snyder states that Christian art borrowed images from the larger culture. Name some of the images that were borrowed. What images does twenty-first century Christianity borrow from the larger culture?

10. One of the images used in Christian art is the *orante*, which refers to a figure with arms lifted up in an attitude of prayer. What posture do you use in prayer? How important is that posture for the act of prayer?

Suffering in the Book of Job and Psalms
A Study of Our Devotional Response to Loss

Robert W. Neff

While we speculate on the question, "Why do people suffer?" the Hebrew Bible does not spend much time answering this question. It deals more directly on how we *respond* to suffering and loss. Many of the Psalms and the book of Job explore the voices of those who suffer and how they deal with many of the losses we experience in life—sickness, betrayal, death of family and friends, social collapse, lack of progeny, separation forced by famine, foreign occupation, or financial ruin.

A majority of the Psalms and the entire book of Job detail in captivating poetry these voices of pain, anxiety, distrust, lament, and dismay. I often marvel at the honest, forthright complaints raised before God found in the Psalms (hymns of praise are far less frequent). And yet these words from the lips of those who are in pain provide the devotional setting for synagogue and church. I believe this is because suffering is accepted as a part of our shared human existence. Job provides the example of the suffering righteous one who demands the attention and interpretation of each new generation of biblical scholars.

The fundamental purpose of this essay is to examine the variety of responses to suffering in the First Testament. How should I as a person of faith respond to what I consider unjust suffering?

What can I say in circumstances that seem unjustified? Why do I feel deserted by God and my friends? What we will discover is that there are a variety of responses to these challenging questions.

Sources of Human Suffering

The Bible does not completely dismiss the causes of suffering. The First Testament opens with an affirmation that God's creation is good (Gen. 1–2). God intends that human beings will have an abundant and fulfilling life. However, by Genesis 3 humans rebel and defy the only commandment given to them—"not to eat the fruit of the tree of the knowledge of good and evil." They eat the fruit of this forbidden tree. This action brings a change in their relation to God and each other. One result is human suffering: the woman will bring forth children in pain and the man by hard labor and sweat will till the soil, yielding little in return. This outcome will be the normal experience for many humans. The First Testament affirms that the universality of human sin has become one of the causes for human suffering.

It's not the only cause of suffering, as the book of Job will attest. In the opening to this story, the reader is told three times that Job is "blameless and upright, one who feared God and turned away from evil" (Job 1:1, 8, and 2:3). Even though Job has lived an exemplary life, the Accuser in the story has a different view of humanity and seeks to demonstrate that Job is corruptible like any other human being. The Accuser believes that every person has a price. If Job suffers, he will turn against God. Job's suffering, therefore, is caused by a disgruntled member of God's heavenly council, who seeks to prove that he knows more about Job than God does. Job loses his family, his wealth, and his standing in the community. Yet Job does not turn against God.

After the first effort fails, the Accuser employs the means of a self-curse, "skin for skin," as a means of trying to undo Job through disease. In resorting to an oath that God must uphold, the accuser exploits a fault line in the universe that requires God to stand behind any oath uttered in a self-curse—a tenet of the Hebrew belief system. The Accuser is betting that Job will turn against God when he suffers in his own body. If Job does not curse God, then the Accuser will give up himself.

What now happens to Job has nothing to do with what God wants for him, but it is the result of a desperate ploy on the part of the Accuser. The cause for suffering in this story is not a human who sins, but rather the design of the universe that has structural fault lines that can be exploited by those forces intent upon doing evil. These fault lines were intended by God for good but have been distorted and used by those desiring evil. Suffering arises independent of a person's moral standing and God's intent for creation.

Why should we begin here? With this last observation on suffering we now know that men and women suffer unjustly and without cause. Both in the Psalms and the book of Job the person who prays to God often does so by professing innocence. For many of us who have grown up in a religious tradition, such a stance of innocence seems impossible. However, it is often the starting point of the petitioner in these biblical traditions. Psalm 22, one that Christians know from the words of Christ on the cross, begins, "My God, My God, why have you forsaken me?" The psalmist does not understand this present situation of suffering because as he/she confesses, "since my mother bore me you have been my God" (v. 10). Surely the selection of this psalm as an appropriate utterance of Christ from the cross underscores this profession of innocence, not only for Christ but for other lamenters who suffer unjustly.

This outlook of unjust suffering is not the only one present in the First Testament. The tradition of wisdom found in Psalm 1 suggests that there is a direct correlation between the actions of the righteous and their prosperity. Those who delight in the law are protected by God "in all that they do, they prosper. . . for the LORD watches over the way of the righteous" (vv. 3, 6a). However, "the wicked are not so, but are like chaff that the wind drives away . . . the way of the wicked will perish" (vv. 4, 6b). The Psalter begins with a confession that there is symmetry in the world, similar to what we discover in Genesis 1 and 2. The lament psalms differ in their outlook. They express the view that prosperity does not always come to the righteous.

We find a similar circumstance in the book of Job with the speeches of Job's three friends. Eliphaz begins with a reiteration of the doctrine found in the first Psalm: "Is not your fear of God your confidence, and the integrity of your ways your hope? Think now, who that was innocent ever perished? Or where were the upright cut off?" (Job 4:6-7). Eliphaz insists that Job will be restored if he is innocent, so he has nothing to fear. This argument is tempered to some degree by Eliphaz's view that humanity is born into trouble and God chastises those whom he loves. Nonetheless, he, Bildad, and Zophar uphold the doctrine that you get what you deserve.

The petitioner often does not agree with the premise of the friends or Psalm 1. Each individual responds differently to his or her unique circumstance of pain and suffering. These responses are not set in philosophical arguments, but are put forth in the context of great pain and loss. As we shall see in the book of Job and the Psalms, not every devout person responds the same way. Some of these voices will seem shrill and jarring, challenging our views of the nature of prayer and how we may address God. Even more distressing for us are the descriptions of the enemies and the request for vengeance against them. Emotional outbreaks and the honest expression of anger are not at all unusual in these prayers. Our more restrained approach to God will be embraced by some, but more often than not we will be challenged by a great many other voices. However, we will begin with an attitude that we expect in prayer—the response of traditional piety to suffering.

The Response of Traditional Piety

Of all the Old Testament characters there is no one more righteous than Job. Despite his piety and devotion, he loses his family, his wealth, his standing in the community, and his health. In all these heartbreaking circumstances, Job does not lose his patience nor does he change the center of his devotion. He does not blame God for his predicament, yet simply confesses, "Naked I came from my mother's womb, and naked shall I return there; the LORD gave, and the LORD has taken away, blessed be the name of the LORD" (1:21). After he comes down with a terminal illness, Job questions rhetorically, "Shall we receive the good at the hand of God, and not receive the bad?" (2:10). When his friends come to visit him, Job sustains his composure even through his suffering and loss. This exemplary behavior is what is expected of a pious man. In these first two chapters Job acts in accordance with the beliefs of traditional Hebrew piety. His friends encourage this attitude toward God and support him at this point in the narrative.

The roots of this piety extend beyond the First Testament itself, and can be found in other cultures in the ancient Near Eastern world as early as the second millennium BC. An individual worshiper who felt he had done no wrong, spoke to his god, "You have doled out suffering ever anew. . . . My God I would stand before you, would speak to you . . . [and] my word is a groan, suffering overwhelms me" (Pritchard 590). In the text itself the worshiper does not raise his voice, become impatient in his suffering, or turn away from his devotion. For this reason the text is often referred to as the Sumerian Job, since it appears to foreshadow the Job that we encounter in the Hebrew Bible.

It is this voice of Job that the writer of the New Testament epistle of James holds up as a model for Christian behavior in the face of great suffering: "Be patient, therefore, beloved, until the coming of the of the Lord. . . . Do not grumble against one another. . . . As an example of suffering and patience . . . we called blessed those who showed endurance. You have heard of the endurance of Job" (James 5:7ff.). Endurance (*hypomonē*) carries the sense of withstanding adversity without complaint and holding firm against any attack.

James has in mind the Job depicted in the prologue (Job 1–2), since he writes about avoiding grumbling and enduring patiently. James may also have Job in mind when he talks about the tongue in James 3. A loose tongue contaminates the whole body, because it, of all the organs of the body, has the power to direct one's whole being. Our task as believers is to tame the tongue and avoid the deadly poison of unbridled speech. Piety defined in this way receives the blows of life patiently and quietly. Control of one's emotions is emblematic of the devout life. This view of piety can be found in the Psalter:

> O LORD, my heart is not lifted up, my eyes are not raised too high; I do not occupy myself with things too great and too marvelous for me. But I have calmed and quieted my soul, like a weaned child with its mother; my soul within me is like a weaned child. O Israel, hope in the LORD from this time on and forevermore (Psalm 131).

As one reads these words, the feeling of quiet and unwavering trust emerges like a child in the arms of a caring and loving mother. This underlying trust can be found not only in this psalm, but in Psalms 127, 128, and 133. If an intrusion comes upon this serenity, the disruption will be overcome by a quiet trust.

My mother exhibited this form of piety her entire life, especially in the face of intense physical and emotional suffering. She was betrayed by her husband. She failed to receive child support and had to provide both income and maternal care for her children. She faced a life-threatening illness in her later years. She became legally blind. Yet in all those years she never became bitter, never disparaged her husband and my father, never turned away from the source of her devotion. She began every day with a prayer for my sister and me, and for many others whom she held close to her heart. When she passed away, my sister and I had been instructed to go to a small chest that would provide us with the final instructions for her funeral service. At the end of the list of her final wishes, she penned these words of comfort to my sister and me, "Weep not for me, my precious ones, I have gone home." My mother embodied a traditional piety throughout her entire life— one that has inspired me, my sister, and many others.

Despite its attractiveness, this model of piety and response to suffering—documented for more than four millennia—is not the only model. In fact, as we look at different First Testament texts this response remains a *minority* voice among responses to suffering.

The Contexts of Lament and Complaint

As we discuss lament and complaint, it will be helpful for us to distinguish between the two. When I lament I want to get something off my chest, however great the loss or pain, so that I feel better. I don't expect a response. In my crying I unload my feeling of distress and may end up feeling better without any change in my external circumstances.

There are no lament departments in large retail stores; they have complaint departments. When I go to a complaint department and raise a concern, I expect that my complaint will be heard and appropriate restoration made. In other words, I, the complainer, expect results to my satisfaction. The circumstances of the lamenter and complainer could be exactly the same, but the *expectation* represented in each style is vastly different. In the complaint I am baring my soul before God with a view that my external circumstances will change, but in lament I am baring my soul before God in the hope of a respectful hearing without a change in my external circumstances. If my store had a Lament Department, I would not expect anything to change. All I would want is for someone to hear me.

Circumstances of laments and complaints from biblical characters can be found throughout the Old Testament. These people ask why they should go on living when life has turned against them. These cries arise out of difficult circumstances, as demonstrated by the following illustrations. "What will you give me," asks Abram, "for I continue childless?" (Gen. 15:2). "If it is to be this way, why do I live?" laments Rebekah in Genesis 25:22 during a difficult pregnancy. After his great victory over the Philistines, Samson cries out in anguish, "Am I now to die of thirst?" (Judges 15:18). Claus Westermann observes that the list could go on. In these biblical narratives, the reader sees the laments and complaints in their primal settings, in a place where life appears at wit's end and to which this form of human expression belongs (90). However, the attitude in prayer may be one in which a person doesn't expect anything to change (lament), or expects a change through a petition for it (complaint).

An underlying assumption in these expressions of suffering is that the individual has done nothing wrong, at least not enough to be treated this way. The great Psalms scholar Sigmund Mowinckel observes there is little room for repentance since the lamenter or complainer asserts that he or she is innocent. In the context of our own tradition this will be quite foreign to our faith stance where confession of sin marks the critical juncture in many Christian worship services. However, as we have already noted, Job is described as a person who is without blemish and yet suffers greatly.

The Response of Lament

By the third chapter of Job, the response of Job has changed drastically. The muted voice of traditional piety has erupted into lament:

> Let the day perish in which I was born, and the night that said, "A man-child is conceived." . . . Why did I not die at birth, come forth from the womb and expire? . . . Why is light given to one in misery, and life to the bitter in soul, who long for death, but it does not come. . . . Truly the thing I fear comes upon me, and what I dread befalls me. I am not at ease, nor am I quiet; I have no rest; but trouble comes (excerpts from Job 3).

Job does not curse God but the day of his birth. His pain has become unbearable. Physical discomfort becomes the focal point for his existence. The clarity of life's meaning has been obscured. The prayer concern rests with the lamenter; in this poem the pain of the first person dominates the entire field. The reader encounters Job's suffering first hand. We cannot escape the intensity of Job's sighs, summarized at the end of the lament in staccato cadence and a relentless pounding—no ease, no quiet, no rest, trouble comes.

Jeremiah shares a similar anguish with Job in tones that mirror in terse fashion his lament:

> Cursed be the day on which I was born! The day when my mother bore me, let it not be blessed! Cursed be the man who brought the news to my father, saying, "A child is born to you,

a son," making him very glad. Let that man be like the cities that
the LORD overthrew without pity; let him hear a cry in the morning and an alarm at noon, because he did not kill me in womb;
so my mother would have been my grave, and her womb forever
great. Why did I come forth from the womb to see toil and sorrow, and spend my days in shame? (Jer. 20:14-18).

This lament concludes a series of six such poems in the book of
Jeremiah. And this one, unlike the others, does not appear to expect any response. Jeremiah seems to have given up and no longer
expects an answer to his prayers. This prophet bares his soul in
sorrow and dismay. He believes he has done everything God has
asked and has been faithful to the prophetic task. Yet he is attacked
by family, friends, and those in power.

The third book[1] of the Psalter ends with a communal lament
over the sacking of Jerusalem and the collapse of the Davidic line.
In an individual lament (Psalm 88), just prior to this communal
outcry, the one who prays finds himself abandoned by God with almost no hope of response:

But I, O LORD, cry out to you; in the morning my prayer comes before you. O LORD, why do you cast me off? Why do you hide your
face from me? Wretched and close to death from my youth up,
I suffer your terrors; I am desperate. Your wrath has swept over
me; your dread assaults destroy me. They surround me like a
flood all day long; from all sides they close in on me. You have
caused friend and neighbor to shun me; my companions are in
darkness (88:13-18).

This individual does not seek forgiveness, sees no end to suffering, and appears to have no hope. He is alone to face the darkness
and God's absence. Walter Brueggemann asserts that Psalm 88 is an
excellent example of unanswered complaint, or lament, in the Hebrew Bible. The speaker addresses what apparently is an empty sky
and an indifferent throne. There are unresolved situations. The

---

[1] The Psalter can be divided into five "books": I (Psalms 1–41); II (Psalms 42–72); III (Psalms
73–89); IV (Psalms 90–106); and V (Psalms 107–150). Each book ends with a section of praise
to God (doxology). In its final form, the Psalter, like the Pentateuch, has five books.

silence of God does not drive Israel away from prayer; it drives Israel to more earnest, intense, passionate prayer" (56).

All three lamenters believe that God has abandoned them and no longer expect answers to their prayers. They are baring their souls in sorrow and raising a chorus of distress. All three protest they have done nothing wrong and cannot explain the inexplicable lack of response from God.

Laments are not just an expression of the past. They arise in the here and now. Take the case of Ann Weems, a writer and poet, who lost a teenage son in a tragic car accident. She was lost in a sea of tears because she knew her son would never return to her. Old Testament scholar Walter Brueggemann encouraged her to write a series of laments to give expression to her feeling of unjustified loss. Over a period of years she composed a series of laments that gave expression to her loss and pain. These laments have now been published[2] and I use them in my own devotional life to give expression to the losses and hurts that I feel—the loss of my mother, close relatives and friends, tragedies like September 11, 2001, and Hurricane Katrina. Her laments continue to have power because she knew she could not have her son back, but by sharing these lamentations she was able to work through her grief. Her laments of deep passion were a path toward healing.

The Response of Complaint

There is a significant change in tone in Job's speech found in chapters 6–7:

> O that I might have my request, and that God would grant my desire; that it would please God to crush me, that he would let loose his hand and cut me off! This would be my consolation; I would even exult in unrelenting pain; for I have not denied the words of the Holy One. What is my strength, that I should wait? And what is my end, that I should be patient? Is my strength the strength of stones, or is my flesh bronze? (Job 6:8-12).

---

[2] Ann Weems, *Psalms of Lament* (Louisville: Westminster John Knox, 1995). Weems uses the lament psalms of the Bible as a model for the poems she writes to express the pain she experienced at the death of her son.

The voice has become angrier, more accusatory, and desires change in one way or another (although it needs to be said, that a similar tone of expression can be found in laments). Patience of any kind has gone out the window. Contrary to the position of traditional piety represented by the three friends who are now aghast at his behavior, Job defends his right to rant and rave—a direct violation of the teaching of traditional orthodoxy. He refuses to be self-contained and controlled. He agrees that he has become angry and believes that this is the only fair response given his situation.

What one finds in the complaint psalms (also in the laments) and those complaints in Job is that in addition to railing against God, the lamenter complains of the enemies who hurl taunts and seek to do the worshiper in. "Many bulls encircle me . . . they open wide their mouths at me, like a ravening and roaring lion. . . . For dogs are all around me; a company of evildoers encircles me (Psalm 22:12-13, 16a). In this case the enemies are not identified, which is true for a good number of lament/complaint psalms. The identification of these figures is widely debated among scholars.

However, there are a number of instances in the First Testament where the enemy is identified. Patrick Miller, in his *Interpreting the Psalms*, rightly directs us to the book of Jeremiah where there is a direct identification of the enemy in the laments of chapters 11 and 12. "Jeremiah's life really is threatened, and the enemy is his family (cf. Ps. 69:8). Alienation from family is not merely a way of expressing total isolation . . . but a reality certainly tied to the way in which Jeremiah's words were perceived as threatening to the priestly establishment of which Jeremiah's family was a part" (60). Miller, in this regard, looks at the life of Hannah (1 Samuel 1–3) where the threat comes from a rival wife who causes her all forms of distress (56ff.).

One may add the theme of betrayal to this circumstance. The writer who is identified in Psalm 3 as David declares, "O LORD, how many are my foes! Many are rising against me" (v. 1). In the title to the psalm we are told that this was uttered when David was fleeing from his son Absalom. One of the most telling descriptions of betrayal by a close friend is found in Psalm 55:

> It is not enemies who taunt me—I could bear that; it is not adversaries who deal insolently with me—I could hide from them. But it is you, my equal, my companion, my familiar friend, with whom I kept pleasant company; we walked in the house of God with the throng (vv. 12-14).

In the book of Job, Job's friends turn on him and accuse him of all kinds of wrongdoing, especially when he fails to respond to their advice in a way that they can accept. Job compares his friends to wet weather streams. In the springtime when everything is fresh and new, they provide needed sustenance. But in the dry times when you really need them, these streams dry up and bring death instead of life. Job argues that his friends are just like unpredictable streams: "My companions are treacherous like a torrent-bed, like freshets that pass away, that run dark with ice, turbid with melting snow. In time of heat they disappear; when it is hot, they vanish from their place" (6:15-17). In essence they bring death. He accuses them of turning on him and forsaking the Almighty by withholding kindness from a friend.

Taunts also arise out of the hostile circumstance of deportation and exile. The enemy is a foreign army or foreign overseer or a neighbor who rejoices in the destruction of Jerusalem. Americans were alarmed when those who relished our demise replayed the annihilation of the twin towers through video reproduction. Psalm 137 recites the satiric request of the oppressors in Babylon, "Sing us one of the songs of Zion!" (v. 3*b*). And in the background is the recollection of the voices of the Edomites at the destruction of the sacred city, crying, "Tear it down! Tear it down! Down to its foundation!" (v. 7). It's hard to accept the reality of defeat, but to be reminded of it through sarcasm and continual abrasion by those who triumphed brings out a heated response like the one found at the end of this psalm: "O daughter Babylon, you devastator! Happy shall they be who pay you back what you have done to us! Happy shall they be who take your little ones and dash them against the rock!" (vv. 8-9).

The Bible does not respond by saying, "You can't talk like that before God." This utterance is surrounded by a series of confessions. In Psalm 136, all twenty-five verses conclude with the words, "for [God's] steadfast love endures forever." God's faithfulness is affirmed in the context of taunting and abuse. In Psalm 138, the confession occurs, "Though I walk in the midst of trouble, you preserve me against the wrath of my enemies; you stretch out your hand, and your right hand delivers me. The LORD will fulfill his purpose for me; your steadfast love, O LORD, endures forever" (vv. 7-8a). In the context of extreme anger and disillusion, the worshiper is not limited in the vocabulary or the feeling that can be expressed to God.

In our own tradition we have been taught to repress our anger and our feelings in worship. I must confess that I was schooled never to raise my voice before God in my prayers; God would not tolerate that behavior. All that changed many years later when I was in my first year at Yale Divinity School. In beautiful, serene Marquand Chapel, we were having a worship service. Bob Spivey was in charge. He had just come from the hospital where his wife had given birth to a baby girl, only to learn that she in all likelihood would die. He prayed with the accusing voice of a distraught father, and berated God at threatening a defenseless child. He begged in his prayer for God to heal his daughter. I thought to myself, "How dare he speak to God in that way!" Years later I must confess that it is one of the few prayers I remember from my student days, and it's not because others were not authentic or elegant. I remember this one because it was the voice of complaint that rose out of the depths of the soul. His daughter lived. The biblical tradition affirms in the tradition of the complaint/lament psalms that God listens to our voices in the harshest of circumstances and does not require that we mute the distress of our suffering.

The Response of Tested Faith

The conclusion of the book of Job looks like a return to a position of traditional piety, but it is not. Therefore, when in 42:6, Job says, "I despise myself, and repent in dust and ashes," this seems contrary to the invitation to Job to gird up his loins like a warrior in Job 38:3 and 40:7. In other words, stop the groveling. Secondly, from the speech from the whirlwind in Job 38–41, Job has an expanded view of God's creative power. Thirdly, Job has already been on a heap of ashes. Does this response simply mean more groveling on his part? I think not. There is another translation suggested by the Hebrew—"Therefore I retract my case and repent *of* dust and ashes." In other words, I am through with dust and ashes; I am going to live life fully. Norman Habel defends this translation, which has been supported by a number of other scholars (575*ff.*). Through lament and complaint, Job has been granted God's creative presence that brings an end to his complaint and remorse (see 42:7*ff.*). And for the rest of the chapter we read that he lives a full life despite all he has lost.

My affirmation of this perspective is derived from the work of one who experienced suffering and oppression in the cultures of Latin America. Gustavo Gutiérrez, in his book *On Job: God-Talk and the Suffering of the Innocent*, writes: "Job is rejecting the attitude of lamentation that has been his until now. The speeches of God have shown him that this attitude is not justified. He does not repent or retract what he has hitherto said, but he now sees clearly that he cannot go on complaining. This means that in his final reply what Job is expressing is not contrition but a renunciation of lamentation and dejected outlook" (87).

Job also overcomes the attitude that God owes him something because of his righteousness. The image of God is trapped by Job's own view of justice—giving in order that God give something back. Gutiérrez writes, "Certain emphases in his protest had been due to the doctrine of retribution. . . . Now that the Lord has overthrown that doctrine . . . Job realizes that he has been speaking of God in a way that implied God was a prisoner of a particular way of understanding justice. It is this whole outlook that Job says he is now abandoning. Only when we have come to realize that God's love is freely bestowed, do we enter fully and definitely into the presence of the God of faith" (87).

What we discover in this journey through the book of Job is a devotion not built on rewards, but on the recognition of God's free gift to us. There is no way that we can gain a hold on God and remove God's freedom in his love and care for us. Again Gutiérrez writes, "The Lord is not prisoner of the 'give me and I will give to you' mentality. Nothing, no human work however valuable merits grace, for if it did, grace would cease to be grace. This is the heart of the message of the Book of Job" (88*ff.*). Devotion is found in the desire for God and a refusal to bind God to a set of principles that the believer defines or controls. God is beyond such a system; otherwise God would not be God.

Job comes to this position while he is still suffering. Job, in the context of suffering, changes his attitude toward God and his friends for whom he now prays. His complaint is now transformed to a mediating presence. Life is not devoid of tragedy or suffering, but even in these circumstances, it is not devoid of the creative presence of God who moves to restore life and surround the anguish of the sufferer. It is this lesson that Job has learned.

Brueggemann, in his book *The Psalms and the Life of Faith*, has captured in his portrayal of the sweep of the Psalter a similar direction in the Psalms. These psalms of lament and complaint which we have encountered through this essay finally come to rest in Psalm 150. Just as Job overthrows his remorse and dejected status, so the Psalter, after sorrow after sorrow, erupts in this way:

Praise the LORD! Praise God in his sanctuary; praise him in his mighty firmament!

Praise him for his mighty deeds; praise him according to his surpassing greatness!

Praise him with trumpet sound; praise him with lute and harp! Praise him with tambourine and dance; praise him with strings and pipe! Praise him with clanging cymbals; praise him with loud clashing cymbals!

Let everything that breathes praise the LORD! Praise the LORD!

Brueggemann writes: "The Psalm expresses a lyrical self-abandonment, an utter yielding of self, without vested interest, calculation, desire, or hidden agenda. This praise is nothing other than a glad offer of self in lyrical surrender to the God appropriately addressed in praise. The Psalter, in correspondence to Israel's life with God when lived faithfully, ends in glad, unconditional praise: completely, and without embarrassment or distraction, focused on God. No characterization of God is given; it is enough that the one to be praised is fully and utterly God and therefore must be praised" (193).

As we observed in the book of Job, the voice of tested faith emerges in the Psalter as well. In this book we find many different individuals within the community giving voice to their hurts, complaints, and sense of loss. By the end of the Psalms, praise erupts without any given reason. The movement through the Psalter that allowed all kinds of statements and misgivings about God comes to rest in the belief that God reigns, even in a world where suffering and disappointment exists.

Job and the Psalms record the voices of human suffering and do not conclude with a firm answer to the causes of suffering on this earth. In expressing heartfelt loss in plaintive cries, not shielding God from anger or hurt or even violent language, the life of faith develops. The lamenter shares the deepest aches and pains of existence in the language of the soul. The one who prays believes not only that God is listening and will respond, but that the believer affirms the flexibility and adaptability of God in relation to one's own circumstance. God's absence will be followed by a deep sense of God's presence. This authenticity in the way one speaks with God allows a level of honesty that is compelling and refreshing. God identifies with those who suffer, and God does not ask for sugarcoating in talking about the way one feels. In such honesty one lays the foundation for renewing one's faith and restoring one's relationship with God. The outcome is not quiescence to the voice of suffering, but the outbreak of the voice of tested faith expressed in three words, "Praise the LORD."

Recommended Reading

Gustav Gutiérrez. *On Job: God-Talk and the Suffering of the Innocent*. Maryknoll: Orbis Books, 1987.

Robert W. Neff. *Voices in the Book of Job*. Covenant Bible Study Series. Elgin: Brethren Press, 2005.

Carol Newsom. *The Book of Job: A Contest of Moral Imaginations*. New York: Oxford University Press, 2003.

Study Questions

Prepare

Read Psalms 1; 22; 55:12-14; 88:13-18; 131; and 137. Also read Job 1; 2; 4:6-7; 6:8-12; 38; and 42.

Take time to clip an article or two from a newspaper or magazine about someone who is suffering unjustly.

Ask

1. I have heard individuals say, "I'm really mad at God right now, but I don't feel I should tell God." Why do you think people respond to suffering this way? What is the proper way to approach God, in your opinion?

2. Neff writes that one of the results of human suffering is human sin. How much of human suffering is the result of poor choices? Chance? Divine origin?

3. The essay refers to "structural fault lines" in "the design of the universe" that can lead to human suffering. When, in your experience, have people suffered unjustly?

4. Psalm 1 seems to state the righteous prosper in all they do, but the way of the wicked will perish. Is that so, in your experience? How would this make people feel who have not prospered? What sort of theology is this?

5. Neff states that one response to suffering—the response of traditional piety—suggests that both good and bad things are going to happen over the course of a lifetime. In some cultures this is described as a "wheel of fortune." All people are on the wheel, and as it spins some fortunes rise and some fall, but ultimately everyone experiences ups and downs. How does this correspond to your experience? Why do some people expect that things will only go well? Why are some outraged when things go poorly?

6. What is the difference between a complaint and a lament, according to Neff? Which more accurately describes your attitude during times of suffering?

7. Have you ever heard anyone lament after the manner of Job 3? Yourself? Another? How are these individuals doing now?

8. Name a national or a regional tragedy that might have called for a lament? Did someone organize worship services after these events to provide a response of prayer? Were the services more of a lament or complaint?

9. By the end of his suffering Job seems to have gained the perspective that he is not alone in his condition. How important is perspective when it comes to suffering and one's outlook for the future.

10. In chapter 42 Job seems to renounce lamentation and have a new outlook. Is that possible for those who have suffered greatly? What do you think motivates people who have suffered terrible wrongs such as genocide and massacre? Job's faith was tested. How does testing change our relationship with God? Between us and the world? Between us and church members?

Love and Desire in the Song of Songs

Christina Bucher

People often ask me why I chose to study the Old Testament, rather than the New, when I did my doctoral work. Perhaps viewing "new" as better than "old," some cannot understand why anyone would want to study the Old Testament. Others will ask why a member of the Church of the Brethren would opt to study the Old Testament. (An oft-repeated claim among Brethren is that "we have no creed but the New Testament.") I reply that the Christian canon includes two testaments, not one; Jesus' Scripture was something close to what Christians today call the "Old Testament"; and the New Testament writers presuppose the writings of the Old Testament. In order to really understand Jesus, the New Testament, and Christian history and tradition, one needs a deep understanding of the Old Testament, the collection of books that I prefer to call "First Testament," "Hebrew Scriptures," or "Tanakh."

I clearly remember what first attracted me to the Hebrew Scriptures. As an undergraduate, I took the standard sequence of Bible introductions: Old Testament in the fall semester and New Testament in the spring. In the fall, I fell in love with both the classical Hebrew language and the Hebrew Scriptures. For the first time in my life, I studied the Bible's historical and cultural context and found answers to questions that had troubled me for several years. The Bible began to make sense to me, once I understood the huge gap in time, culture, and language between the origin of the biblical texts and the time of my reading them.

Having struggled as a child with my perception of the Bible's demand for perfection, which I thought both Jesus and my church posited as a necessary condition of discipleship, I loved the fallibility of the characters who inhabit the stories of the Tanakh. Many of the leading figures had committed much graver sins than I had ever even contemplated, yet there they were in Scripture: Moses, the lawgiver, who had killed a man, and David, Israel's king and God's beloved, who had committed adultery. Others exhibited less serious flaws: Elisha, who apparently had quite a temper, and Jacob, who seriously deceived his father.

I loved (and still love) the earthiness of the First Testament people and the playfulness of many of the stories. At Bethany Theological Seminary, I had the good fortune of studying the Hebrew Scriptures with Bob Neff. Under Bob's tutelage, my appreciation of the Hebrew Scriptures deepened. I became further convinced that the church needs its First Testament as much as it needs its Second Testament, because Christianity's thought and practice are grounded there. The relationship between the testaments is complex, just as the relationship between various teachings within the New Testament is complex. On some topics, the Hebrew Scriptures provide welcome insight that is either absent or assumed in the New Testament. This volume of essays investigates what the Hebrew Scriptures offer on some of these topics. This particular essay explores views of love and desire in the Song of Songs and ways in which these views contribute to our understanding of both human nature and Christian spirituality. What we learn from Song of Songs about human nature, and human sexuality in particular, is neither comprehensive nor complete. Nevertheless, it does offer a scriptural affirmation of human sexual desire.

At a second level of reading, influenced by certain traditions of Christian spirituality, we can deepen our experience of God and our understanding of the divine-human relationship.[1] For centuries Christian interpreters have read Song of Songs metaphorically as a

---

[1] "Christian spirituality" refers to expressions of the lived experience of Christians, as opposed to discussions of doctrine. Christian spirituality can be found in devotional and mystical writings, hymns, liturgy, and the visual arts.

celebration of divine-human love. And although this mode of reading was out of favor for much of the twentieth century, a metaphorical reading of Song of Songs links positively to several new directions in Christian theology and spirituality. In what follows, I will first explore the "plain sense of the text"[2] and what the Song has to say about love and desire. Then, I will propose reading Song of Songs metaphorically, outlining implications of such a reading for Christian theology and spirituality today.

What Does Song of Songs Tell Us about Love?

Let him kiss me with the kisses of his mouth![3]

Song of Songs 1:2*a*

What a shock to the unsuspecting reader who opens the Bible to the first chapter of the Song of Songs (also known as "Song of Solomon"). Often overlooked, the eight chapters of the Song of Songs can be found roughly three-quarters of the way through the First Testament, tucked in between Ecclesiastes and Isaiah. In these chapters we discover love poetry, written largely in the form of dialogues between an unnamed man and woman, in which they express their love for one another and their desire to be together. Anyone handed this collection of poetry without being told the poems can be found in the Bible would certainly take them to be a celebration of human sexual attraction and a poetic description of sexual desire. So, what is a book like this doing in the Bible?

The central Hebrew term for love in the Bible is *'ahav*, a word that has a range of meaning that is about as broad as that of the English word "love." The Hebrew term has both verb and noun forms (the noun is *'ahavah*). The verb can have both personal and impersonal objects; you can love both "people" and "justice." For instance, the Hebrew *'ahav* can refer to the love of parents and

---

[2] I follow early Christian tradition in contrasting plain sense (or literal sense) and spiritual sense. By plain sense of the text, I mean the grammatical sense that is accessible to anyone who reads carefully and attentively. By spiritual sense, I point to a second meaning that reveals truths about our relationship with God.

[3] All translations from the Hebrew are mine, unless otherwise noted.

children (Gen. 25:28, "Isaac loved Esau"). In Leviticus 19, however, it is the term used in the commands to love neighbors (v. 18) and sojourners (v. 34). The term can also be used in the context of international political relationships. For example, King Hiram of Tyre is called a "lover of David" in 1 Kings 5:1.[4] In addition to being used of human love, the Hebrew 'ahav describes the love of humans for God (Deut. 6:5, "you shall love the LORD, your God"). Less frequently, the term is used of God's love for people. In Song of Songs the verb 'ahav and the noun 'ahavah are used in the context of sexual love.[5]

In Song of Songs, both verb and noun forms of this word occur frequently, along with other related vocabulary. The woman refers to the man as "the one I love" (1:7, 3:1-4). She announces that "his banner over me is love" (2:4b) and proclaims that she is "sick with love" (2:5). In several verses, the noun 'ahavah may refer to expressions of love or to lovemaking:

> May he kiss me with the kisses of his mouth!
> For your *lovemaking* is better than wine (1:2).

> How beautiful is your *lovemaking* my sister, bride,
> How much better than wine is your *lovemaking*,
> The scent of your oils is better than any balsam perfumes (4:10).

In addition to talking about their love and lovemaking, the man and woman refer to each other with terms of endearment. The man usually refers to the woman as "my darling" (Hebrew *ra'yati*, which can also be translated "my lover" or "my companion"). She calls him "my beloved" (*'dodi*, which some versions translate with "my lover").

Ancient peoples identified feelings and emotions with different parts of the body more than moderns do. Westerners today speak of the heart as the locus of feelings, even though we know that anatomically the heart has the function of pumping blood through-

---

[4] 1 Kings 5:15 in the Hebrew text.
[5] For more detailed information on this term, see Jenni and Westermann, Vol. 1, 45-54, and Gowan 306-308.

out our bodies. We send heart-shaped cards on Valentine's Day, not to suggest the recipient should see the doctor for a stress test, but to express love and affection. The association of "heart" and "affection" does not appear in the Bible, at least not frequently. In the Bible, the heart is associated primarily with decision making and understanding. We can see this identification of heart and will in references to the "hardening" of Pharaoh's heart in the exodus story. When it says that Pharaoh hardens his heart, it means he refuses to let the people leave Egypt.

In Song of Songs, we see a similar association of heart and will, or decision making. In 4:9, the man describes the way in which his lover affects him, using a verb formed from the Hebrew noun for "heart" (*lev*).

> You have *captured my heart* (*libavtini*), my own, my bride.
> You have captured my heart with one glance of your eyes,
> With one coil of your necklace (4:9).

The verb translated here as "captured my heart" occurs only a few times in the Bible, which makes it difficult to determine its true sense in our passage. Formed from the noun meaning "heart," the verb has two possible meanings. Some translations imply the verb has a privative meaning: she has taken away his heart (his will), leaving him weak and unable to resist. Words such as "stolen," "captured," and "ravished" communicate the privative sense. By contrast, however, the verb could also have an intensifying meaning, having to do with "giving" or "increasing" heart (will), motivating the lover to act, and perhaps sexually arousing him. This may be an example of Hebrew wordplay where both meanings are operative: the lover *both* cannot resist his beloved *and* becomes sexually aroused by her. Duane Garrett tries to capture the ambiguity with "you leave me breathless" (194). Othmar Keel suggests that it means something like "you drive me crazy" (162).

In four distinct poems, the lovers express their admiration for each other: 4:1-7; 5:10-16; 6:4-10; and 7:1-7. Scholars often refer to this type of poem as a *wasf*, a term borrowed from Arabic culture, where it refers to a type of love song in which one lover describes his or her beloved's appearance. Each of these poems conveys the sense of delight experienced by the lover who contemplates the beloved. In 5:10-16, the woman praises the man. In the other three poems, he praises her. In his commentary on the Song of Songs, Othmar Keel explains the function of the poems of admiration.

> One of the central experiences of love is the lover's tendency to see all things beautiful and desirable as reminders of the beloved, finding in her or him their unity and meaning. The beloved gives the world not only a new radiance but also a meaningful center; yet, at the same time, the beloved becomes the lover's whole world (24).

Love Is Strong as Death

Although the majority of the book's poems are in the form of speeches directed by one lover to the other, the book contains one poetic statement *about* love (8:6-7). This passage begins with the woman's request to her beloved:

> Set me as a seal upon your heart,
> As a seal upon your arm.

Ancient Near Eastern people wore seals as rings on their fingers or as bracelets on their upper arms (armlets) or as necklaces hung on a cord around their necks. These seals had several functions—both symbolic and real. They were somewhat like passports, ID cards, or credit cards in that they verified the identity of the owner. Like these modern forms of identification, ancient seals were precious possessions. As such, they stood for the owner's commitment and integrity (as in Genesis 38, where Judah leaves his seal as a "pledge").

A declaration about love, stated as a comparison, follows the woman's request.

> For Love (*'ahavah*) is as fierce as Death.
> Jealousy (*qin'ah*) as hard as the Grave.
> Its sparks, sparks of fire,
> A mighty flame.
> Many waters are not able to cover Love (*'ahavah*),
> Rivers cannot flood over it.

Here, love is compared to death and found to be death's equal in terms of ferocity. We all know death to be that powerful force that none of us can resist. Even the Christian hope in resurrection acknowledges that all humans will die. Resurrection offers new life by overcoming death, not by getting rid of it. Jesus really died. Even he could not avoid death.

How can love be as strong as death? Ellen Davis suggests that love protects us from the fear of death. Love teaches us to yield to the other, which becomes "the best preparation for what Christians have traditionally called a holy death" (*Proverbs, Ecclesiastes, and the Song of Songs* 297).

If love is as fierce as death, jealousy is as hard as the grave. The Grave, translated from the Hebrew term *she'ol* is a synonym for death in the Hebrew Scriptures. It is sometimes left untranslated as "Sheol" and can also be translated "Underworld" (but does not suggest punishment or torment). Although some translators prefer the term "passion," the Hebrew term *qin'ah* is probably best translated "jealousy." It is surprising to find such a positive statement about "jealousy," which is often a negative character trait. The term is used to characterize God in the Hebrew Scriptures, suggesting that in certain contexts we can view jealousy positively. Davis asserts that jealousy is acceptable when it occurs in defense of the covenant relationship between God and Israel (*Proverbs, Ecclesiastes, and the Song of Songs* 298).

Translators vary on the meaning of the phrase I have translated "a mighty flame." The Hebrew word *shalhevetyah* contains a reference to God, if we separate "*yah*" from the rest of the word. If so, this is the only direct reference to God in the entire book. The words *shalhevet yah* mean "flame of Yah," with Yah being a short form of the name "Yahweh." We see this short name for God in the Psalms' command to praise God (*halelu-yah*, "praise Yah,"). An alternate translation (and the one I favor) is to take the particle *yah* as a suffix that indicates intensity. If we follow this line of thinking, the phrase then means "a mighty flame" (NIV), "a raging flame" (NRSV), "a raging fire" (GNT), or "a most vehement flame" (KJV, RSV). Although I translate the phrase "a mighty flame," the allusion

to God in the Hebrew reminds us that God's love can be like a raging fire. This double meaning is hard to capture in English translations, but it is immediately apparent in the Hebrew. We may also
be reminded of appearances of God in the Bible that are connected
to fire: the burning bush that is not consumed (Exodus 3:2), fire
upon Mount Sinai (Exodus 19:18), and "what looked like fire" in
Ezekiel's vision (Ezek. 1:27), to name a few.

From fire, we shift to water. Both fire and water represent el-
emental powers of the natural world. Despite all our technologi-
cal skill today, we cannot totally avoid the destructive power of fire
and water. In dry seasons people living in the western part of the
United States flee their homes as wildfires encroach upon space
that humans had marked out for dwelling, while those who live
along the Eastern Seaboard and Gulf Coast must sometimes abandon their homes during hurricane season. In the Bible, water is
both a source of life and a cosmic force that sometimes threatens
life (as in the great flood of Noah's time). Our poet here proclaims
that love contains within itself power equal to fire and the ability
to withstand raging waters.

To conclude this brief unit, we find an aphorism about love.

> If anyone offered all their wealth in exchange for love,
> It would be utterly scorned (8:6-7*b*).

As is often the case with wisdom literature, this saying is elusive. My
translation takes the saying to mean that it is impossible to purchase
love. "You can't buy love" seems to be the thrust of the saying. The
second half of the saying translated word for word is something like
this: "they would utterly scorn him [or 'it']." Since it's not clear who
"they" are, it might mean that "people" (in contemporary terms this
might refer to "consumerist society") would scoff at anyone who was
willing to give up his or her wealth in order to gain love. It is also un-
clear whether the final pronoun refers to the individual ("him") or
to the wealth ("it"), or to both the man and his wealth. My translation suggests that it is the attempt to buy love that is scorned. This
seems to fit best with what precedes. Just as love cannot be overcome by the powers of the natural world (fire or water), it also

cannot be bought. The Contemporary English Version suggests this with its simplified translation: "Love cannot be drowned by oceans or floods; it cannot be bought, no matter what is offered."

We discover in the Song of Songs an affirmation of human sexuality and the power of love. Love has the ability to drive a person "crazy" with desire. Love has power that makes it a match even for death. And, although you might wish to, you cannot buy love. So far, so good. The poems of Song of Songs praise human love and sexuality. There is one problem, however. Much of the book focuses on the loss, absence, and anguish of being separated from the beloved.

What Does Song of Songs Reveal about Desire?

The recurring problem in Song of Songs is that the two lovers are kept apart, either by circumstances or by the efforts of others. Perhaps surprisingly to some readers, we discover upon close inspection that much of the book describes the experiences of *absence* and *separation*. Rather than describing the experience of intimacy, many of the poems depict the anguish of loss. Song of Songs explores the feeling of desire—the desire to overcome the separation from the beloved.

The word *ēros*, one of several Greek terms for love, has to do with love's desire. Biblical scholar Tod Linafelt discusses the concept of eros that he sees in Song of Songs.

> Eros is finally a dialectical movement between these poles of absence and presence, lack and plenitude, longing and consummation. That is, one's experience of eros exists in a tension that can only ever be resolved in a provisional way, since to come down once and for all on either side would mean the end of eros, absence without hope and presence without qualification being equally a threat to erotic love (253).

Much of the Song of Song's poetry has to do with eros, desire for that which is missing. At first, "desire" may strike some readers as falling more on the sinful side of the equation. Although the Bible condemns envy and lust, desire itself is not condemned. Some sexual desires or expressions may be considered wrong, but sexual desire itself is not wrong (Gowan 104-105). In a discussion of biblical wisdom literature, Ellen Davis argues that desire is viewed as something good if the object of desire is good.

> In using the language of love and desire, the sages alert us to the hidden but essential connection between what we want and what we may come to know. Through holy desire, we may indeed gain what Israel called wisdom: true, realistic knowledge of God, ourselves, and the world. But we may also waste our desire, by turning it to things that are unworthy of us, or harmful to us. . . .
>
> The key insight is this: desire is never spiritually neutral. It either sharpens our perception, so that we see ourselves and the world in something of the same way God sees, or else it distorts our understanding of our God-given situation in the world ("Wisdom, Desire, and Holy Love" 8).

Rather than beginning with the Hebrew vocabulary for terms of desire, we start by looking at expressions of desire in the poems. In the absence of the beloved, the woman expresses her desire to find him and to be close to him. In 3:1-4, she describes a search she undertakes for her beloved. Although it is not clear if this passage refers to an actual search the woman undertakes or to a dream that she has, the passage describes a situation in which the woman bemoans her separation from her lover and expresses her desire to be close to her beloved.

> Upon my bed every night
> I seek the one I love,
> I seek him, but I do not find him.[6]
> I shall arise and go about the city,
> In the streets and squares,
> I will seek the one I love.

---

[6] Many versions translate the Hebrew perfect verbs in this passage with a form of the past tense in English. I have translated the verbs with a present tense in English to suggest that this may be an experience (dream or waking thoughts) that recurs. This is supported by the plural form of the noun "nights" with the attached preposition "in," which can be translated "every night."

> I seek him but I do not find him.
> The guards find me—
> The men who go around the city—
> "The one I love—have you seen him?"
> Scarcely have I passed by them
> When I find the one I love.
> I seize him and do not let him go,
> Until I bring him to my mother's house,
> To the room of she who conceived me.

The lovers' desire for each other is also articulated through the many expressions of desire for physical intimacy. In the opening poem, the woman expresses her longing for her lover's kisses.

> O, may he kiss me with the kisses of his mouth,
> For your lovemaking is better than wine (1:2).

Similarly, he expresses the desire to be in her presence, where he can see and hear her:

> My dove in the clefts of the rock,
> In the hiding place of the mountain track/cliff.
> Show me your form,
> Let me hear your voice,
> For your voice is sweet,
> And your form lovely (2:14).

Perhaps surprisingly, the book, which is richly ambiguous and filled with double entendres, ends not with a description of consummation or communion, but with an expression of desire.

> Flee, my beloved, and make yourself like a gazelle
> Or the young of the deer upon the mountains of spices (8:14).

Although it is possible that she is instructing her lover to flee *from* her, it seems more likely that she is calling him to flee *to* her. But the book ends without telling us if he does so, and thus the book ends on a note of desire, not consummation, and hope, not fulfillment.

In addition to these descriptions of desire, Song of Songs contains the vocabulary of desire. We find in Song of Songs three occurrences of a "formula" of mutual love. In 2:16, the woman declares, "My beloved is for me, and I am for him" (or, "My beloved is mine, and I am his"). The second occurrence, in 6:3, reverses the statement. She declares, "I am for my beloved, and my beloved is for me" (or, "I am my beloved's, and my beloved is mine"). The third occurrence, in 7:10,[7] introduces the Hebrew word *teshuqah*, "desire," into the formula. "I am for my beloved, and his desire is for me."

Based in part on this vocabulary term, biblical scholar Phyllis Trible connects Song of Songs to the story of Adam and Eve in the garden and suggests that Song of Songs redeems the "love story gone awry" of Genesis 2–3. Noting that one of the two other occurrences of the noun *teshuqah* in the Hebrew Bible is in Genesis 3:16, where the woman is told, "Your desire (*teshuqah*) shall be for your man, but he shall rule over you," Trible proposes that the woman's statement, "I am for my beloved, and his desire is for me," restores mutuality to male-female relationships.

> In Eden, the yearning of the woman for harmony with her man continued after disobedience. Yet the man did not reciprocate; instead, he ruled over her to destroy unity and pervert sexuality. Her desire became his dominion. But in the Song, male power vanishes. His desire becomes her delight. Another consequence of disobedience is thus redeemed through the recovery of mutuality in the garden of eroticism. Appropriately, the woman sings the lyrics of this grace: "I am my lover's and for me is his desire" (160).

Song of Songs and the Experience of Loss

Reading the poetry of Song of Songs carefully, we discover that the book explores the experience of loss and separation as much as it describes the experience of love itself. Although it may be sexually explicit in some of its language, the book is not a sex handbook. It does not give instructions, prohibitions, or rules on how to engage in lovemaking. Rather, it explores the intensity of desire and anticipation. It describes the anguish of separation and loss.

---

[7] 7:11 in the Hebrew text.

The vision of the Song of Songs is not a tragic one, however. Rather, this drive towards the union of lovers characterizes comedy understood in its classic sense.[8] Biblical scholar Bill Whedbee explains, "Comedy typically *celebrates*: it can affirm love and life even in the midst of separation and death" (276). Paradoxically, the poems celebrate love yet do not ignore or dismiss the reality of separation and loss.

The ability of the poetry in Song of Songs to express the anguish of separation became abundantly clear to me a few years ago when I led a Bible study with a group of older adults. At the outset, I wondered how these readers in their 60s and 70s would take to the book. I had read Song of Songs with college students in their late teens and early twenties, and I knew how they typically responded (with pleasure and surprise, for the most part). But here was a book that tradition has suggested King Solomon wrote in his youth about two "youthful" lovers. As I talked about the themes of love and loss, I looked around the group and noted individuals whose partners had recently died. Suddenly, the theme of "separation from the beloved" became intensely real in a new way. I read the book with new eyes, seeing that it could strike a chord with both young lovers anticipating the joys of intimacy and older lovers experiencing the loss that death brings to a relationship.

At one level, Song of Songs speaks to us about human love, sexuality, desire, and loss. The emotions the lovers in Song of Songs experience are age-old emotions. Thus, we find in Song of Songs affirmation of our human experiences. Sexual love is good. Desire is good when the object of desire is good. The experience of separation and loss from the one we love is universal, but love has such power that it can overcome the fear of separation and death. As we reflect more deeply on the poetry of Song of Songs, we may begin to see that this book also speaks to us of our experience of God— of our love for God, our desire for spiritual intimacy, and our sense of God's absence, which we hope will be overcome.

---

[8] In its classic sense, comedy refers to a dramatic work whose plot line contains a happy resolution of the work's thematic conflict.

A Theological Reading of Song of Songs

Only recently have we read the Song of Songs as poetry that describes the experience of a man and a woman who are sexually attracted to each other. For two millennia, Jews and Christians read the book theologically. Early on, Jewish interpreters saw in the Song's poetry a description of God's love for the covenant people. (Scholars disagree on how early the theological reading began within Judaism.) Christians have followed this line of interpretation, but identified the lovers variously as Christ and the church or Christ and the individual Christian. Christian mystics read the text as a dialogue between the soul and Christ. In the medieval period, the lovers were sometimes identified as Jesus and Mary, where Mary symbolizes the church or the "ideal Christian."

In the twentieth century, the pendulum swung sharply in the opposite direction, especially with the discovery of ancient Egyptian love poetry that parallels the poems of the Song of Songs in content and structure. For much of the twentieth century, biblical scholars rejected the traditional theological interpretation and labeled it "allegorical." At a time when many biblical scholars were searching for "original meanings," twentieth-century scholars preferred to interpret the Song of Songs as a collection of love poems that celebrate human, sexual love, which they thought to be the original intention of the poetry. More recently, biblical interpreters have suggested that our interpretation of the Song does not have to be either/or. Rather, we can recognize multiple levels of interpretation as valid. It can be both/and. Biblical scholar Ellen Davis describes these multiple levels of interpretation in the following way.

> Because healing must occur at multiple levels, the language of the Song of Songs plays simultaneously upon several registers. It speaks about human love in language as exuberant, and at the same time delicate, as has ever been written. It speaks also, as the mystics have always seen, about love between the human soul and God (*Proverbs, Ecclesiastes, and the Song of Songs*, 232-233).

Reading the Song of Songs theologically, we understand that our experience of human, sexual love tells us something about the love of God—both God's love for us and our love directed to God. We are familiar with the imagery of God as "father" in the Bible, which allows us to think of the ways in which parents relate to children and children to parents. We are also familiar with the imagery of God as "king," and the ways in which ancient Israelite kings were expected to provide for their people. A theological reading of the Song of Songs offers another model for understanding the way in which God and humans relate to one another—that of lovers. In her book *Models of God: Theology for an Ecological, Nuclear Age*, theologian Sallie McFague proposes just that. She offers three new models of God: God as mother, God as friend, and God as lover. In using the term "model," McFague suggests two things. First of all, we construct the way we talk about God by using metaphor. Ancient Israelites used the metaphor of "king," which worked for them, but may not work so well for us today, if we think a constitutional democracy is a better form of government than a monarchy. Second, the term "model" implies a more permanent construction than the term "metaphor." She describes a model as "a metaphor with 'staying power'" (34).

The notion of God as lover suggests a different relation between God and humankind (or God and world). As we see in the love poetry of the Song of Songs, lovers value and appreciate each other. They love each other not out of duty or demand, but out of love, desire, and attraction. Similarly, God as lover implies that our response to God is intrinsically, rather than extrinsically, motivated. We respond to God out of love, not fear. Like the beloved in the Song of Songs, God has an allure that attracts us. We want to know God and to be known by God. What better way to think about our desire for spiritual intimacy with God than the model of God as lover? To borrow Jeremiah's language, our relationship with God is inscribed upon our hearts (Jer. 31:33). We *desire* a covenant relationship with God. It is not something that has to be forced upon us. A model of God as lover helps us recognize that we don't have to be coerced into loving God.

Theologians Wendy Farley and Catherine Keller also seek to reclaim *eros* (desire) for the church. In her book *The Wounding and Healing of Desire: Weaving Heaven and Earth*, Farley speaks of "Divine Eros."

> Love is the fullest form of spiritual existence, the most perfect self-manifestation of spiritual beings. It arises from the erotic energy that is uniquely embodied in each person. To love and be loved, unencumbered by the terrors of the passions and the tyranny of the ego, is the spontaneity of spirit in its freest expression. We are rivers of erotic power that have become hopelessly clogged by the flotsam and jetsam of life. The infinitely tender work of the Divine Eros is to enable this river to flow clear and strong (119).

Drawing upon her process thought mentors Alfred North Whitehead and John B. Cobb,[9] Keller develops the view that *agapē* and *erōs* are complementary, not antagonistic as Swedish theologian Anders Nygren had argued. In the early twentieth century, Nygren proposed that only *agapē* love is truly Christian, and that *erōs*, being self-centered, turns one away from God. Firmly rejecting Nygren's view, Keller claims that *erōs*, God's creative love, *lures* us into becoming who we really are. *Agapē*, God's responsive love, relates to us as the persons we have become. *Erōs* attracts, lures, and invites. *Agapē* responds, feels, and receives. Keller describes divine *erōs* and *agapē* as "different gestures of divine relationality—yet their motions are in spirit inseparable, in constant oscillation" (99).

Replacing the model of "all-powerful God," Keller proposes a God who is neither omnipotent nor impotent. Clearly not a coercive God, this God is One who invites and lures. This God is alluring, rather than commanding. Keller asks, "Is love to be measured by power? Or is power to be measured by love?" (94). She answers her questions by explaining her shift from power to love.

---

[9] Grounded in the process philosophy of Alfred North Whitehead, which views reality as in flux, process theology emphasizes God's immanence, relationality, love, vulnerability, and suffering. Rejecting the notion of a coercive God, process thought promotes the view that God works through persuasion. Process theologians include John B. Cobb, Jr., Bruce G. Epperly, Catherine Keller, and Marjorie Hewitt Suchocki.

> When it comes to the gospel standard, the answer is unambiguous. The New Testament never says, "God is power." It does say, "God is love" (1 John 4:8). Therefore the power Christians attribute to God must meet the standard of love—even the high standard of what we call "Christian love." Not vice versa. . . . It is not that power needs love to balance it out, that the sternly lordly power of divine domination is softened and complemented by the gospel of love. It would rather be that love is the power, the energy, the style of influence, of God (94).

Reading Song of Songs theologically, we find support for McFague's model of God as lover. We find the erotic energy that Farley associates with Divine Eros. And we find additional biblical support for Keller's proposal that our relationship with God is defined by love, not by power. A theological reading of Song of Songs supports a different understanding of the dynamic relationship we experience with God. With help from the Song of Songs, we recognize God's allure, rather than feeling threatened by God's power.

In addition to providing us with a different model of God, Song of Songs offers spiritual support to those who experience the absence of God, what the mystics call "the dark night of the soul." Just as the woman searches in the night for her lover, but does not find him (Song 3:1-4), so, too, do we often experience the absence of God in our lives. We seek God, but we fail to find God. We may learn from Song of Songs to persevere despite our sense of God's absence. We trust that "many waters cannot quench God's love." We live in hope and in the expectation of God's return. Writing about pastoral care, especially to those who struggle with depression, Carol L. Schnabl Schweitzer claims that Song of Songs teaches that "from the depths of the darkest abyss that depression represents, there is an absolute love that reaches toward us" (287).

Jesus Spirituality

The model of God as "lover" may seem radical to all but those who have studied Christian mysticism.[10] Christian mystics have used this

---

[10] Christian mysticism refers to those aspects of Christian faith and practice that have to do with the preparation for and direct experience of God's transforming presence. Some Christian mystics found that the language and imagery of God as lover expressed well their experience of God's intimate presence in their lives. Both male and female mystics describe their marriage to God.

language, but it has been off-limits in most contemporary Christian God-talk. By contrast, the language of Jesus as lover or bridegroom is more familiar and perhaps more comfortable to some. Christ as the bridegroom of the church can be found in the letter to the Ephesians and is well-developed in Christian theological tradition. Bridal imagery also appears in Christian hymnody, which is one expression of Christian spirituality. I offer a few examples as illustrations of the tradition that speaks of Jesus as lover, bridegroom, and friend.

Charles Wesley, the eighteenth-century leader in the Methodist movement, portrays Jesus as the individual Christian's true lover in the well-known hymn "Jesus, Lover of My Soul."

> Jesus, lover of my soul, let me to Thy bosom fly,
> While the nearer waters roll, while the tempest still is high.
> Hide me, O my Savior, hide, till the storm of life is past;
> Safe into the haven guide; O receive my soul at last.

Ida A. Guirey's early twentieth-century hymn "Jesus, Rose of Sharon" identifies Jesus as the rose of Sharon (from Song 2:1), and the refrain focuses upon the believer's love of Jesus.

> Jesus, blessèd Jesus, Rose of Sharon,
> Bloom in radiance
> And in love within my heart.

In an Easter hymn from the nineteenth century, Jackson Mason develops the theme of Christian hope for resurrection. Mason directly quotes Song 2:10-13 in the hymn.

> O voice of the Belovèd!
> Thy bride hath heard Thee say,
> "Rise up, My love, My fair one,
> Arise and come away.
> For lo, 'tis past, the winter,
> The winter of thy year;

> The rain is past and over,
> The flowers on earth appear.
>
> "And now the time of singing
> Is come for every bird;
> And over all the country
> The turtle dove is heard;
> The fig her green fruit ripens,
> The vines are in their bloom;
> Arise and smell their fragrance;
> My love, My fair one, come!"

The hymn concludes with an expression of hope and desire for both new life and spiritual intimacy with the Lord.

> Lord, let us feel Thy presence
> And rise and live and bloom.

Another nineteenth-century hymn, by Charles W. Fry, explores the model of "Jesus as friend," using language and imagery from Song 2:1.

> I have found a friend in Jesus, He's everything to me,
> He's the fairest of ten thousand to my soul;
> The Lily of the Valley, in Him alone I see
> All I need to cleanse and make me fully whole.
> In sorrow He's my comfort, in trouble He's my stay;
> He tells me every care on Him to roll.

Fry's hymn downplays the explicit language of erotic love that we find in Song of Songs. It stresses that Jesus as our friend is always with us, thus resolving some of the tension we find in Song of Songs. We see that most clearly in the line, "He will never, never leave me, nor yet forsake me here."

Unlike Fry and other hymnists, Johannes Scheffler (also known as "Angelus Silesius"), a sixteenth-century writer, does not seem troubled by the erotic language of the Song of Songs. Some of Scheffler's poems are collected under the title *Heilige Seelenlust* ("The Soul's Holy Desire"). Poems from *Heilige Seelenlust* can be found as hymn texts in early Pietist hymnbooks, including the early

Brethren hymnbook *Das Kleine Davidische Psalterspiel der Kinder Zions (The Little Davidic Psalter of the Children of Zion)*.

Many of the hymns of the *Little Davidic Psalter* reflect the mystical tradition and its use of the language and imagery of the Song of Songs (Durnbaugh 30-31). In the introduction to her work on Brethren hymnody, Hedda Durnbaugh describes the dual influences on Brethren hymnody of mysticism and Pietism.[11]

> A product of mysticism and Pietism was a certain type of Jesus-hymn which reflected both the secular erotic poetry and the Baroque reaching for the infinite. The result was religious poems about Jesus, which had themes of mystical eros and/or mystical union and language which borrowed heavily from the Song of Solomon (6).

The following poem from *Das Kleine Davidische Psalterspiel* emphasizes the theme of the individual Christian's separation from the beloved Jesus and alludes to Song 3:1-4 and the woman's search for her beloved.[12]

> Where is Jesus, my desire,
> My beloved and my friend?
> Where then has he gone to?
> Where might he be found?
>
> Oh, I am calling from pain and hurt!
> Where then is my Jesus?
> I have no rest in my heart,
> Until he is near and with me.
>
> My soul is clouded over,
> With many sins and trespasses.
> Where is Jesus, whom my soul loves,
> And longs for day and night?

---

[11] Similarly, Bernard McGinn notes, "mysticism found a place among the Free Church traditions nourished both by the Radical Reformers and (strangely enough) the Catholic Quietists" (24). Although mysticism may not be strongly represented in contemporary Anabaptist and Radical Pietist groups, McGinn and Durnbaugh both comment on its historical influence on those traditions.

[12] My thanks to Amy Milligan, who translated this poem from the German.

Oh! Who gives me dove-wings,
That I could at any time
Fly over mountains and hills,
Searching for my Jesus?

He takes away my sin and hell,
He takes away my fear and distress.
He rejoices my soul,
And helps me out of all distress.

From now on I will not give up,
Will search for him more and more,
In the forests, in the streets,
I will seek him here and there.

Most beloved Jesu, let yourself be found,
My soul cries out to you.
Wink to me with your eyes.
Quickly let me be with you.

In this hymn text, influenced by mysticism and Pietism, the twin themes of love and desire that we see in Song of Songs are used to express the Christian's deepest devotion to Jesus. Although some Christians may initially find McFague's model of "God as lover" uncomfortable, Christian hymns indicate that the model of "Jesus as lover" has a strong footing in Christian spirituality. Reflection upon this tradition of Jesus spirituality may foster greater openness to the theological propositions of McFague and Keller, especially within Anabaptist and Pietist denominations that emphasize the centrality of Jesus to the understanding of God and God's revelation.

Song of Songs for Today's Church

In this essay, I have proposed that Song of Songs encourages us to think more broadly about the meaning of love within a Christian context. This can happen at two distinct, but interrelated, levels. On one level, Song of Songs affirms human sexual desire and erotic love, which should be a welcome support for those who have sensed the church's ambivalence with regard to human sexuality. In addition to this support for sexual desire, Song of Songs mirrors our experiences of loss and separation from those we love. Although the book offers no direct solutions to the problem of loss, the Song acknowledges our grief.

On a second level, we find in Song of Songs a resource for theological and spiritual reflection. When we imagine God as lover, we realize our own true selves as persons who desire intimacy with God. We abandon the desire for an omnipotent God in favor of a God who invites. Like the lover in the Song of Songs, we long to hear God's voice of invitation. This is also true within the tradition of Jesus mysticism, or Jesus piety, which speaks of Jesus as the soul's beloved. Finally, a theological reading of Song of Songs better equips us for the "dark night of the soul," when we feel abandoned, even by God. With Song of Songs as guide, we live in hope and desire that the dark night of winter shall pass and that we shall hear the voice of the turtledove and know once again the presence of God in our lives.

Recommended Reading

Song of Songs

David M. Carr. *The Erotic Word: Sexuality, Spirituality, and the Bible.* New York: Oxford University Press, 2003.

Ellen F. Davis. *Proverbs, Ecclesiastes, and the Song of Songs.* Westminster Bible Companion. Louisville: Westminster John Knox, 2000.

The July 2005 issue of *Interpretation*, with essays on Song of Songs by Chip Dobbs-Allsopp, Daniel Grossberg, Tod Linafelt, and Carol L. Schnabl Schweitzer. See, especially, Linafelt's essay, "The Arithmetic of Eros," and Schweitzer's discussion of Song of Songs in relation to pastoral care.

Process Theology

Catherine Keller. *On the Mystery: Discerning Divinity in Process.* Minneapolis: Fortress Press, 2008.

Marjorie Hewitt Suchocki. *God Christ Church: A Practical Guide to Process Theology.* Revised ed. New York: The Crossroad Publishing Company, 1989.

Study Questions

Prepare

Play some of your favorite instrumental music. Read Song of Songs aloud on your own from a modern translation.

Think about love songs that have been important to you at different stages in your life. Make a list of these songs, and if possible bring a recording of your favorite love song to the session.

Ask

1. What are some of the ways that the church has read the Song of Songs? What was your reaction to the book prior to this session? Bucher asks the question, "What is a book like this doing in the Bible?" How would you answer this question?

2. Bucher catalogues ways in which the Hebrew term for love is used in the Old Testament. List and discuss some of these ways.

3. What is the difference between the way our society uses the image of the heart and the way it is used in the Hebrew Bible? What image would you use for the place of these understandings?

4. Song of Songs 8:6-7 is treated as a special passage. Compare Bucher's translation with the translation in your Bible. Discuss some of the differences. The word *jealousy* usually has a negative connotation. Under what circumstances is it a positive term, in Bucher's opinion?

5. While physical love between a man and a woman is described in rich terms in the Song of Songs, Bucher points out that *desire* seems to be more a factor than actual *consummation*. What is the place of delay of desire both in the Song of Songs and in human interactions as you have experienced them? Does this idea of "desire, not consummation, and hope, not fulfillment" have any application to your understanding of either God's kingdom or the ministry of Jesus?

6. How do you respond to the idea of a God as a lover? Is this a comfortable image? Is this an image you have encountered in

sermons or Bible studies? Bucher writes that the notion of God as lover means that God and humankind "love each other not out of duty or demand, but out of love, desire, and attraction." Is this your experience of God?

7. Share some of the love songs that were important to you. You might share them in one of two ways. If you have a recording, play it, and then invite people to name the tune or sing along as soon as they recognize it. Or you might simply name the song and see how many know it and can sing a few lines of it. Discuss why the song attracted you. Does it still do so?

8. The ancient Bible expert Rabbi Akiva, whose wisdom was celebrated by other rabbis, once said: "The entire universe is unworthy of the day on which the Song of Songs was given to Israel. For all the writings are holy, but the Song of Songs is the holy of holies." Why do you think a revered Bible expert would make a statement like this? Do you agree or disagree with this statement? Of all the books of the Bible, which do you consider the "holy of holies"? Why?

9. Ancient Bible commentators spoke of Songs of Songs as an allegory about the love between God and the people or Christ and the church. Modern commentators focus solely on the human love story in the book. Bucher suggests that it is important to consider both love stories when reading Song of Songs. Were you brought up to consider the human relationship with God as a love story? If so, in what way? If not, why? Are you comfortable with the idea of both love stories playing a part in the interpretation of this book?

10. Bucher discusses the matter of love and loss. She suggests that love is stronger than loss. What comfort is to be found in contemplation of love when one has lost the object of love? Has the church provided adequate comfort or insight in times of extreme loss?

Daniel: Piety, Politics, and Perseverance

David M. Valeta

The book of Daniel presents readers with many interesting co-nundrums. It is one of the most popular books in the Hebrew Bible, containing stories and images that vividly connect with the human imagination.[1] At the same time, the book has spawned countless de-bates over interpretive issues. The book of Daniel illustrates themes of personal piety in relationship to public witness that Brethren and other Anabaptists wrestle with continually in their attempt to be faithful disciples of Jesus Christ.[2] This essay is a small contribution to the ongoing conversation between this biblical text and the call-ing of the church to live faithfully in every age.

Piety

Daniel is one of those biblical figures that you want your children

---

[1] Christians generally use the designation Old Testament. The use of the term Hebrew Bible recognizes that Jewish and Christian communities both value these writings, and my use of this term recognizes the ecumenical and interfaith commitments of Robert W. Neff. See the interview with Neff in *The Responsibility People*, edited by William McKin-ney (217-18).

[2] I am struck with a sense that this text is a particularly appropriate one to explore in the context of a collection of essays in honor of Robert W. Neff. The book of Daniel explores the intersection of personal faith and public responsibilities. Neff's professional life exem-plifies the intertwining of serious academic study and the engagement of biblical texts with a commitment to bring those texts to life in service to the church. (See his 1998 essay, "The Bible, Devotion, and Authority," 75.) I am reminded of his statement from a 1983 article on biblical authority, "I have never seen my role as denominational executive and biblical scholar as two separate worlds. Both tasks have been fostered by my study of the Bible" ("Taking Biblical Authority Seriously," 15).

to emulate. The basketball skills of Michael Jordan inspired a promotional campaign centered on the phrase "I want to be like Mike!" and Daniel could easily fit into such an ecclesiastical marketing strategy (Rovell 95-122). A quick survey of representative scenes from Daniel highlights the pervasiveness of the theme of piety. Chapter 1 recounts how Daniel and his friends are forcibly removed from their homeland to exile in Babylon, and are placed in a program of royal training to become useful subjects to King Nebuchadnezzar. They show their resolve not to be fooled by the material benefits of royal promises and provisions by refusing to eat at the king's table (v. 8). Their decision to stay pure and loyal to their God results in the gifts of divine knowledge and skill as well as the ability to interpret dreams and visions (v. 17).

These talents are immediately useful as the king has a dream in chapter 2 that his servants cannot recount to him or interpret while Daniel is able to do both. Daniel and friends are royally rewarded for their abilities, and the king praises their God (2:46-49). Kings in the book of Daniel usually give intemperate orders, and in chapter 3 Nebuchadnezzar demands that everyone worship a golden statue. While Daniel is curiously missing from this scene, his three friends carry on in fine Danielic tradition; they remain loyal to their God and are saved from the fiery furnace.

Daniel returns and exhibits his mantic and visionary gifts in chapters 4 and 5, particularly in his ability to interpret the writing on the wall. Again, Daniel is handsomely compensated for his work (5:29). Chapter 6 decisively rounds out the depiction of Daniel as pious hero when he survives a night in the den of the lions after resolutely continuing his practice of prayer before an open window.

While the genre of the literary material changes in Daniel 7–12, our hero continues to receive revelations from God and his position as a pious, faithful servant of the Lord is confirmed. Daniel is steadfast and heroic, a person you want to imitate.[3]

---

[3] "Daniel in the lion's den" has been a favorite subject in the western cultural tradition, including pop culture. For example, it has been interpreted for children through the successful VeggieTales series of Bible story animations. For those not familiar with VeggieTales, visit www.bigidea.com.

Religious communities read and interpret their sacred texts in ways that are beneficial to their life together. Reading Daniel or any part of the Bible for the purposes of spiritual growth and the strengthening of an individual's relationship with God is an important part of the Christian tradition. Brethren have recognized this and denominational Christian education materials, for example, rightly emphasize such themes. Sometimes, however, individualistic spiritual readings that are so much a part of Christian tradition can overshadow other important understandings of a text.

Brethren and other Anabaptists have long recognized that Christian faith is not simply an individual spiritual journey.[4] The Scriptures contain resources to help us not only navigate our way through life in a dangerous world but work for systemic change and become an advocate for others. I would like to explore this aspect through another reading of the Daniel materials that highlights the political nature of this book.

Politics

I want to begin this section of my analysis of Daniel with a quote from Neff's contribution to a volume subtitled *Narrative Forms in Old Testament Literature*: "Imprecision in the classification of literary genres has caused an increasing restiveness among form critical investigators of the Old Testament" (Neff 1985, 17). Form criticism in biblical studies is an attempt to analyze and classify texts according to their genre.[5] To use an example from New Testament studies, a reader intuitively knows that there is a difference between the four Gospels and the letters of Paul. Gospels tell stories, have lots of narrative material with dialogue, and easily capture the imagination of the reader. Letters are more formal, contain

---

[4] For an example of a Brethren approach to politics and the Scriptures, see Robert W. Neff's short essay on "The Biblical Basis for Political Advocacy."

[5] To read more about form criticism, you may consult the following: Douglas A. Knight, "Genre in the Old Testament," in *Mercer Dictionary of the Bible* (Macon, GA: Mercer University Press, 1991), 322-323; Marvin A. Sweeney, "Form Criticism," in *To Each Its Own Meaning*, ed. S. L. McKenzie and S. R. Haynes (Louisville: John Knox Press, 1999), 58-89; and Gene M. Tucker, *Form Criticism of the Old Testament* (Philadelphia: Fortress Press, 1971).

greetings, and are often topical and generally short and to the point.

Genre confusion has plagued Daniel studies for centuries, and this has obscured a proper understanding of the political nature of the book, particularly the narratives of Daniel 1–6. An exploration of genre issues and other formal features is a critical task that will help us fully appreciate the political nature of the entire book of Daniel.

Genre, Language, and Social World

Interpreters of Daniel encounter a perplexing assortment of genres, languages, and ideological viewpoints within the book that frustrates attempts to discern a coherent hermeneutical strategy. A quick reading of the book of Daniel reveals two primary literary forms (narrative and vision), two different languages (Hebrew and Aramaic), and two competing viewpoints on how one should live under foreign domination (collaboration with existing rulers or hostility toward such rule). The first two dichotomies of literary form and language are easily observable but difficult to explain.

This confusion over genre is not surprising. Genre recognition has been a particularly vexing issue in studies of the book of Daniel for a number of reasons. Daniel is often identified as the best example of apocalyptic literature in the Hebrew Bible because of the vivid visions of the second half of the book. One popular formal argument is that apocalyptic literature from that period of history often has a narrative context and Daniel 1–6 provides the introductory material for the otherworldly visions. Daniel 7–12 exhibits the characteristics of apocalyptic literature in both form and content, but apart from the dream and vision reports of Daniel 1–6 the narratives are not apocalyptic in nature.

The entire book is most often classified as an *apocalypse*, a type of writing that many believe has implications for the coming end of the present age and prophecies for the age to come. Daniel and other biblical writings such as Revelation, Ezekiel, Zechariah, and certain passages from the Gospels and the letters of Paul are classified as apocalyptic writings that give detailed scenarios for the future.[6] The nature and purpose of apocalyptic literature is an important area of contemplation for Christians today, yet that is not the sole focus of this study.[7]

The root meaning of apocalypse is "to reveal," which includes revelation of the nature of God and the divine realm. Such revelation can encompass visions, dreams, encounters with otherworldly beings, journeys to the heavens or the netherworld, and similar fantastic occurrences. The classification of the book of Daniel as apocalyptic literature, while suggestive and partially helpful, has not answered all the interpretive puzzles posed by this book.

The presence of two major languages in Daniel that do not correspond to accepted generic boundaries is one of the thorniest questions in academic study of Daniel. The court tales of Daniel 1–6 and the apocalyptic visions of Daniel 7–12 are divided into the Aramaic section of Daniel 2:4*b*–7, sandwiched by the Hebrew sections of Daniel 1–2:4*a* and Daniel 8–12. This perplexing and persistent problem admits no adequate solution. The existence of Aramaic and Hebrew in Daniel has puzzled scholars for centuries. Recent proposals highlight the possibility that the use of two languages lends authenticity to the account and contributes to the literary artistry in the composition of Daniel. The use of both Hebrew and Aramaic, as well as a smattering of Greek, is intentional, and it serves both artistic and ideological purposes. This new movement in Daniel studies that highlights its multilingualism is going in the right direction.

The discussion concerning the social world and ideological viewpoint of the book finds a majority of modern interpreters in agreement. Most concur that the apocalyptic visions of Daniel 7–12 are more negative toward the kingdoms and rulers of this world, while the stories of Daniel 1–6 hold open the possibility of

---

[6] Dispensational hermeneutics (i.e., the interpretive strategy of dispensationalism), study Bible texts such as the Scofield Reference Bible, and popular writings such as Hal Lindsey's *The Late Great Planet Earth* and the more recent Left Behind series focus on the apocalyptic aspects of the book of Daniel.

[7] A short, succinct, and helpful exploration of the nature and purpose of apocalyptic literature is found in the Good Ground Bible Studies session on Daniel and Ezekiel, titled *Cracking the Code* (Ramirez 6-14).

fruitful accommodation and collaboration with foreign authorities. Early interpreters noted this positive appraisal of exilic cooperation, but had difficulty reconciling this perspective with their understanding of Nebuchadnezzar as one of the most despicable foreign kings to conquer the peoples of Israel and Judah. Today, the discrepancy is often not even acknowledged. The juxtaposition of positive and negative attitudes toward a foreign ruling authority in one book is a puzzling construction.

Form- and source-critical studies of Daniel 1–6 have often characterized these stories as examples of "success in the court" or "lifestyle in the Diaspora" narratives modeled on a tradition of court tales that was popular in the ancient Near East. The protagonist in these tales is successful in various adventures through the use of skill and faith, and the presence of these types of stories in various cultures gives evidence of the popularity of this genre. Many scholars argue that the basic overall political stance of these stories is one of loyalty, optimism, and accommodation toward the ruling powers.

A second related interpretation identifies these court narratives as hero stories. For example, this understanding is based in part on the recognition of structural affinities between the stories of Daniel and other examples of hero stories that are common in folk literature, both in the ancient Near East and in other cultures throughout history. These structural resonances confirm for many interpreters the judgment that the primary purpose of these stories is to celebrate the exploits of Daniel and his friends and lift them up as examples of piety and cunning in the midst of a dangerous foreign land. The four heroes are celebrated as paragons of virtue, moral superiority, and wise living.

Reading Daniel 1–6 in this way, however, seems problematic when the court tales are compared with Daniel 7–12. The "success in the court" interpretation of Daniel 1–6 describes a mostly benign, nonjudgmental relationship with a conquering foreign system, while the apocalyptic section has a much more negative tone toward the ruling powers. This predominant understanding of the purpose of the Jewish court legends has undergone reassessment in the last few years. Interpreters are identifying a darker, more judgmental tone to these court tale narratives (Smith-Christopher 20-22). There is an increasing appreciation for the novelistic character of these stories and their ability to creatively express the frustrations and hopes of oppressed peoples. Recent work by Larry Wills (30-39) and Erich Gruen (137-88) is sensitizing us to the novelistic character of these narratives and how embellishment, invention, and humor are integral parts of these stories.

A second awareness driving a reassessment of these tales is the increasing recognition of the oppressive realities of social and political life for persons and cultures living under the sway of occupying and colonizing powers. Postcolonial discourse and analysis of biblical passages is an essential analytical tool for understanding the social dynamics and context of a given text. A case can be made that the social and political realities of exile create an atmosphere where covert and creative resistance is the best and sometimes only option available to those who disagree with the ruling powers. I believe such a reading is the key to understanding Daniel 1–6, and the way forward to seeing the entire book as a unified whole.

Menippean Satire

Is there a genre designation that can suggest solutions to the various conundrums outlined above and also provide an interpretive paradigm that unifies the message of the book of Daniel? One way forward is to explore the book of Daniel as *menippean satire*.[8] Mikhail Bakhtin was a Russian literary theorist who produced much of his work during the time of the Soviet Empire. His life (1895-1975) in Russia and the Soviet Union was marked by periods of upheaval and exile that often paralleled this contentious period of history. His writings were at times unpublished for many years, destroyed, or lost. In some ways, he is the ultimate survivor of a period of time in Russian history where the struggles of authoritarian Soviet dogma with the constant yearning of the human spirit to be free and have individual choice parallels many of the concerns of

---

[8] For a fuller discussion of Menippean satire see Valeta, 55-66.

his life and erudition (Green 11-26). There are some obvious connections with the political circumstances of the Daniel material and the life of oppression under Soviet rule.

Bakhtin analyzes various precursors of the modern novel that exist in classical antiquity and includes writings he calls *serio-comical literature*. There are three basic characteristics of the serio-comical. First, despite the great external diversity of these writings, they share a connection to carnivalistic folklore or carnivalized literature. The primary ritual of the carnival was the mock crowning and subsequent dethronement of the carnival king. Kingly imagery, therefore, is important. There are often banquets and other trappings of royalty. Bakhtin uses the carnivalesque to refer to the opposition between the official and popular cultures of a society.

In such literature, alternative voices and literary constructions challenge the monologic voice of control and open the possibility of other sources of power. Carnavalized literature questions and critiques accepted norms and constructions of power and control. Serio-comical works are not impressed with legends or the authority of the epic (or the authority of the monologic propaganda power structure, that is, whatever the king wants), but instead create imaginative scenarios for the exploration of new ideas, often critiquing the status quo. Their focus is on the present.

Secondly, they employ a variety of styles, languages, and voices—serious and comic—that creates an atmosphere where accepted power arrangements are brought into question.

Thirdly, they share a commitment to the exploration of truth. Bakhtin includes writings such as the Socratic dialogues and menippean satire as ancient exemplars of serio-comical literature.

Menippean satire usually consists of a blend of prose, verse, and poetry. It is often in the form of a loosely constructed narrative or an ironic essay that delivers a message of judgment. A wide variety of literary and rhetorical devices are available for satiric writing. Beast fables, dramatic incidents, fictional experiences, sarcasm, irony, mockery, and exaggeration are only a few of the ways an author might employ the satiric wit. Bakhtin extrapolates a list of fourteen characteristics of the genre, which he now calls the menippea:[9]

1. Comic elements;
2. A freedom of plot and philosophical inventiveness;
3. A use of extraordinary, fantastic situations or wild parodic displays of learning to test the truth;
4. Some combination of both crude and lofty imagery, settings, and themes;
5. A concern for ultimate questions;
6. Scenes and dialogue from the earthly, heavenly, and netherworldly realms;
7. Observation of behavior from an unusual vantage point;
8. Characters who experience unusual, abnormal moral, and psychic states;
9. Characters who participate in scandals, eccentric behavior, and/or inappropriate speech;
10. Sharp contrasts and oxymoronic combinations;
11. Elements of social utopia;
12. A variety of inserted genres within the work;
13. A multi-styled, multi-toned, or multi-voiced work that is dialogic based on inserted genres, voices, and languages;
14. A concern with current and topical issues.

The combination of these seemingly heterogeneous traits creates the unique quality and organic unity of menippean satire. This list contains a large number of the characteristics that exist in the fully developed novel, which led Bakhtin to understand menippean satire as a manifestation of the growing novelistic impulse in the Hellenistic period (Bakhtin 107-24).[10]

From this list, one can note that the connection the Daniel stories have with a number of the key characteristics of menippean satire is quite noticeable. The book of Daniel includes fantastic

---

[9] Menippean satire originates with the Greek cynic Menippus of Gadara in the third century BCE (Valeta, 57-58).

[10] The Hellenistic period is 333-63 BCE. In those years, Greek civilization spread throughout much of the ancient world.

scenes and characters such as the fiery furnace incident, the transformation of the king into a wild beast, the writing on the wall, the
lion's den, the Ancient of Days, the four great beasts, the battling
ram and goat, and the great angels Michael and Gabriel. The presence of multiple kings and their advisors at court also lend to the
carnivalistic feel of the stories.

Furthermore, the Daniel stories are an edited product that
doubtless draws upon earlier precursors that coalesce in the Hellenistic era, a time when Judaism was threatened by overt and dis-
guised outside forces and philosophies. Additionally, Hellenistic
Judea was filled with polyglots, people who spoke and/or read
some combination of Aramaic, Hebrew, and Greek, making the
dialogic process found in the literature of this place and time more
pronounced. Consequently, a careful study of the Daniel narratives in light of Bakhtin's understanding of genre, the novelistic
impulse, and menippean satire helps us understand better the political implications of these tales.

Menippean Satire and Daniel

How then does menippean satire operate in the book of Daniel as
a critique of the politics of empire? A brief survey of the Daniel
material will illustrate the utility of such a reading.

One of the most conspicuous techniques is the use of the *Leit-
wort*, or leading word, which is the recurrence of a word or phrase
that sets the tone for a passage. Word and phrase repetition is not
a sign of authorial weakness, or poor editing. It is an important
component of the overall rhetorical strategy that highlights the
chief concerns of a composition.

In chapter 1, the root of the word for "king" or "rule" (*melekh*)
occurs in various forms over twenty times. This is a chapter seemingly about royal privilege and power, and yet the entire chapter
describes various scenes of resistance and subversion. In Daniel 1,
King Nebuchadnezzar is portrayed as a conqueror of both the political and cultic power centers of Judah as he defeats King Je-
hoiakim and plunders the sacred articles of the temple.

Then the finest of the deportees are chosen for special education and training for imperial service. From the beginning Nebuchadnezzar appears to be in control, but the reality is that the
king's servants collude behind his back and help the Hebrew heroes
subvert the wishes of the king. The repetition of the verb "give"
(*nathan*) three times in this chapter, each time with God as the subject who controls what happens in the story, indicates that there is
an ironic undercurrent at work throughout the chapter.

The king may claim to be all-powerful, but the story indicates
something quite different. The public transcript indicates that the
king's desires are completely fulfilled, for indeed the conscripts are
trained and in the end presented to the king for royal approval. As
far as the king knows, his orders have been totally followed and
completely obeyed. However, the reader also learns that Daniel
and his three friends negotiate with the king's servants to change
the terms of their subjugation. Many posit that the Hebrew heroes' concerns about diet stem from piety and a desire to remain
ritually pure.

While purity is certainly an issue, another likely motivation,
one that is apropos to the political nature of this chapter, is the
motivation to resist the royal edicts whenever possible. The author reinforces the attitude of resistance in this chapter by a continued use of the Hebrew names of the heroes (Daniel, Hananiah,
Mishael, Azariah) over their new imperial names (Belteshazzar,
Shadrach, Meshach, Abednego). Their actions have the political
consequence of setting themselves apart from the king's agenda
and the Babylonian training table (Chia 17-36). Their resistance
takes the form of the trickster hero, which James Scott defines as
one who makes his way through a treacherous environment of enemies not by strength but by wit and cunning (162-66).

This resistance is covert and invisible to the king, yet it is pow-
erfully subversive and indicative of the true relationship between
the king and his subjects. The delicious denouement of this story
is that the king knows nothing of this subterfuge, and deems the
four Hebrews to be better servants than even his most trusted
countrymen (Daniel 1:20-21). This commendation by the king

adds to the irony of this chapter; the heroes are in effect rewarded for their subversive behavior. Thus the public transcript of this story attempts to affirm the king's sovereignty, while the hidden transcript reveals that his conquered subjects resist surrendering their identity in a variety of ways. This is a chapter primarily about power and control, not dietary scruples or royal advancement for willing noble captives.

In Daniel 2, there is the first of many fantastic images, as well as a change in language from Hebrew to Aramaic. Nebuchadnezzar experiences trouble sleeping, a common malady of troubled monarchs, and his sleeplessness indicates his lack of control over even his own life. He has an incomprehensible dream of a grotesquely shaped statue, and it is Daniel, not his own court advisors, who comes to the king's rescue.

In this dream interpretation story there are a number of word-play techniques that heighten the ambiguity and playfulness of the narrative. When the king asks the counselors to tell the contents of the dream to him, he uses a form of the verb "to know" (*yada'*) in verses 3, 5, and 9. His counselors respond many times with a form of the verb "to declare" (*chavah*), a technical term with the nuance "to interpret." The shifting use of these synonyms highlights the cross-purposes of the king and his advisors. Once they begin to understand each other, the advisors cannot believe the king is asking them to interpret the dream without telling them its content. The king threatens to annihilate all of them. This wild swing of action and emotion is characteristic of each of the court tales and underlines the satirical nature of these stories.

A second synonym wordplay is the varied use of the words "interpretation" (*pesher*) and "secret" (*raz*). While the king and his advisors frantically search for an interpretation (*pesher*), it is God through Daniel who provides the hidden answer (*raz*) to the mystery, creating an ironic contrast between the supposed knowledge of the counselors and the true knowledge from on high.

Also, there is the use of lists of multiple synonyms in order to heighten the hyperbolic quality of this story. These include lists of sages (vv. 2, 10, 27), rewards (v. 6), rulers (v. 10), power (v. 37), shattering (v. 40), and homage (v. 46). This is a technique that is used in many instances throughout the court tales of Daniel. Even though the dream interpretation is less than positive for the king, Nebuchadnezzar responds with effusive praise of Daniel and his God (2:46-49). This response is overblown and outside of expected royal behavior, and it serves as a satirical barb against the king. Kings are not expected to praise the gods of their captives. Throughout this chapter, the king finds that the usual royal solutions do not work, and he must rely on outsiders to solve his problems.

Another issue to consider concerning Daniel 2 is the change to the use of Aramaic. The use of Aramaic is intentional, expressing a certain ideological perspective. Bakhtin developed a concept known as *heteroglossia*, or the presence of multiple conflicting voices in a text. This is indicated by the presence of different ideological voices in the text, and occasionally it is obvious by the presence of two different languages in the text.

Heteroglossia, expressed through the use of Hebrew and Aramaic, is a double-voiced discourse that expresses the intentions of characters in the story and the refracted intentions of the author. The book of Daniel uses Aramaic, the "official" language of the royal court, in some very "unofficial" ways to express humor and satire toward the king and his empire. In particular, the author expresses his judgment of king and empire through the use of wordplay techniques in the "official" language. Thus, the use of Aramaic is itself an act of satire. The persistent use of wordplay techniques in this chapter and throughout the book of Daniel demonstrates that the text is a highly complex creation designed to judge king and empire.

Daniel 3 provides some of the best examples of the rich use of wordplay techniques to make fun of the king. This chapter is a highly structured rhetorical masterpiece that highlights the impotence of the king. First, there is the hyperbolic description of the ironically tottering statue that represents the power of the empire (vv. 2, 3, 5, 7, 12, 14, 18).

Secondly, the repeated use of lists of government officials (vv. 2, 3, 27), musical instruments (vv. 5, 7, 10, 15) and subjects of the king (vv. 4, 7, 29, 31) is a wordplay technique that highlights the ludicrousness of this scene. Thirdly, there is the contrast between the verbose royal proclamations and the simple refusal of the three to do the king's bidding (vv. 16-18). This results in an enraged king who then orders them to be burned alive. The contrast between a wildly reactive king supposedly in control and the calm demeanor of his prisoners is starkly ironic.

Fourthly, the furnace scene is filled with a veritable smorgasbord of menippean-like satirical events. The fire is kindled seven times hotter (vv. 6, 11, 15, 17, 19, 20, 21, 22, 23, 26), so hot that the king's soldiers are consumed by the intensity of the heat. However, the fire does not harm the three heroes. They are unbound and walking freely with a fourth person whose appearance is described "like a son of the gods." The expected outcome of gruesome death by fire is ironically transformed into a time of deliverance as well. When they come out of the furnace, the crowd inspects their bodies, hair, and clothes as if they are examining the men for lice. The requisite conversion prayer of a supposedly transformed king follows as the final touch of a preposterous and laughable portrait of a king who vacillates and is easily swayed.

The menippean construct suggests an intriguing solution to a textual issue in Daniel 4. Daniel 4:1-3, the opening verses of most modern translations, appears as the final three verses of Daniel 3 in the Masoretic text of the Hebrew Bible.[11] The inclusion of these three verses in chapter 4 in modern translations supports the identification of the form of the chapter as a royal letter or epistle. A detailed discussion of this issue is beyond the purview of this study, but the possibility of the inclusion of such an official form of royal correspondence, particularly in light of the contents of this letter, fits well with a menippean use of a form in a satirical manner.

First, the king in this royal communication issues effusive praise of the Hebrew God. No such document exists in history.

---

[11] The Masoretic text (MT) is the traditional Hebrew text that is used as the basis for modern translations of the Hebrew Bible. The term is derived from the Hebrew word *masorah*, which means "tradition." Chapter and verse numbers in English translations do not always agree with divisions in the MT.

The chapter then recounts another troubling dream that only Daniel is able to interpret. The rise and the fall of the great tree in Daniel 4 sets forth the antithesis of human and divine kingship in no uncertain terms. The synonyms "great" (*rav*) and "mighty" (*taqaf*) [vv. 8, 17, 19, 27, 33] and "king" (*melekh*) and "rule" (*shallit*) [vv. 14, 22, 23, 29, 31] are used to establish this contrast.

Nebuchadnezzar boasts of his greatness, but his words are hollow compared to the great God of heaven. The interpretation comes true as Nebuchadnezzar brags of his greatness from the roof of the royal palace only to be turned into a beast of the field. The king is humiliated and degraded beyond human boundaries, and this depiction severely ridicules and parodies the might of imperial earthly sovereignty. The final verse of the chapter ends the letter with another satirical prayer of praise of the Hebrew God. The king never seems to learn the lessons of limits of human royal sovereignty.

Chapter 5 contains numerous wordplays, including the well-known writing on the wall. In verses 2 and 3, there is an example of the literary device known as *phrasal repetition*, where entire statements are repeated with small but important changes. The reader learns that Belshazzar causes the temple vessels to be brought forth in verse 2, but verse 3 adds that these vessels are from the house of God. The narrator subtly introduces his point of view with the addition of these words.

A graphic instance of wordplay is the loosening (*mishtarayin*) of the knots (*qitrey*) of the king's bowels in verse 6. This may be the most satirically funny scene in the book as the king literally soils his pants before a thousand of his subjects (Wolters 117-22)! Then the same words are used in verses 12 and 16 to describe the ability of Daniel to "loosen the knots" of interpretation of the riddle.

In verse 12 it is the queen mother who informs the king of Daniel's abilities, and the advice coming from a female character adds to the sarcasm of the scene. There is no doubt here that the king is being severely ridiculed. Then in the interpretation of the writing on the wall in verses 26-28, there is the extended punning structure where three weights (*mene', teqel, ufarsin*) are used as three acts of evaluation (*menah, teqiltah, perisat*) in order to make three judgments against the king. A final wordplay is the fact that the weighing (*teqel*) of the king's actions results in the death (*qetil*) of the king![12]

The description of the pit of ferocious creatures in chapter 6 is one of the most memorable in the book of Daniel, and fits well with the many other fantastic scenes depicted in the book. The king hurries down to the den, hoping against hope that Daniel has been saved (v. 20). Daniel, indeed, has been rescued from the mouths of the lions, and the king rejoices in his deliverance (vv. 20-24*a*).

As in Daniel 3, God saves the condemned because he is both faithful and innocent of real wrongdoing (v. 23). As in Daniel 3, his body is closely inspected and found to be unharmed (v. 24*b*). Because the advisors have falsely accused Daniel of acting against the king's interests, they are subject to the same penalties to which Daniel would have been subject if proven guilty—death in the lions' den. The conspirators are thrown to the lions.

Verse 25 notes that the ones who had slandered (literally "eaten the pieces") Daniel are themselves devoured by the hungry felines—not only the 123 conspirators but also their wives and children. The tables are turned against the king's officials. Their plot ends in their own death. The fact that the wives and children are also thrown to the lions indicates, once again, a fantastic overblown situation so reminiscent of menippean satire. The lions overpower or rule over them (*shalat*), a term associated with sovereignty throughout the Aramaic portion of Daniel. This is a nice wordplay that encapsulates the power struggle present in the entire book. Ultimately, God rules over all.

Perseverance

Ultimately, God rules over all. This is the bridge that connects the two sections of the book of Daniel and becomes the overarching

---

[12] See Rembrandt's wonderful depiction of this scene, *Belshazzar's Feast*. 12 May 2009. Art and the Bible. http://www.artbible.info/art/large/95.html.

theme of the entire book. The apocalyptic materials of Daniel 7–12 have obvious generic differences with the stories of Daniel 1–6, but there are continuities that help connect the sections structurally and thematically. Now it is Daniel who is receiving the dreams and visions, and the interpretation comes from a messenger of God. The fantastic images continue, including images of beasts, the Ancient of Days, the Son of Man, a battle between a goat and a ram, and the intervention into human history of the angels Gabriel and Michael. The setting has changed from the adventures of Daniel and his compatriots in the courts of the various kings to a wider setting of conflict and confrontation on earth and in the heavens. The stakes are high, the dangers are great, but the resources to meet those situations are even greater.

A satirical reading of the narratives of Daniel 1–6 provides a clear parallel with the apocalyptic section of Daniel 7–12. An attitude of judgment toward kings and empires unifies the entire book. There is also the possibility that humor and satire may also provide a bridge between these seemingly two disparate sections. Two recent studies point to the possibility of reading the apocalyptic section in a satiric and humorous way.

First, James Charlesworth explores the popular nature of the folklore and iconography of apocalyptic literature (5-29). He suggests that there is a humorous and satiric quality to many of these stories. One possible setting for such stories may have been around the campfire, a place for good storytelling, for laughter at the incongruities of life, and for stories that help listeners make sense of the world. The fantastic images, the larger-than-life nature of apocalyptic stories, and the struggles between good and evil are all indicators of the popular nature of these stories and the attempt to come to terms with the larger themes of human existence.

Secondly, E. Alan Perdomo argues that apocalyptic literature, by using vivid symbolism to represent historical realities, can also be understood as an expression of protest by an oppressed people against the status quo (163-73). He suggests that there are parallels specifically between Daniel 7 and examples of satirical protest in Latin American literature. Through apocalyptic satire, people are given relief and hope because the enemy is cut down to size. The present sufferings under the reign of brutal rulers are seen as finally under a control beyond themselves, both human and divine.

Daniel 7 provides two brief examples. The four beasts are portrayed in vivid and terrifying language, but the reality is that they are but dwarfs when they are compared to the Ancient of Days and the celestial court. The so-called little horn arrogantly boasts of being powerful, but finds itself easily subdued by the Ancient of Days despite its bluster. Walter Wink reminds us that apocalyptic literature is always a protest against domination (103). It is an alternative act of the imagination that confronts the myth of redemptive violence[13] that permeates our cartoons and our foreign policy (Wink 13-31).

Many strategies are necessary to cope with living under the sway of the kingdoms of this world. Paramount, of course, is faithfulness to God and the ethics of God's kingdom. Like Daniel and friends, one must pray at the window, refuse to bow down to idols or statues or anything else that is put in the place of God, and know that God will be with those who are faithful, no matter how hot the furnace or how fierce the lions.

It is not surprising that the Daniel stories were often referred to in the witness of the Anabaptist martyrs recounted in *The Martyrs Mirror*. When the values of the kingdom of God are affirmed, one can participate and support the principalities and powers of the world. At other times we are called to be a witness for the alternative reality of the kingdom of God, to be an advocate for the sovereignty of the Prince of Peace. Sometimes it is important to resist overtly, other times covertly. Individuals and communities make such decisions based upon their best understanding of the call of God and their understanding of Scripture. Sometimes laughter at oneself and at the powers of this world is the only way to make it through. Laughter in the face of oppression disarms the powerful and gives hope and the will to persevere.

---

[13] The myth of redemptive violence advocates the victory of order over chaos through the means of violence.

Conclusion

One of the clearest continuities throughout Daniel is the fact that kings and empires are not as powerful or as strong as they appear. God is ultimately in control, and this is reason for hope. Followers of Jesus are called to be faithful advocates of an alternative reality toward politics as normal, and to persevere in their commitment to make the kingdom of God a reality in this world.[14] The book of Daniel uses humor and irony, and techniques of menippean satire, to cut kings and kingdoms down to size. A satirical reading of the book of Daniel establishes that the stories in Daniel 1–6 are critical of kings and empires and thus are thematically linked with the apocalyptic section of the book. There is a consistent and persistent message of judgment that is woven throughout the book. The message disrupts controlling authorities and voices. It challenges easy claims to truth. It offers a hilariously subversive resistance to empire and any who support it. The stories we tell at our dinner tables, around the campfires at church camp, from our pulpits, and through the microphones at Annual Conference are vital to our ability to persevere.

---

[14] See Robert W. Neff's discussion of political advocacy, which for Brethren is grounded in the life and teachings of Jesus of Nazareth (Neff 1987, 205-07).

Recommended Reading

Daniel Berrigan. *Daniel, under the Siege of the Divine*. Farmington, PA: Plough Publishing House, 1998.

John J. Collins. *Daniel: A Commentary on the Book of Daniel*. Hermeneia. Minneapolis: Fortress Press, 1993.

Danna Nolan Fewell. *Circle of Sovereignty: Plotting Politics in the Book of Daniel*. Second ed. Nashville: Abingdon Press, 1991.

André Lacocque. *Daniel in His Time*. Studies on Personalities of the Old Testament. Columbia: University of South Carolina Press, 1988.

Paul M. Lederach. *Daniel*. Believers Church Bible Commentaries. Scottdale, PA: Herald Press, 1994.

David M. Valeta. *Lions and Ovens and Visions: A Satirical Analysis of Daniel 1–6*. Sheffield: Sheffield Phoenix Press, 2008.

Study Questions

Prepare

Read the book of Daniel. How much of the first six chapters is familiar? How much of the final six chapters is familiar?

Find the reproduction of Rembrandt's *Belshazzar's Feast* at www.artbible.info/art/large/95.html and take time to examine it prior to coming to the session. Draw a picture of your favorite story from Daniel.

Ask

1. When someone mentions the book of Daniel, what sorts of things do you think of? In what context is the subject brought up, if at all? How often have you heard Daniel mentioned in sermons?

2. In recent work Bob Neff has talked about the importance of a book's placement in the canon, the order in which it appears in the Bible. The book of Daniel appears among the Prophets in the order that appears in Christian Old Testaments, and among the Writings (which includes Psalms, Proverbs, Job, Esther, and other books with wisdom and stories) in the Hebrew Bible used by Jews. Does this make a difference? What does it say about the Hebrew view of Daniel? What conclusions can you draw from the way it should be interpreted?

3. Valeta writes that the "root meaning of apocalypse is 'to reveal,' which involves revelation of the nature of God and the divine realm." How does this definition affect the meaning of apocalypse as is understood in the society? Has Daniel been presented to you as a book that is obscure or clear?

4. Read and react. Valeta refers to a passage in *Cracking the Code* that reads: "Most people have the impression that the apocalyptic portions of the Scriptures are deliberately obscure and that only those with superior knowledge and understanding can decode them. The opposite is true. Apocalyptic documents are written to make it clear to God's people living under oppression

that the present tribulations cannot last and that God, despite all appearances, remains active in human history." The passage goes on to suggest that North Americans don't "get" apocalyptic literature because they are not oppressed.

5. Valeta says that the book of Daniel seems to offer two different viewpoints toward the way to resist an oppressive government. Identify and contrast the two. What is the safest way to resist an overwhelming power? What is the most effective?

6. A *menippean satire* is an extended piece told in the style of a narrative or novel that has many targets of ridicule. Often it is about something other than what it appears. It was the choice of style for authors such as Mikhail Bakhtin who wrote under an oppressive regime. Name some of the elements of menippean satire as identified by Valeta. How are they used in the book of Daniel? If Daniel is considered satire instead of or as much as prophecy, what is the effect on the reader?

7. What is the place of dreams in the book of Daniel? How does this compare to your own view of dreams? Have you ever had a vivid or profound dream that affected your outlook on life or your choice of a way to live?

8. The author refers to Rembrandt's depiction of *Belshazzar's Feast*. Discuss the visual aspects of the piece. Describe each person's expression. Which one matches what you think your reaction would be? Compare the pictures you drew prior to the session. Which stories from Daniel seemed to intrigue the group?

9. "Daniel and the lion's den" seems to be one of the most popular stories from the book of Daniel. What are your memories of the story when you were young? Did your story version or biblical retelling include the slaughter of the false prophets and their families, including the children? How do you react to story elements such as this? According to Valeta, how does this work within the story as a satire?

10. Valeta refers to Walter Wink's assertion that "apocalyptic is always a protest against domination." As a group, can you think of ways that societies oppressed under dictatorships would take comfort in Daniel? What parts of Daniel should provide comfort to people in Western societies? What parts would condemn us as members of Western society?

Prefiguring Fulfillment
Brethren Approaches to the Old Testament

Jeffrey A. Bach

The Schwarzenau Brethren, who began with the baptism of eight adults in late summer 1708, treasured the Scriptures from their origins. The Old Testament was vitally important to the Brethren, although Brethren have typically read the Old Testament as pointing toward and being fulfilled by the New Testament. This in no way meant that Brethren, who often call themselves a "New Testament church," commit the Marcionite heresy of discarding the Old Testament.[1]

The following essay explores how Brethren have made important use of the Old Testament through their history up to the early twentieth century. This examination of a sample of Brethren writers will show that Brethren generally valued the Old Testament as inspired Scripture and tended to interpret it typologically, absorbing influences from interpretive trends around them (such as dispensationalism in the nineteenth century). Typological interpretation of the Bible goes back to ancient times and sees commandments and teachings and events in the Old Testament as

---

[1] In the second century, Marcion of Sinope contended that the God of the Old Testament was not the same as the God to whom Jesus witnessed. He also held that of the early Christian writers, only Paul truly understood the gospel. Accordingly, he rejected the entire Old Testament and accepted as authoritative only ten letters of Paul and an edited version of Luke's Gospel.

revealing God's activity in their own right, while at the same time pointing toward a future teaching or event in the New Testament. As Justo González has written, "a typological interpretation sees the meaning in the earlier event itself, whose historicity it does not deny" (91). In typological interpretation the "stress lies on the event itself—and not the words—prefiguring other events." The exploration in this essay concludes with the early twentieth century, as other articles in this volume deal with modern approaches to the Old Testament. For this essay, Old Testament refers to the sixty-six books of Hebrew Scripture that twentieth- and twenty-first-century Protestants generally consider canonical. This definition is not absolute, because in the eighteenth century some Brethren quoted books of the Old Testament Apocrypha. The term "Old Testament" is used because it is the most common term that Brethren of the eighteenth and nineteenth centuries used to denote these books of Scripture.

Old Testament Interpretation before Higher Criticism

Until the twentieth century, Brethren read the Old Testament with a pre-critical approach. Many Brethren believed that Scripture is inspired by God and can be read and understood by common members of the church with the aid of faith. In using a typological approach, Brethren often viewed the Old Testament as "prefiguring" the New. Certain details or events in the Old Testament were seen as pointing toward events in the New. There is virtually no evidence among Brethren writers prior to the spread of modern biblical scholarship for trying to read the Hebrew Scriptures for their own sake and in their own light. Since the eighteenth century, some Brethren have tried to understand meanings of words and context better, but without much extensive recourse to scholarship. Brethren have also valued highly the role of the community of believers interpreting Scripture together under the guidance of the Holy Spirit. Prior to the twentieth century, Brethren rarely trusted individual interpretation, nor did they regard interpretation as the sole domain of an academically trained rank of professionals. Still, throughout their history, Brethren have valued the insights of leaders and teachers in interpreting the Bible.

Frequent quotations from the Old Testament and some quotations from the Old Testament Apocrypha in early Brethren writings demonstrate that the early Brethren valued the Old Testament highly as sacred Scripture. Their typological interpretation is understandable, given the large percentage of early Brethren who came from Reformed backgrounds. Calvinism had taught a continuity between the Old and New Testaments. Calvin believed that the "ceremonial" law of the sacrificial system was not binding in the new covenant under Jesus Christ, but the moral elements of the Old Testament were binding. Still, Calvinism saw in the New Testament a greater fulfillment of the Old.

Alexander Mack, Sr., built his case for adult baptism by immersion with several Old Testament references of prefiguring. The rescue of Noah from the flood revealed "a prefiguration [*Vorbild*] of the water baptism of the New Covenant" (Mack, ed. Eberly 46). The rescue of Israel from the Egyptians at the sea and Levitical rules for washing to be cleansed from leprosy likewise "prefigured" adult baptism by immersion for Mack.

Outer Practice and Inward Faith

While the early Brethren typically interpreted the Old Testament as prefiguring the New, they were not purely literalists. Along with the correlation between the Old and New Testament, Mack saw an important correlation between *outer practice* and *inner faith*. For the early Brethren, the "outward Word" was the written Scripture. Equally important but inseparably linked to the outward Word was the inner spiritual experience of the living Christ, the "inward Word." According to Mack, "the outward and inward Law retained the same meaning," as the stone tablets of the Ten Commandments point toward the New Covenant "written in each believer's heart . . . by the Holy Spirit" (Mack, ed. Eberly 85). That which is "inwardly written by the Spirit of God is completely identical with that which is outwardly written in the New Testament," wrote Mack (Mack, ed. Eberly 85).

The Brethren broke with some of their Radical Pietist friends such as Hochmann von Hochenau by insisting that personal divine revelation could not render some teachings of the New Testament unessential. The Brethren rejected any notion of a continuing revelation, as they feared that prophets of the Community of True Inspiration might allow.[2] Mack acknowledged that "the Scriptures are only an outward testimony" of things "taught and commanded by the Holy Spirit" (Mack, ed. Eberly 83). However, "all believers are united in it, for the Holy Spirit teaches them inwardly just as the Scriptures teach them outwardly" (Mack, ed. Eberly 83). Thus the early Brethren saw a unity in inspiration of the Old and New Testaments, and interpreted the differences by explaining that the Old prefigures the New.

Conrad Beissel

The close link between inward and outward Word helped most of the early Brethren avoid the excessive use of allegorical interpretation common among Radical Pietists. With allegory, particular details of a biblical passage could be taken out of context and expanded to fill any meaning desired. This was especially typical in Jacob Boehme's two expansive allegorical commentaries on Genesis, his *Aurora*, the first of his works, and his two-volume *Magnum Mysterium*, his final large work. Conrad Beissel, founder of the Ephrata Community in 1728, was especially absorbed with Boehme, and drew some Brethren to join him, including two of Mack, Sr.'s sons (Alexander, Jr., returned to Germantown in 1748).

A good example of the difference between Brethren interpretation and Beissel's allegorical interpretation of Scripture was the matter of circumcision in Genesis 17. Mack rejected the Calvinist interpretation that circumcision was an Old Testament basis for infant baptism. Instead he reinterpreted circumcision on the eighth day after birth as the basis for waiting for spiritual rebirth to receive

---

[2] The Radical Pietist group known as the Community of True Inspiration was founded in 1714 in southwestern Germany by Eberhard Ludwig Gruber and Johann Friedrich Rock. In the nineteenth century, members of the Community emigrated to the United States. They eventually settled in Iowa, and are known today as the Amana Society.

adult baptism (Mack, ed. Eberly 50). Beissel followed Boehme's allegorical reading to interpret circumcision as proof of God's displeasure with procreation, thus using the story to endorse celibacy (Beissel 194). Accordingly, the early Brethren steered away from the excesses of allegorical interpretation of the Old Testament found among some Radical Pietists.

Michael Frantz

Michael Frantz, an important elder at Conestoga in Beissel's neighborhood, reinforced the link between inward and outward Word and the Old Testament prefiguring the New. Frantz left a rhymed confession of faith after his death in 1748, which Christopher Saur II published in 1770. Dale Stoffer noted the importance of the inner and outer meanings of Scripture in Frantz's work (97). Frantz explained how the outer leads to the inner in the practice of feet-washing, alluding to the role of inward and outward Word, along with Old and New Testament.

> The outer points to the inner,
> Otherwise it is the letter [of the Word] which can only kill,
> The outer has only shown that later the person has submitted.
>
> But now, according to God's counsel,
> One does not merely wash away the body's dirt;
> One makes a covenant of good conscience,
> And builds upon the foundation of Christ (10-11).

Frantz interpreted the marriage of Adam and Eve typologically to prefigure the relationship of a believer's soul to Christ in spiritual marriage. He portrayed the New Testament prohibition of divorce as fulfilling and superseding the Old Testament allowance for divorce, citing Christ's words that divorce was formerly allowed only because of human hardness of heart (15).

In his treatment of worldly authority and peace, Frantz emphasized the difference between the Old and New Testaments, rather than the unity. When a difference appears between the testaments, he upheld the New Testament as superior because it reveals Jesus who fulfills the Old. Frantz wrote, "the entire New Testament does not belong in secular rule, it belongs in Christ's passion, [where] suffering will bring comfort and strength" (22-23). In the paragraphs immediately following this assertion, Frantz upheld Jesus' teaching to turn the other cheek as superseding the Old Testament custom allowing an eye for an eye. To offer one's cheek to one's enemy, rather than overpower the enemy, is "the mind of Christ" (22-23). While the Old Testament allowed for "waging war against their enemies," Christ's congregation "should be completely defenseless" with regard to the outward sword (24).

Frantz employed this same approach to reject observing the seventh day as a sabbath, as the Ephrata Community practiced. The sabbath "is commanded in the old covenant completely plain and clear," wrote Frantz, but "the Son of Man is the Lord of the Sabbath" (28). According to Frantz, "Christ is the end of the Law, because he has received a New Testament from his Father," which is sealed in Christ's blood (29). Thus Jesus Christ and his new covenant supersede the commandment to observe the seventh day.

Alexander Mack, Jr.

More evidence for how Brethren interpreted the Old Testament in the eighteenth century comes from Alexander Mack, Jr.'s open letter about when to practice feetwashing in the order of the love feast. The letter was printed with the second edition of his father's treatise, *Rights and Ordinances*, published in 1774. Mack, Jr., who had been elected to ministry at Germantown in 1748, wrote that the Old Testament must be interpreted in light of Jesus Christ, with a reading that seeks love and peace among the faith community who interpret the Scriptures together. In the letter, Mack, Jr., first established the practice of feetwashing in the Old Testament. He cited its use as a hospitality gesture before meals, and as a part of ritual purification for priests prior to serving in the temple (32). The act of Jesus to wash the disciples' feet at the Last Supper fulfilled what was prefigured in the Old Testament and established it for subsequent generations of Christians to practice. "The prefiguration of the devout fathers prior to the Law and under the Law coincide exactly," Mack wrote (468).

Jacob Stoll

A unique approach to the Old Testament came from another elder at Conestoga, Jacob Stoll. In 1806 he published *Spiritual Little Spice Garden for Souls Seeking Salvation*. The book is a collection of 114 poetic devotions based on short passages from the Bible. Eighty-one of the devotions are based on Old Testament verses, and twenty-five of those devotions come from texts from the Minor Prophets, including Hosea, Joel, Amos, Obadiah, Jonah, Micah, Zephaniah, Haggai, and Malachi (68-95). The devotions, which are reminiscent of Gerhard Tersteegen, are completely spiritual reflections with little connection to a literal reading of the text. No other book by a Brethren author takes up so many Bible passages, especially from the Old Testament, in such a thoroughly spiritual manner.

Sarah Righter Major

Although very few writings of women from among the Brethren have come down from the eighteenth or first half of the nineteenth century, one letter from Sarah Righter Major indicates some of her approach to the Old Testament. In 1835, after she had begun to preach publicly when invited, she wrote a letter to one of her critics. In it, she stated her belief that while the man was created first, she believed that woman was made "equal to him" (229). In her own kind of typological interpretation, Sarah cited the prophecy from Joel that Peter quoted in his Pentecost sermon as being fulfilled in the New Testament by the coming of the Holy Spirit. The Spirit's power for women to prophesy is still in effect in the church. Again alluding to a typological interpretation, Sarah wrote that "there is much in the Old Testament about holy women, in the old and new church of Moses and of Christ" (230). The equality of women to men in creation and the gift of the Holy Spirit enabling women in the Old Testament to speak messages from God find their fulfillment in the New Testament, with the Holy Spirit empowering women to pray and prophesy. Sarah found warrant for her ministry in these stories.

Creative Hermeneutics and Dispensationalism

In the mid-nineteenth century, Peter Nead and B. F. Moomaw, two prolific Brethren authors, illustrated both a continuity of the typological approach to the New Testament employed by eighteenth-century Brethren, and new interpretive influences from dispensationalism.

Peter Nead

About the same time that Sarah Righter Major wrote to her critic, Peter Nead embarked on his writing career among the Brethren. In 1834 he published *Primitive Christianity, or, a Vindication of the Word of God*, the first of many efforts to explain systematically the faith and practices of the Brethren. Raised in a Lutheran family, Nead joined the Methodists in early adulthood. In 1823 he learned of the Brethren and was baptized in 1824. He and his wife settled in her family home in Rockingham County, Virginia, in 1825. They moved to the Dayton, Ohio, area in 1848. He expanded his initial book in *Theological Writings on Various Subjects; Or a Vindication of Primitive Christianity as Recorded in the Word of God*, published in 1850. The core of Nead's approach to biblical interpretation was already present in the first edition of 1834.

Like Brethren writers of the eighteenth century, Nead had high regard for the Old Testament, which he saw as prefiguring the New. Old Testament sacrifices were good in their era, wrote Nead, because "it was by the law of sacrifices that the great Atonement [sic] which Christ, the Son of God, made in his own body, was prefigured or shadowed forth" (Nead 1834, 16). The first purpose of the law in the Old Testament, according to Nead, was to show that God is righteous and holy. Its second purpose is to show people that they fall far short of God's righteousness and are unable to attain God's righteousness on their own. For Nead, this second purpose of the law is to convince people to seek Christ's atonement (Nead 1834, 14-15). This view is similar to part of Martin Luther's understanding of the law, and may well have been part of Nead's childhood religious formation in his Lutheran household. Nead distinguished between the *moral law*, consisting of the commandments regarding

human behavior, and the *ceremonial law*, consisting of commandments related to sacrifices, the priesthood, and rituals. The moral
law reveals the "knowledge of sin," and the ceremonial law reveals
"the expiation from sin." Nead called the ceremonial law the
"Levitical dispensation." According to Nead, the ceremonial law
was binding only until the coming of the Messiah, Jesus Christ, who
fulfilled it in his own death, making it "null and void" (Nead 15). In
these views Nead was close to Calvin's views in the *Institutes of the
Christian Religion* on the distinction between moral and ceremonial
law, and the purpose of the moral law (Calvin 354-55, 364, 453).

Nead brought some new emphases to biblical interpretation
among Brethren. In *Baptism for the Remission of Sins*, first published
in 1845 and incorporated as Part II of his *Theological Writings* in
1850, Nead developed a concept of dispensationalism in interpreting the relationship of the Old Testament to the New Testament.
He still viewed the Old Testament as typologically foreshadowing
the New. However, he included a framework of dispensations in
which God acted in varying patterns with humanity. According to
Nead, the first dispensation was the age of Adam and the ancestors.
The second age was that of Abraham and the Jewish people. The
third dispensation was the Christian dispensation, beginning with
Jesus Christ's ministry and his crucifixion and resurrection. The
fourth and final dispensation was that of the Millennium (Nead
1850, 355-356). According to Nead, each of the first three dispensations lasted approximately two thousand years. Each dispensation evidenced corruption overtaking God's people. Yet a faithful
remnant always remained to experience God's saving work.

Nead saw the Brethren as this faithful remnant in his time. He
admonished them to observe the distinctive practices, including immersion baptism in the names of the Trinity, feetwashing, the Lord's
Supper (the love meal of love feast) and communion, the holy kiss,
as well as nonconformity and nonresistance. These teachings would
preserve their faithfulness while awaiting the coming of Christ and
the final dispensation of the return of Christ. Nead's dispensationalism may have come from influences from the emerging Adventist
movement, which was popular in mid-nineteenth-century America.

Thus, he brought some new influences into Brethren biblical interpretation at the very time he sought to systematize and preserve what was distinctly Brethren.

B. F. Moomaw

About a generation younger than Nead, Benjamin Franklin (B. F.) Moomaw, an elder in Botetourt County, Virginia, wrote and preached in defense of Brethren faith and practice. Moomaw had been a Baptist, as were his father and oldest brother. He became convinced that the Brethren faith of his mother was closer to the New Testament and joined the Brethren around 1840. Two of his brothers and two of his sisters followed him into the church (Moomaw 1867, 45). He diligently opposed slavery and advocated the Brethren peace witness before, during, and after the Civil War. He published a collection of three treatises in 1867. One dealt with immersion baptism; another addressed the Lord's Supper and spiritual new birth. The third essay was presented in the form of a dialogue defending nonresistance.

Moomaw upheld the importance of the Old Testament, and yet contrasted the "old covenant" with the new. In his essay on baptism, he wrote that baptism "supercedes [sic] the Jewish dispensation" and its "rights and ceremonies with the ordinance of circumcision," which he assigned to "the Jewish polity" (Moomaw 1867, 8). According to Moomaw, in Jesus Christ "the law of Moses is now superceded [sic]" and the "seal" of the old covenant with Abraham, namely circumcision, ended (Moomaw 1867, 9). Baptism became an "ordinance belonging inclusively to Christ" in the new covenant established for Christians. Rather than finding a spiritual interpretation for circumcision as Mack, Sr., had done, Moomaw simply dismissed its importance.

Moomaw combined his contrast of the two testaments with the familiar typological interpretation of the Old Testament to explain the Lord's Supper, the love meal eaten at love feast. Advancing the argument of Peter Nead that the Lord's Supper was not a Passover meal, Moomaw wrote that the Passover foreshadowed Christ as the Passover Lamb, not the meal that he instituted with his followers.

"Christ is the anti-type of Passover, taking the place of the type" (Moomaw 1867, 156-157). The *type* refers to the commandment or item in the Old Testament that is fulfilled in a corresponding commandment or item in the New Testament, known as an *antitype*. In this case, Christ as Passover Lamb fulfilled the purpose of the Passover. Christ initiated the love meal as something new, not as a counterpart to the Passover. For Moomaw, as for Nead, the Lord's Supper would find its fulfillment in the future marriage supper of the Lamb in Revelation (Moomaw 1867, 164).

Moomaw's treatise on nonresistance addressed objections he often heard from Christian supporters of war that God commanded wars in the Old Testament. They charged that if there is a unity between the testaments, then Christians could and should fight. Moomaw approached this difficult problem for Brethren pacifists by contrasting the two covenants. He first introduced his treatise by pointing out that the ancestors of faith (Abraham, Isaac, and Jacob), the law, and the prophets all pointed toward a "coming priest after the order of Melchisadec [sic], the King of Peace," referring to Melchizedek's title as "King of Salem" [King of Shalom] (Moomaw 1867, 223). Thus, although Moomaw would contrast the two testaments, he opened his argument by presenting the peacefulness of Jesus Christ as the promise of the Old Testament.

Moomaw made a clever interpretive move in dealing with wars in the Old Testament. He conceded that if God commands war, then God's followers should fight. He agreed that David, a warrior, was called a "man after God's own heart." Nevertheless, David, "having shed blood abundantly, was not permitted to build the temple, the house of God" (Moomaw 1867, 225). Moomaw reinforced this point with his typological interpretation of the Old Testament. He saw the temple as an antitype for Christ's church, which is the new temple of God in the New Testament. "So, as the antitype was composed of material unstained by human gore, so the temple, the type, must be build [sic] by hands free from blood" (Moomaw 1867, 225). As the temple could not be built by one whose hands were bloodied by warfare, so the church of Jesus

Christ could not be sustained by those who fight and kill. Thus Moomaw used the Old Testament itself to undermine the potential example of David to support Christians going to war.

Moomaw answered the claim that God would allow for wars of self-preservation by citing Ezra (chapter 7) as evidence that God provided protection for those rebuilding the temple. Moomaw claimed that "the heart of the king" or other rulers is ultimately in God's hands, and God can turn the heart as God wills (Moomaw 1867, 228). Moomaw turned to the story of Shadrach, Meschach, and Abednego in the book of Daniel as evidence that even when a king or ruler commanded something contrary to God's will, believers should have no fear in refusing to obey wrong commands (Moomaw 1867, 233).

Moomaw replied to the claim that God commanded war in the Bible by stating that the two "dispensations" of Old and New Testament cannot be arbitrarily mixed. Not only did Moomaw draw contrasts between the old and the new, he also argued that the new was a consummation of God's kingdom, and "all wars and fightings are opposed to the spirit of the gospel." Indeed, killing was the result of sin, for which he cited the story of Cain's murder of his brother after Adam and Eve's first sin (Moomaw 1867, 240, 244). Jesus Christ fulfilled the "moral law by perfectly obeying it in his life, suffering and doctrine." The law "as understood under the former dispensations" was quite different from the moral law as "practiced by Christ and the Apostles" (Moomaw 1867, 249-251). Moomaw cited the antithesis of "eye for an eye" from the Old Testament with the command to "resist not evil" in the Sermon on the Mount. "The law is changed," wrote Moomaw. In the Old Testament "wars were permitted," but "in the New Testament they are forbidden" (Moomaw 1867, 257).

B. F. Moomaw cleverly combined the Brethren use of typology with an interpretive contrast between the covenants. Thus, he used Old Testament passages to critique war that found their fulfillment in Christ's teaching of nonresistance and peace. He showed some of the cleverest uses of these hermeneutical approaches to preserve the importance of the Old Testament for Brethren, and still defend the distinctive, New Testament-grounded teachings of the Brethren.

"No Creed but the Bible"

Not quite a decade after Moomaw's three treatises, a new spate of writers defending distinctive Brethren teachings drew on the thought of Nead and Moomaw, giving new contours to old arguments. Stephen H. Bashor, an active evangelist who sided with the Progressives in the Brethren divisions of the 1880s, wrote a little book defending Brethren practices. Titled *The Gospel Hammer and the Highway Grader, or Rubbish Cleaned from the Way of Life*, the book was published in 1878, just six years after his baptism and three years after his election to ministry at the Whitesville congregation (near St. Joseph, Mo.).

The book seems reflective of what may have been his preaching style. Bashor opened by citing Isaiah 35:8-9, about the path or way of God on which only the holy ones will travel. With this introductory passage he set the stage to contrast the Old Testament and the New Testament, arguing that the two covenants are different (7). Like Nead and Moomaw, Bashor argued against circumcision as a sign of the covenant similar to infant baptism, because circumcision pertained only to the "Abrahamic covenant" (33-40). Similarly, he employed the contrast between the testaments to separate the Lord's Supper (the love meal) at love feast from the Passover. Like Moomaw, he argued that the meaning of Passover was fulfilled in Christ, who replaced it with a new celebration. Nevertheless, Bashor attempted to preserve a connection between the testaments. "Christ has no power to change the law and hence could not change it," wrote Bashor. However, Christ did have "the power to fulfill it as it stands" (68).

Interestingly, Bashor concluded his book by claiming that Brethren have "no creed but the Bible," and that the Bible is the "only rule of faith and practice" (102-103). The "Bible and the Bible alone" is the only "safe guide to heaven and eternal felicity." With these words he echoed some of the concepts of Henry R. Holsinger, whom Bashor knew well. The Progressives adopted the

motto, "the Bible, and nothing but the Bible," rather than emphasizing just the New Testament (Holsinger 529).

Defending Nonconformity with the Old Testament

Matthew M. Eshelman created a unique interpretation of the Old
Testament to set the framework for his defense of Brethren
nonconformity in his book, *Nonconformity to the World; or, A Vindication of True Vital Piety*, published in 1874. Eshelman, born near
Lewistown, Pennsylvania, had grandparents who were Brethren,
although he did not join the church as a young man. He enlisted
in the Union army in the Civil War. Afterwards he moved to Illinois, and in 1871 he joined the Methodists. However, he was baptized into the Sugar Creek congregation of Brethren (southern
Illinois) in 1873. He moved to Lanark in northern Illinois, where
he was elected to the ministry. He was involved in the beginnings
of McPherson College in Kansas and later Lordsburg College
(La Verne) in California, although he remained skeptical about
higher education in religion. In 1892-1893 he associated with
Brethren Church (Progressive) congregations, and then returned
to the Church of the Brethren. He went back to the Brethren
Church after 1906. *Nonconformity*, his first book, shows a vigorous
defense of Brethren plainness at a time when controversy over
dress was one of the tensions pulling the Brethren apart. Eshelman later favored the Progressive approach.

His book opens with two sections introducing the Old Testament and the Jews as a people set apart as a distinctive people bound
to obey specific commands from God. Eshelman used this as the
basis for introducing nonconformity as a marker of the Brethren as
God's distinct people, set apart to be a holy priesthood of believers.

According to Eshelman, God made creation and the first humans good. After the first transgression, which Eshelman blamed
on Eve, God provided a succession of covenants, "each covenant
more perfect than its predecessor" (5-9, 13-15). Each covenant had
a sign associated with it (the rainbow with Noah and circumcision
with Abraham). In calling Abraham, God chose a people to be exclusively God's own. By "clinging to the covenant, Abraham and

his descendants became a distinct people" (16). Using the typological interpretation, Eshelman wrote that "step by step," God "prepared the way for the shadow and through the shadow and the patterns the Redeemer brought the image to sight" (17). In this case, the "image" refers to the New Testament teaching that was prefigured in the "shadows" of the Old Testament.

In the covenant of the law made with Moses at Mount Sinai, God gave regulations for the Israelites to build a sanctuary—the tabernacle—where they would worship God. In order for them to do this "holy work" of worship, God required them "to be dressed in garments unlike other people" (26). The peculiarity of dress, to which Eshelman referred as the special tassels (fringes) and ribbons required by the Mosaic law, was commanded so that the people would "look upon it and remember the commandments of the Lord and do them" as a people nonconformed to the world (27).

Eshelman attributed the "fall" of Israel to their turning to foreign gods and marrying foreign women. He cited numerous quotations from Isaiah, Jeremiah, Hosea, Amos, and Judges condemning Israel for falling "into the pit of worldly popularity, which is idolatry." They discovered "some of the 'non-essentials,' and among the number was the matter of dress" (34-36). When the Israelites removed their "badge of distinction, the fringe and the ribbon," they had nothing to look at to remember to keep the commandments of God (36). Thus, while Eshelman combined typology with an interpretation of successive dispensations or covenants, he actually based the Brethren teaching of nonconformity on the Old Testament covenants creating a set-apart people who were given distinctive dress to remind them of their distinctive commands.

In the third part of his book, which is by far the longest, Eshelman condemned a host of worldly pleasures that marked conformity to the world, including silken and fashionable clothing, entertainments such as playing cards, attending fairs, holding teas, "strawberry parties," and attending testimonial dinners with joking and frivolous stories. He also denounced raised platforms and

pulpits in meetinghouses. Here he claimed that the stand for
Solomon's bronze laver was not justification for a raised stand for
preachers [see 2 Chron. 6:13; 28:18], and that Ezra's pulpit was for
proclaiming the law in the street, not for worship in the temple
[Neh. 8:4] (139-143). Eshelman did not mention the account in
Ezra of the consecration of vessels of gold and silver to be used as
holy objects within the temple.

Some readers might regard Eshelman's detailed recommenda-
tions for nonconformed living with a bit of humor, and complain
that his use of the Old Testament was forced. However, he attempted to bring the Old Testament to bear on an important aspect of Brethren faith at a time when it was charged with emotional
controversy. He sought to use the Old Testament to emphasize the
importance for Brethren to live visibly as God's witnesses in the
world.

S. N. McCann, a Church of the Brethren missionary to India and
Bible teacher at Bridgewater College, turned Eshelman's grounding
of nonconformity in the Old Testament on its head in his book *The
Lord Our Righteousness*, published in 1896. McCann studied at the
Brethren Normal School (later Juniata College) and at the Southern
Baptist Theological Seminary. McCann wrote that Israel was chosen to be "elect, not by works but by God's unfolded plan of salvation" (41). Good works "coupled with obedience of ordinances and
ceremony" cannot make a person righteous. "Our only righteousness is Christ, our substitute," who is the "sin offering" for the whole
world (15, 41).

Redefining Typological Interpretation

A Brethren minister and educator from Ohio, Quincy Leckrone,
wrote on redemption by grace and distinctive Brethren teachings
in his book, *The Great Redemption*, published in 1898. His book
marked the start of a movement away from a fully typological approach to the Old Testament, using a concept more like metaphor
or symbol for understanding the First Testament. He still retained
the importance of the Old Testament for Brethren and interpreted
it in light of the New Testament. However, he wrote that "the law

was figurative, the meaning, Metaphoric [sic] and the sacrifices symbolic" (281).

Although he did not mention Israel or the Old Testament specifically, Leckrone wrote that when God made a covenant with the chosen people, God "required of those accepting it obedience to some external rite which he [God] himself pointed out." This rite was a "sign," or "seal" with a specific material "token." Baptism and water were the "seal" and "token," respectively, for the new covenant, corresponding to water used for purification in the old covenant (32). Feetwashing, according to Leckrone, was no longer a "non-essential" matter for Christians than was washing in the Jordan River for Namaan by command of Elisha. Although Namaan thought that the rivers of Syria would be just as good as the Jordan for cleansing his leprosy, the Jordan was necessary according to Elisha's directions. Leckrone used this Old Testament story to support New Testament practices of the Brethren.

Leckrone also drew from Peter Nead and B. F. Moomaw in defending the Lord's Supper as a necessary practice for Christians, rather than being an outmoded Passover. Like his predecessors, he identified Christ as the "antitype of the Paschal lamb and at his death the Passover was fulfilled." The "supper that he instituted" was a "new institution" (117). Leckrone added to this familiar Brethren interpretation another distinction that appeared already in an essay that John Kline wrote about the Lord's Supper, which was published in Peter Nead's *Theological Writings*. Leckrone repeated that the Lord's Supper is "a type of what is to come," pointing "forward to the final marriage feast" when believers are "forever united with the Lamb, the Son of God" (117, 124). For Leckrone, the communion of bread and cup pointed back to Christ's death on the cross, while the Lord's Supper—the love meal—pointed toward a future fulfillment.

In defending nonswearing, Leckrone faced more difficult Old Testament precedents. He pointed out that God never "allowed false swearing," but did allow that people "might swear by His name (Deut. 6:13)." Leckrone resorted to contrasting the two testaments to disallow swearing. "Since the fulfillment of the law and prophets" is in Jesus Christ, "the former dispensation has passed away" (119-120). He used the same line of argument to defend the Brethren peace teachings (230-232). While the old Brethren patterns of typology and contrasting the Old Testament as different from the New were still at work in Leckrone's writing, he began a small shift toward the language of symbol and metaphor to soften a formal typological interpretation.

Rosenberger and Biblical Inspiration

Sometime after 1914, Isaac J. Rosenberger published *The Holy Spirit*, a collection of essays that originally appeared in *Gospel Messenger* in 1914. A widely traveled evangelist who was as prominent as Stephen Bashor, Rosenberger had attended Baldwin Wallace College in his native Ohio. While his book dealt with the Christian concept of the Holy Spirit for which he advanced evidence from the Old Testament, the work illustrates a reading of the Old Testament through the New Testament, although without a strictly typological approach. Rosenberger saw the Holy Spirit present in creation with a life-giving role in the Spirit of God moving upon the waters and the "breath" of God giving life to the first human, which Rosenberger claimed recurred in the vision of the valley of dry bones in Ezekiel (11-18).

Rosenberger read evidence of the Holy Spirit in the Old Testament. He saw three "endowments" of the Holy Spirit there. The first was the gift of divinely given strength, represented by Gideon and Samson. The second endowment of the Holy Spirit was wisdom, for which Rosenberger named specifically Moses and Joshua. Curiously, he did not mention Solomon or Job in this connection. The third endowment was prophecy, illustrated by Elisha, Samuel, Moses, and, interestingly, Balaam, who was unable to curse the people God blessed (22-31).

Perhaps most instructive in Rosenberger's book is his view of scriptural inspiration. Rosenberger saw a kind of unity between the testaments. He believed that the Old Testament prophets had been able to see into the future, and that many of their prophecies had already been fulfilled. This was evidence for him of the inspiration of the Scriptures. His understanding of Old Testament references appearing in the New Testament, and New Testament writers quoting passages from the Old Testament likewise confirmed for him the inspiration of Scripture. While admitting that some books of the Bible showed the personality of their authors, Rosenberger held to a view of plenary inspiration of the Old and New Testaments. By this he meant that both testaments were fully inspired by the Holy Spirit (45-59). By his own admission, Rosenberger was influenced by other writers on the topic and his book is not uniquely Brethren. Still he offers an insight into an early twentieth-century attempt to explain the inspiration of Scripture. Rosenberger differed from earlier Brethren writers in seeing a greater unity in the inspiration of the testaments. He did not differ in the Brethren approach of reading the Old Testament through the New.

The Effects of Biblical Criticism

One final book from the first part of the twentieth century illustrates the transition under way as biblical criticism began to influence Brethren biblical interpretation, especially in the institutions of higher education. This development was not inevitable, nor was it the culmination of all previous Brethren interpretation. Rather, the development came as some Brethren were exposed to new trends in scholarly interpretation. D. W. Kurtz wrote *The Gospel of Jesus*, published in 1936, during his five-year presidency of Bethany Biblical Seminary during the depths of the Great Depression. He had studied at Ohio Northern University, Juniata College, and Yale Divinity School. He had served Brethren congregations in Brooklyn and Philadelphia and taught Greek at Juniata. He was president of McPherson College from 1924-1927. In some ways, other Bible teachers in the Church of the Brethren, such as E. G. Hoff, son of Bethany founder E. B. Hoff, and to lesser extents Floyd Mallott and W. W. Slabaugh, might better illustrate in their teaching some glimpses of the emerging influence of biblical criticism among Brethren. Mallott's posthumous exposition on Ecclesiastes, *Is Life Worth Living?* merits its own analysis, but falls outside the scope of this survey. Because none of these three men had published any-thing of substance prior to 1936, Kurtz's book will serve simply as an illustration. To be sure, none of these individuals represented a full development of historical criticism of the Bible. Their careers at Bethany in the 1920s and beyond indicated changes coming among some Brethren from new scholarship.

While *The Gospel of Jesus* is not about the Old Testament, Kurtz's treatment of the Old Testament signaled a change for Brethren. He contrasted the way God is portrayed in the two tes-taments. The Old Testament portrayed God as "the Strong One, the Almighty, King and Judge." Jesus, however, gives a "fuller rev-elation, making it clear that the Creator and Sustainer of the uni-verse" is also "our Father, whose real character embraces holiness and redemptive love." Echoing Protestant liberalism, Kurtz im-plied a dichotomy between an Old Testament image of God as "strong" and a New Testament image of God as "loving" (25-26). In a later chapter, Kurtz wrote that the gospel of Jesus brings free-dom, which is "self-determination" (35). Although never "free from the moral law," a Christian "is free from the Jewish cultus [sic] law, that is, the keeping of days, months and seasons; and the sacrifice of sheep and goats; the Jewish Sabbath with its many re-strictions; and the ritual observance of cleansing, formulas and prayers and fasts" (36). Kurtz wrote that life in Christ was obtained "entirely apart from the law, and it made one free from the cultus of the law" (37). For Kurtz, the "law was never to be the way of sal-vation, only to make one conscious sin" and aware of the need for salvation (69). Kurtz emphasized the difference between testa-ments so strongly that he effectually diminished the importance of the Old Testament. This development was new in the Church of the Brethren. Prior to the twentieth century, Brethren had gone to lengths to retain high regard for the Old Testament, even as they created explanations when it seemed contrary to their distinctive practices taken from the New Testament.

Kurtz found the most valuable truth in the Old Testament to be the ideal of vicarious suffering, which he saw most clearly in Isaiah 42:13–53:12. Yet Kurtz used this passage for another chance to talk about Jesus, rather than interpret the text in its context. Despite all of the emphasis on Jesus in Kurtz's book, Paul was ultimately the hero. Without saying so directly, Kurtz clearly favored the Pauline interpretation of Jesus. Strongly shaped by his education at Yale and the period he studied at the German universities of Leipzig, Berlin, and Marburg in 1908-1909, Kurtz had a modern Protestant—namely, Lutheran—reading of Jesus. Although Kurtz's book is not about the Old Testament, its reading of Jesus seems remote, if not cut off, from Jesus' Jewish context and Judaism's sacred writings. The book is a sign of how Protestant liberalism was affecting views of the Old Testament among Brethren with higher education. Kurtz is illustrative for the role of the Old Testament at Bethany during the first half of the twentieth century. With the hiring of Robert W. Neff in 1965, the seminary had its first teacher fully trained in modern exegetical methods for studying the Hebrew Scriptures. While this era of change is beyond the scope of this article, Neff set new terms for studying the Hebrew Bible at Bethany in ways that changed how many Brethren would look at and study the Old Testament.

Conclusion

While this brief overview of Brethren approaches to the Hebrew Scriptures concludes in the early twentieth century, one can say that historically the Brethren highly valued the Old Testament. Brethren typically avoided literalizing the Old Testament, often preferring to interpret it as prefiguring the New. During the twentieth century, the rise of higher critical methods of interpretation added new perspectives, but did not replace all other understandings of the Hebrew Scriptures in the Church of the Brethren. Members continue to interpret the Hebrew Bible in a variety of ways, many shaped by influences from outside the Brethren. Some members of the Church of the Brethren continue to value the role of the gathered community of believers in interpreting the Old Testament. Members of the church should not expect that only one approach to Scripture will eliminate all others. Likewise, members of the Church of the Brethren should not expect that the church will surrender all interpretation to an elite group of biblical specialists. Nevertheless, Brethren have always valued skilled, faithful teachers who will share tools with the faith community to interpret and engage meaningfully and prayerfully with the Old and New Testaments. How blessed we are when we have teachers among us who help us to hear, believe, and practice the Word of God.

Recommended Reading

Donald F. Durnbaugh. *Fruit of the Vine: A History of the Brethren, 1708-1995*. Elgin: Brethren Press, 1997.

Marcus Meier. *The Origin of the Schwarzenau Brethren*. Philadelphia: Brethren Encyclopedia, 2008.

Dale R. Stoffer. *Background and Development of Brethren Doctrines 1650-1987*. Philadelphia: Brethren Encyclopedia, 1989.

Study Questions

Prepare

Think of the most recent sermon you heard based on the Old Testament. Make a few notes about the subject and points made along the way. Did the preacher use the Old Testament to point to Christ? Was the Old Testament text used as a bad example in comparison to the New Testament? How much background on the Old Testament text was given?

If you or your church has a copy of *The Complete Writings of Alexander Mack*, leaf through the pages and note with pencil where there are quotations from the Old Testament. Which books are quoted? Are the quotations used to back up New Testament passages? Do they stand on their own?

Questions

1. Bach states that the early Brethren all respected and used the Old Testament, but often read it as "prefiguring" the New. Describe and discuss Bach's outline of Calvinist beliefs about the Old Testament.

2. An allegory is a representation of an abstract or spiritual meaning through concrete or material forms. How did some allegorically link circumcision and baptism, and what was the Brethren response?

3. Bach mentions several figures from Brethren history, including Alexander Mack, Jr., Sarah Righter Major, and Peter Nead. Compare and contrast their approaches to the Old Testament as reflected in their writings. Do any of these approaches resemble your own?

4. What was meant by Peter Nead (and others) when it comes to dispensations? How did this guide his interpretation of the Old Testament?

5. B. F. Moomaw is described as saying that Jesus superseded the Law of Moses. How did his Old Testament interpretation address the challenge of Christians who insisted that the Bible sanctions war? How did he view King David versus Jesus?

6. One often hears that Brethren have no creed but the New Testament. Stephen H. Bashor is quoted as saying that the Brethren have no creed but the Bible. Which statement do you lean closer to? How have you heard it expressed? How did Bashor connect the love feast with Old Testament history and practice?

7. Bach focuses on Matthew M. Eshelman's unique interpretation of the Old Testament, especially with regards to a controversial issue of his day—nonconformity in dress. Are there any contemporary issues that you have addressed by turning to the Old Testament? How authoritative would you consider the Old Testament when it comes to contemporary issues?

8. What progression does Bach see between the work of Isaac J. Rosenberger and D. W. Kurtz? What were their views of the inspiration of the Hebrew Scriptures? Do you think that Kurtz downgraded the Old Testament, and do you think it is downgraded in the church today?

9. If you attended Sunday school and church as a child, think back on the Old Testament stories you heard from the pulpit or in the class. Did you enjoy these? Which, if any, were your favorites? Were there some that bothered you? Explain why. Was the Old Testament regularly preached or taught? Does the approach you heard fit into any of the typologies mentioned in Bach's article? Consider these same questions with regard to your experience as an adult who attends Sunday school, Bible studies, and worship.

10. As a group, compare the notes you prepared about the most recent sermon you heard based on the Old Testament. Did the preacher use the Old Testament to point to Christ? Was the Old Testament text used as a bad example in comparison to the New Testament? How much background on the Old Testament text was given? Do you enjoy Old Testament sermons?

Brethren Ordinances and Old Testament Practices

Denise D. Kettering

Should Brethren eat roasted lamb or beef at love feast? Should congregations use leavened or unleavened bread at communion? Should only elders practice anointing? These questions have plagued Brethren at various points throughout their history. At first glance such questions may appear trivial, and yet they arose again and again at Annual Meeting[1] as Brethren congregations tried to develop a unified approach to their church ordinances.

Part of the dilemma for Brethren was how to treat the relationship between their ordinances and the Old Testament and its practices. Historically, the Brethren tradition has ordinances, such as baptism and the love feast, that are firmly rooted in the teachings of Jesus; however, these practices also reflect ancient Israelite customs and rituals found in the Old Testament. In the Church of the Brethren, it has not always been popular to stress these connections to the Old Testament. As Robert W. Neff stated, "To be an Old Testament-toting Church of the Brethren person was not easy, but I felt I had a calling to make the Old Testament live in the Church of the Brethren" (Neff 15). The conflicted nature of the Brethren relationship to the Old Testament becomes increasingly

---

[1] Since 1927, the annual gathering of the Church of the Brethren has been called Annual Conference (Slabaugh 33).

clear when one compares Brethren ordinances and Old Testament customs and rituals. While the early Brethren acknowledged the connection between Brethren and Israelite practices, later Brethren interpreters distanced themselves from Old Testament traditions. Despite this mixture of approval, the Brethren ordinances of baptism, love feast, the holy kiss, and anointing adopted elements of Old Testament customs and rituals. Interestingly, Brethren practices exhibit parallels in meaning and execution with practices found in the Old Testament.

Brethren have always focused on the New Testament as the primary source for theology and practice. Even while using the apocryphal books—Sirach, the Wisdom of Solomon, Tobit, and so forth—in a limited fashion, the Brethren relationship to the Old Testament has remained more complicated. Brethren have consistently interpreted the Old Testament in light of the New Testament, and the New Testament has been viewed through the lens of Jesus Christ's commands and example. While Alexander Mack, the first Brethren leader, emphasized continuity between the Old and New Testaments, he always privileged the New Testament (Gardner 9-11). This interpretive schema persists among some of Mack's successors today, as demonstrated by the pamphlet "Basic Beliefs within the Church of the Brethren," published by the Brethren Revival Fellowship: "If one is to have a true understanding of the will of God, he must always accept the New Testament interpretation of the Old Testament. What was seen only vaguely (in the Old Testament) in *the dim starlight* of promise and type, is now seen clearly (in the New Testament) in the *bright sunlight* of God's complete and perfect revelation in Christ." Thus, envisioning the Old Testament as a prefiguring of the New Testament has been the predominant interpretive approach used by Brethren.

Historically Brethren have used the Old Testament selectively. Brethren interpreters have tended to emphasize the Law (Genesis, Exodus, Leviticus, and Deuteronomy) and the Prophets (Isaiah, Jeremiah, Ezekiel, Daniel, Hosea, Joel, Amos, Micah, and Jonah), avoiding the historical books (Joshua, 1 and 2 Samuel, 1 and 2 Kings, and 1 and 2 Chronicles) because of their bloody battles and ritual sacrifices (31-32). In relationship to Brethren ordinances, this trend in biblical reading was no different, as citations in theological texts and Annual Meeting minutes appear most frequently from the Law and the Prophets.

The lives of the ancient Israelites were shaped by customs and ritual practices. Israelite rituals defined membership in their community, developed a communal memory, and served as reconciling devices in both festival celebrations and everyday life. The institution of circumcision served as a defining mark and initiation ritual into the community of the chosen (Gen. 17:1-11). Feetwashing and the kiss were social customs employed in the Old Testament as signs of hospitality and reconciliation. The Law developed even more ritual actions. Washing and ablutions gained particular significance because of the Law's emphasis on ritual purity, categories of clean and unclean.

One of the established Israelite festivals, which continued to hold great significance for the people of Israel, was the Passover.[2] God ordered the Israelites to commemorate the passing of the angel of death over the houses of the Israelites as a festival to the LORD—"a lasting ordinance" (Exodus 12:14). On the first day of the festival, the Israelites removed the yeast from their homes and for seven days they could only eat unleavened bread. The culmination of the festival was a feast that entailed eating lamb and bitter herbs quickly with their sandals on and their staff in hand to symbolize their preparation before fleeing Egypt.

For Brethren, an ordinance is a religious ritual that was ordered or instituted by Christ for the church to follow. Traditionally, Brethren ordinances provided corporate experiences in which a brother or sister did not stand alone before God (Lehman 58). There is not, however, a single consistent list of Brethren ordinances in official documents. While most Brethren agree that baptism by immersion and the three-fold practice of love feast and communion are ordinances, there have been disagreements about

---

[2] The Passover festival is often combined with the Feast of Unleavened Bread, and the two festivals are treated as one holiday in some passages of the Bible.

whether practices such as anointing the sick for healing, the laying on of hands, and the holy kiss should also be identified as ordinances (Flora 976-980). *The Brethren's Card*, first published in the 1920s in an effort to outline briefly the significant elements of Brethren identity, explained that the Church of the Brethren observed the following New Testament rites:

> Baptism of penitent believers by trine immersion for the remission of sins (Matt. 28:19; Acts 2:38); feet-washing (John 13: 1-20; 1 Tim. 5:10); love feast (Luke 22:20; John 13:4; 1 Cor. 11:17-34; Jude 12); communion (Matt. 26:26-30); the Christian salutation (Rom. 16:16; Acts 20:37); proper appearance in worship (1 Cor. 11:2-16); the anointing for healing in the name of the Lord (James 5:13-18; Mark 6:13); laying on of hands (Acts 8:17; 19:6; 1 Tim. 4:14). These rites are representative of spiritual facts which obtain in the lives of true believers, and as such are essential factors in the development of the Christian life (Brown 2005, 9).

While it is clear that all of these practices are rooted in New Testament passages, there are four ordinances—baptism, the love feast, the holy kiss, and anointing—that drew on Old Testament rituals and practices and, in some cases, presented troublesome correlations for later Brethren.

Baptism

The Israelites had many uses for water in their rituals, including prescribed washings for a variety of purposes. When Jacob prepared his household to visit the shrine of God in Bethel, he made everyone purify themselves by washing first (Gen. 35:2). The people prepared at Mount Sinai for God's revelations by washing themselves and their garments. Priests had to wash before making sacrifices. Lepers also went through a specific ceremonial cleansing before they could resume full participation in community life. Touching a dead person or animal as well as menstruation required washing before gaining readmission to community activities. There were three kinds of ablutions: washing hands, washing hands and feet, or full immersion. Full immersion was used after the healing of a leper, for uncleanliness, or on the Day of Atonement (Simmons 36-69).

Over time, immersion also became an initiation rite in Judaism. Three men served as sponsors and took the naked initiate to a pool where he stood up to his neck in water. The sponsors recited the commandments to him, he promised to keep them, a benediction was pronounced, and finally he was fully submerged. Christ gave the command to baptize, but he did not dictate a particular mode of baptism. The New Testament established the ordinance of baptism, which mirrored the purification of the Jewish initiation service (Simmons 43). Thus, the Brethren practice of immersion drew strongly on previously practiced Jewish rituals that branched out from Old Testament roots.

In his *Rights and Ordinances*, Alexander Mack, Sr., identified several instances in the Old Testament that prefigured the practice of water baptism. He identified signs of the water baptism at the beginning of the tabernacle community: "Moses had to make a large laver or vessel before the tabernacle where the priest Aaron and his sons were to wash themselves first before they could go into the tabernacle (Exodus 18:20; 40:12). This was also a strong prefiguration for the water baptism which was commanded by Jesus" (Durnbaugh 1958, 349). Mack drew a parallel between the purification and washing rituals established in the Old Testament community and the Brethren practice of adult baptism. Just as the priests could not enter the tabernacle without being washed and purified first, a person could not completely be part of Christ's church without receiving water baptism. He also cited the Mosaic Law on how healed lepers had to wash their bodies in water, women had to bathe in water, and other purifications were necessary before worship and full participation in the community (Lev. 14:8-9). All of these purification rituals foreshadowed the water baptism ascribed in the new covenant through Christ. Mack even noted that it was customary for Jews to receive outward cleansing and purification under the law, so that baptism was not new for the New Testament Jewish community (Durnbaugh 1958, 350). Thus, Mack connected Brethren baptismal practice with Old Testament cleansing rituals. The Old Testament purification rites prepared the Israelites to go before God, and likewise Christian baptism prepared the believer to join the Christian congregation and go before God (Durnbaugh 1958, 355). For Mack, the washing rituals of the Israelite community prefigured the practice of Christian baptism.

Despite the evident correlations between Old Testament cleansing rituals and baptism, Brethren interpreters more frequently focused on a connection between baptism and circumcision. While still in Germany, one of the original Brethren members, Andreas Boni, challenged the Frenkendorf pastor Jacob Maximillian Meyer on the issue of infant baptism. Boni claimed that he could not find any evidence for infant baptism in the New Testament. He further challenged the prevalent early modern correlation between infant baptism and circumcision.

As the sign of the covenant, circumcision was prescribed for every male when they were eight days old (Gen. 17:9-14). Many theologians identified circumcision as a foreshadowing of Christian baptismal practices. If the membership sign of the old covenant was implemented in infancy, then it seemed logical to infer that baptism—an initiation rite into the new covenant—should likewise take place in infancy. Thus, the Brethren had to deal with this issue in an innovative way in order to participate in the theological debates of early modern Europe. According to Meyer, Boni argued, "Some say [infant] baptism was introduced instead of circumcision, when one circumcised the children on the eighth day. This was valid under the Law, but we live under grace. It is useless to say that baptism shared with the infants as a sign of the covenant of God, because they do not understand it. He maintained these opinions persistently" (Durnbaugh 1958, 90). Thus, one early Brethren response was to differentiate Old Testament obedience to the Law and the New Testament notion of grace, placing the two concepts in opposition to one another. From this opposition he extrapolated that the Law required initiation as an infant, and grace required membership as an adult. This idea appeared in the writings of contemporary Radical Pietists. For example, Ernst Christoph

Hochmann von Hochenau wrote to Alexander Mack on July 24, 1708, that he found no warrant for the baptism of children in the New Testament because Jesus did not institute the practice (Durnbaugh 1958, 111).

In his tract *Answers to Gruber's Basic Questions*, Alexander Mack also addressed the relationship between baptism and circumcision. He stated that Christ created a new covenant for believers so that they did not need to adhere to the rules of the old covenant: "Just as circumcision did not concern children before the eighth day— to have circumcised before that time would have even been a violation of circumcision—the baptism commanded of believers does not concern children before they are able to profess their faith. The eighth day of circumcision is a prefiguration of this" (Durnbaugh 1958, 333).

Thus, while Mack drew a parallel between the eighth day circumcision and baptism as initiatory rites, he did not deem the age of the initiates to be of primary importance. Instead, he stressed that the "eighth day" is the "first day of the new creation of a person," implying that for the Christian the whole childhood preceded the "eighth day" adult baptism upon profession of faith (Durnbaugh 1958, 334). Essentially Mack emphasized that boys who died before their circumcision or uncircumcised females were not banned from participating in the community or salvation. Likewise, those Brethren children who died before receiving baptism would not be condemned, negating the need to baptize infants. Thus, the eighth day for Mack became the time when believers professed their own faith (Brown 1983, 153). Water baptism did not save, rather Christ saved; baptism was instead an act of obedience to Christ. "Mack placed the locus of baptism more around a loving and obedient response than on baptismal regeneration, the view that the act of baptism has saving efficacy" (Brown 1983, 153). Thus, Brethren recognized both the cleansing rituals of the Old Testament and circumcision as rituals that pointed forward to the practice of baptism and incorporated similar meanings. Purification rituals, like baptism, cleansed from sin. Circumcision, like baptism, initiated a person into communal membership. The early Brethren understood the connections between certain Old Testament rituals and the Brethren ordinance of baptism.

Love Feast

After baptism, the most important Brethren ordinance was the love feast. With its focus on community, imitation of Christ, and servanthood, it stands at the heart of Brethren identity. This ritual encompasses much about the Brethren way of life and their self-understanding. The love feast consists of three parts: feetwashing, a meal, and the partaking of communion. All of these rituals, we need to note, have ties to the Old Testament.

The preparation required for love feast in many Brethren congregations during the eighteenth and nineteenth centuries in some ways mirrored the Jewish preparation for the Passover. A deacon would visit each baptized member to ensure that he or she still stood in proper relationship to God and the faith community. In preparation for the visit, church members would often clean their houses as a sign of spiritual cleansing and preparation (Stayer 202). This practice mirrored the way that Jewish families would clean their houses, making sure that all the yeast had been removed from the home before the beginning of Passover. This cleaning process prepared Jews and Jewish homes for the coming of the Passover, and likewise for Brethren it prepared Christians for the reception of the love feast.

Feetwashing

The Brethren practice of feetwashing referenced episodes in the Old Testament that portrayed feetwashing as a purification ritual and hospitable custom. For example, Brethren authors noted that priests had to wash their feet before serving in the temple. Further, in biblical times, hosts offered water to their guests so they could wash their feet. Wealthy hosts might provide a slave to wash the guest's feet as an act of hospitality. When Jesus knelt to wash the disciples' feet, he girded himself with a towel, emulating a slave. This action added a symbolic quality to the notion of servanthood that became so important to the Brethren practice of feetwashing.

In a 1774 open letter appended to an edition of Mack's *Rights and Ordinances* and *Basic Questions*, Alexander Mack, Jr., used Old Testament resources to explain the roots of the Brethren feet-washing practice. After openly acknowledging the difficulties many people had with the practice of feetwashing, he explained why Brethren adhered to this practice. While the bulk of the letter substantiated his position by building on New Testament references, he started with the Old Testament by claiming that "the ancient devout fathers practiced feetwashing after the Law." He cited Genesis 18:4; 24:32; and 19:2 to make his argument. In Genesis 18:4, Abram received three visitors at Mamre, and upon seeing them he called for water to be brought so that the visitors could wash their feet. Likewise in Genesis 24, when Isaac's servant arrived at Laban's house and met Rebekah for the first time, water was brought as a welcome to wash the guest's feet. Finally, Lot offered hospitality to the two angels when they came to Sodom—in the form of water to wash their feet (Gen. 19:2). Thus, according to Mack, Jr., the Israelites performed feetwashing as a practical and symbolic act. He did not even marshal all of the evidence available from the book of Genesis to support his claim. For example, Joseph sent for water so that his brothers could wash their feet when they arrived as an act of hospitality and welcome (Gen. 43:24).

Further, Old Testament evidence demonstrates that the patriarchs were not the only ones to practice feetwashing. Priests practiced feetwashing, too. Namely, Aaron and his sons had to wash their hands and feet before they could serve in the tabernacle (Exodus 40:31-32). There was a special basin designated for this washing. God commanded Moses to,

> Make a bronze basin, with its bronze stand, for washing. Place it between the Tent of Meeting and the altar, and put water in it. Aaron and his sons are to wash their hands and feet with water from it. Whenever they enter the Tent of Meeting, they shall wash with water so that they will not die. Also, when they approach the altar to minister by presenting an offering made to the LORD by fire, they shall wash their hands and feet so that they will not die (Exodus 30:18-20).

Washing the feet was such an important preparation for the priest that it required a special basin explicitly for that purpose. While Mack did not cite the construction of the basin as an important precedent for the Brethren feetwashing practice, he did cite the implementation of the practice when Aaron and his sons first entered the tabernacle as evidence for the importance of feetwashing in the Old Testament. This act of feetwashing was primarily an act of obedience to the Law and a preparation for service. Finally, he cited the example of Abigail washing David's feet as his last piece of Old Testament evidence to support the long custom of feetwashing (1 Samuel 25:41). Mack, Jr.'s survey revealed that Old Testament feetwashing practices related to hospitality and service, but he does not specifically discuss whether feetwashing also served a purifying function in preparation for communion.

Mack, Jr., even noted that these stories also influenced the placement of feetwashing in the love feast order of service, namely that "the devout fathers performed feetwashing before the meal" (Durnbaugh 1967, 464). So, not only was there a precedent established in the Old Testament for the act itself, but there was a precedent in the placement of the feetwashing at the beginning of the love feast service.

Love Meal

Within both the Passover feast and the Last Supper, the actual meal—the food—had symbolic meaning (Ramirez 20). Alexander Mack complained in his *Rights and Ordinances* about the communion customs of his day: "Some hold 'the Lord's Supper' in the morning, others, at noon, but none have it as a supper. When an evening or a noon meal is to be held, there must be something to eat! But there the people go to their so-called 'supper' and return from it hungry and thirsty. Some do not even receive a bit of bread and a little wine, but at the same time are filled with great extravagance of clothes, sensual, debauchery, selfish pride and the like" (Eberly 62).

Mack saw few parallels between the communion practices of his day and the biblical narrative of the Last Supper. In reaction, he proposed a different mode of the Lord's Supper, one that included a meal. It should not surprise us to find that Mack connected this love feast to the Old Testament Passover meal. According to Mack, only worthy recipients could receive either the Passover or the love feast. Just as those who wanted to receive Passover had to be prepared properly, those who received the Lord's Supper must be baptized correctly and in right relationship with God and the Christian community (Durnbaugh 1967, 363). The Brethren always maintained the need for this actual feast, even reiterating at the 1848 Annual Meeting that scriptural evidence indicated a supper was eaten by Jesus and the disciples the night that Jesus instituted communion (*Minutes* 100). Yet, the Meeting did not indicate that the meal eaten at the Last Supper was the Passover meal. Thus, while Mack comfortably drew parallels between the Passover and Lord's Supper, later interpreters ignored these connections.

In a letter between Alexander Mack, Jr., and Johann Preisz (1752-1829), Mack, Jr., commented on the importance of the Lord's Supper and drew direct correlation to the Passover. Particularly, he expressed interest in the blessings offered by Jesus at the Last Supper. He acknowledged that "the good Master gave separate thanks and concluded the Passover" (Durnbaugh 1967, 233). Jesus gave thanks in accordance with the close of the Passover meal. This proves that the younger Mack recognized that the origins of this thanksgiving were derived directly from the Passover celebration.

The traditional love feast meal consisted of bread, broth, rice, lamb or beef, butter, and water (Stayer 204). One of the interesting aspects of this memorial supper in Brethren history is the attempt to distance this Christian celebration from the Jewish Passover meal. As early as 1827, congregations had already raised questions at Annual Meeting about whether or not the meat used for the meal should be lamb or beef. At first glance, it would seem quite natural that lamb should be used, given the recognition by the early Brethren that the basis for this meal was the Passover feast.

The 1827 Minutes confirm this position, declaring that it was "most agreeable" to use mutton, "as it has been always customary with the ancient brethren" (*Minutes* 51). The Meeting did, however, urge patience with those who used beef for the meal and did not identify this as an area to apply church discipline. The issue arose again in 1853 when a query asked whether churches could "put away the lamb" at the Lord's Supper and use beef instead. The Meeting reiterated that lamb would be better, "but inasmuch as Christ has made us free from the ceremonial law, and as there is no command in the New Testament that it must be so, we should bear with each other in love in such matters" (*Minutes* 137).

Apparently the problem did not go away and presumably caused divisiveness between congregations. Some churches began to shift away from using lamb to beef for the love feast meal. In 1855, only two years later, the issue arose again. The query was whether congregations that used beef instead of lamb could continue to commune with the church. Meeting responded that each person should submit to the order of the church where they lived, but that they should also allow for differences in this matter and obey Paul's admonition in Colossians not to judge each other based on what they ate or drank and bear with one another rather than see this as a divisive issue (*Minutes* 151).

Here two distinct groups appeared. One group tried to uphold the earlier Brethren practice, which recognized the Passover roots of the meal, and another group wanted to move away from what they interpreted as Jewish customs. The desire of this latter constituency became clear in the 1858 minutes when a query was brought to Meeting about whether it was in line with biblical teaching to use beef instead of lamb in the Lord's Supper. This time the Meeting simply answered "It is" (*Minutes* 174). In a few years, this issue moved from a mere toleration of beef to the point where it became advisable to use beef instead of lamb. This action further differentiated the Passover and Brethren practices.

In 1863, the shift away from lamb became even clearer when a congregation queried whether "it is contrary to the gospel to have lamb's meat at the Lord's Supper" (*Minutes* 217). Here, the question indicates a complete turnaround from the earlier position. Lamb, once the favored and normative meat for the love feast, became increasingly seen as questionable fare. The Meeting determined that it was not contrary to the gospel to have lamb, and members should bear with each other because there was no "precept or example of what the supper did or shall consist" (*Minutes* 219). This statement completely ignores the Passover roots of the Last Supper, demonstrating the move from the earlier Brethren position that recognized the Passover roots of the love feast to a position that claimed there was no indication in the text that connected the Passover to the meal.

Communion

A similar debate took place over whether Brethren should use leavened or unleavened bread. Clearly the Old Testament text highlighted the use of unleavened bread at the Passover. The Gospels suggested that Jesus used unleavened bread at the Last Supper. In the 1870 minutes, a query raised the problem, "Why is it that the brethren use leavened bread at their love feasts? Had we not better take the example of Christ and the apostles, and use unleavened bread?" The response to this question shows perhaps the most interesting self-conscious attempt by the Brethren to distance themselves and their Christian celebration from the Old Testament and its Passover customs.

Meeting responded, "We do not believe it right to keep the Jewish customs" (*Minutes* 290). This blunt answer clearly attempted to reject the Old Testament practices tied to the Passover, even though it also meant distancing from the Gospel accounts of the Last Supper and completely ignoring Jesus' connection to Judaism. Interestingly, despite the admonition to abandon unleavened bread and use leavened bread in order to differentiate between Brethren and Jewish customs, it appears that many congregations continued to use unleavened bread. The 1906 *Inglenook Cookbook* contained several recipes for unleavened communion bread and none for a leavened bread specifically for communion use. Thus, while the Meeting may have wanted the Brethren to move away from the practices of Judaism and the Passover feast, many congregations apparently continued to use unleavened bread. To this day, many Brethren congregations continue to use unleavened bread during communion, drawing on recipes passed down through generations of deaconesses.

Annual Conference struck one final blow in the nineteenth century against any correlation between the love feast and the Passover. The 1880 Minutes exhibit a deliberate attempt to quash the connection with the question, "What shall be done with brethren that teach that Christ ate the legal Passover on the night in which He instituted the bread and wine?" The question suggested that church discipline should be meted out for drawing this connection. The answer reveals how far the Brethren had moved from their early founders' recognition of the connectedness between the Old Testament Passover feast and the Brethren practice of love feast: "Such teachers should cease to teach so, as it is not the teaching of God's Word. And if they will not cease doing so they should be dealt with according to Matthew 18" (*Minutes* 374). The answer assumed the need for disciplinary action on the basis that the teaching violated the meaning of the meal.

When one makes a critical review of New Testament ordinances, it does appear that there are clear foundations in Old Testament practice. Brethren, on the other hand, have had an ambiguous relationship with those very Old Testament echoes in Christian practice. The service of communion was prefigured in the Old Testament when Melchizedek, the King of Salem, brought out bread and wine and offered it to Abraham, saying, "Blessed be Abraham by God Most High, Creator of heaven and earth. And blessed be God Most High, who delivered your enemies into your hand'" (Gen. 14:18).

Bread was offered to Abraham's visitors at Mamre, and Lot offered bread to his visitors in Sodom. Bread was also a vital part of the sacrificial system. The book of Leviticus described the type of bread to use: "If he offers it as an expression of thankfulness, then along with this thank offering he is to offer cakes of bread made without yeast and mixed with oil, wafers made without yeast and spread with oil, and cakes of fine flour well kneaded and mixed with oil" (Lev. 7:12). Thus, bread became an important part of the offering and sacrifice alongside animals and grain. Wine was often a drink offering. All of the elements of the love feast contained clear connections to customs and rituals found in the Old Testament, yet the Brethren had a conflicted relationship with the Old Testament roots of the meal. While the early Brethren acknowledged that there was a connection between the meals, later Brethren spurned these connections, expressing an increasing desire to move away from Old Testament rituals.

The Holy Kiss

The holy kiss came into use in a variety of ways for Brethren: during the communion service, as a greeting, and as part of church discipline. Yet, despite the attempt to make the kiss correspond to Paul's New Testament language of greeting, the kiss actually modeled Old Testament uses as a gesture of reconciliation, greeting, or departure. When Joseph's brothers arrived in Egypt after so many years apart, he kissed them in welcome and greeted his father the same way (Gen. 45:15; 50:1). When Moses and Aaron met in the desert, they kissed. Thus, the kiss served as a greeting among family members. Esau welcomed Jacob back with a kiss and embraced him as a sign of reconciliation after having been estranged for years (Gen. 33:4). The book of Ruth portrayed the kiss as a gesture used before a departure. When Orpah departed from her mother-in-law, she kissed her as a gesture of greeting and kindness (Ruth 1:14). The kiss was even used in conjunction with anointing Saul (1 Samuel 10:1). While these uses mostly involved family members, the Old Testament uses of the kiss demonstrate a wide range of options. For Brethren, the notion that the church was the family of God connected the Christian practice to these Old Testament uses.

Brethren had several uses for the kiss in their family of God. Two uses mirror Old Testament events: as a greeting and as a tool for reconciliation. Brethren members kissed in greeting not only when they met for church or other religious gatherings, but also when they visited each other or met when they were about their business. The kiss served as a greeting among members, but it also became a sign to outside observers that the Brethren met each other in peace and brotherhood.

The second use of the kiss related to how the Brethren used the kiss in reconciliation practices. The 1840 Annual Meeting stipulated how congregations should reintroduce members who had undergone church discipline, and the kiss played a central role in the reconciling process. When a person was ready to reenter the community, congregational members of the same sex would greet the reconciled member with the hand of fellowship and the kiss, while members of the opposite sex would offer a handshake (*Minutes* 71). The kiss symbolized a reunification of the church family and welcomed the previously excluded or disciplined member back into proper relationship. Just as Esau forgave Jacob and welcomed his return, the Brethren offered a similar ritual to separated brother and sisters. It is interesting to note, however, that the Old Testament is never mentioned in reference to this use.

Anointing

Just as the holy kiss held many meanings, anointing in the Old Testament was used for a variety of events. The Brethren focused predominantly on the use of anointing in healing. Anointing and the laying on of hands in the Brethren world were frequently connected, although the laying on of hands had multiple purposes that did not always relate to healing. The laying on of hands enabled the Holy Spirit to flow into a person. There were three uses for this practice: (1) after baptism as a blessing, (2) when setting an elder apart through a special blessing and consecration to the office, and (3) for healing of the sick. The anointing service, based on James 5:14, involved two elders placing oil on the head of a sick person and praying for healing (Lehman 56-58).

The practice of anointing had deep roots in the ceremonial life of the Israelites. Anointing in the Old Testament was frequently used to consecrate people or items for holy use. For example, the high priest and sacred vessels were anointed with oil in order to prepare them for sacred use (Exodus 29:29; 30:26). The special anointing oil was made from a combination of olive oil and spices (Exodus 30:22). Moses used this oil to consecrate the tent of meeting, the table and utensils, the priestly garments, and Aaron and his sons. The Law testifies to the holy and sacred nature of this oil: "It shall not be poured on anyone's body, nor shall you make any like it in the same proportion; it is holy, and it shall be holy to you. Whoever shall mix any like it or whoever puts any of it on a layman shall be cut off from his people" (Exodus 30:32-33). The oil consecrated generations of priests by recognizing their special status in the community as members anointed to do the work of the Lord. The oil held a special position in ritual life by setting other things apart as sacred from everyday life.

The Old Testament credited anointing with several other uses. For example, it also had medicinal and healing qualities (Psalm 109:18; Isaiah 1:6). Anointing could be employed for hospitality purposes too, such as offering guests oil as a way to refresh and invigorate the body (Deut. 28:40; 2 Samuel 14:2; Ruth 3:3; Psalm 104:15). Finally, priests and kings were anointed as they entered their new position as religious or political leaders. The most frequent use of the term in the Old Testament is to refer to kings or priests as "the anointed." No crown was required in the Israelite community; instead, the requirement was to be anointed by the high priest as a symbolic "crowning" (1 Samuel 16:13; 2 Samuel 2:4). Successive generations of kings received anointing as witnessed in the books of Kings and Chronicles. Prophets also received anointing with holy oil to signify their role as chosen spokespersons for God (1 Kings 19:16; 1 Chron. 16:22; Psalm 105:15). Jesus instructed the disciples to anoint for healing when he sent them out to minister (Mark 6:13). This mandate drew on the existing practice within the Jewish tradition of anointing for healing. The early Christians also practiced anointing (James 5:14-15). Yet, after the early church period anointing faced continual regulation, relegating it to a practice carried out only before death. Finally, the sixteenth-century reformers almost completely eliminated the practice. The Brethren adopted the practice for physical healing and spiritual uplifting—forgiveness of sins, strengthening of faith, and comforting the mind (Bowman 54-56). Yet, this is one area where the whole range of meanings from the Old Testament was not adopted by the Brethren.

Annual Meeting addressed the issue of anointing multiple times. In 1812, the problem was whether anointing could be administered at the request of a brother or sister. Annual Meeting stated:

> It might be administered to them, provided they would not seek further help from an earthly physician; and if it should so be that the Lord would raise them again to health, and they should fall sick again, and think the Lord would call them away, and they ask again to be anointed, we would have not right from the word of God to refuse them, and it should be left to those brethren's wisdom who are called to do as the anointing will teach them (*Minutes* 30).

In this case, the practice of anointing most closely resembled the earlier Christian practice that involved anointing with oil as a last rite. It was a last resort for the sick, rather than a method of healing that could be used in conjunction with medicine.

The 1827 Minutes described the practice of anointing as it should be practiced among the Brethren. First the participants should sing a few songs and then unite in prayer. The service stipulated that there must always be "two brethren" present. One would extend his hand and the second would pour oil into the first brother's hand. The first brother would put the oil on the head of the person being anointed while reciting the appropriate verses from James 5:14. Then both brethren would lay their hands upon the head of the sick person and pray over them again. This practice grew almost exclusively out of the New Testament as the Old Testament accounts usually involve one person performing the anointing service (*Minutes* 196-197).

In this arena, one of the most important issues for Brethren was whether or not the anointing needed to be performed by ordained elders or not. An 1850 decision stated that only bishops or ordained elders should perform it, differing from the 1827 decision discussed above (*Minutes* 120). This issue simply would not resolve itself. After deferring the issue at several conferences in the late nineteenth century, a study committee returned to the 1893 Meeting with a report on the question. The study committee determined that "elders" could be anyone who had authority in the church, therefore including lay church officials or deacons. Thus, anyone duly authorized by the church could perform anointing (*Minutes* 572-573). Unlike in the Old Testament when priests or prophets typically performed anointing, here the conclusion was that one need not be ordained to practice anointing. Thus, there is more divergence between the Old Testament ritual and the Brethren ordinance regarding who could administer the ritual. The practice of anointing in the Old Testament predominantly set people or objects apart into the sacred realm. The Brethren practice centered on healing and therefore differed from many of the descriptions of anointing found in the Old Testament, yet the practice itself of placing oil on the head, laying hands on the head of the one to be anointed, and then offering a prayer differed little.

Conclusion

While the Church of the Brethren has tended to rely on the New Testament as a guide for theology and practice, there are certainly Old Testament precedents that influenced the creation of the ordinances followed by the Brethren. It is true that the Brethren drew particularly on the practices of Jesus to establish their ordinances. In doing so, they also drew on the Jewish practices that Jesus knew and followed.

Baptism drew on initiation practices present in the Jewish community, as well as notions from the Law related to being clean or unclean. The love feast modeled the Passover meal, and feetwashing was a frequent practice that held a special significance in part because of the historical precedence of service it represented. The Israelite community employed anointing to designate something as sacred, and as a method for healing purposes. The New Testament practices that shaped the Brethren movement often stemmed from Old Testament festival practices and preparations for holy rites.

In summary, the Brethren have had a conflicted relationship with the Old Testament roots of their rituals. Early Brethren acknowledged that the Old Testament practices had prefigured Christ's institution of the rituals, giving significance to the Old Testament meanings for the rituals. Later generations of Brethren, however, did not view the Old Testament rituals as warmly. In fact, some tried to limit the connections between Old Testament and Brethren practices. Despite their efforts, it remains a fact that baptism mirrors the cleansing rituals instituted in the Law, feetwashing was always an act of hospitality and service, the Passover meal provided the menu for the love feast, the holy kiss was an important reconciling gesture, and anointing was a powerful way to invoke the sacred. The meanings behind these rituals—hospitality, commemoration, and reconciliation—were prominent themes that gave these ritual actions their power and authority. Such concepts made these rituals vital and so important that generations of Brethren believers and their practical and symbolic roots reach back through Jesus to the religious life found in the Old Testament.

Recommended Reading

William Eberly, ed. *The Complete Writings of Alexander Mack.* Winona Lake, IN: BMH Books, 1991.

Denise Kettering. "'Greet One Another with a Holy Kiss': The Evolution of the Holy Kiss in the Church of the Brethren." *Lines, Places, and Heritage: Essays Commemorating the 300th Anniversary of the Church of the Brethren.* Ed. Jeff Bach and Steve Longenecker. Bridgewater, VA: Penobscot Press, 2008:197-212.

Frank Ramirez. *The Love Feast.* Elgin: Brethren Press, 2000.

James W. Simmons. "Baptism in the Early Church." *Brethren Life and Thought* 7 (1962): 36-46.

Study Questions

Prepare

Jot down some of the customs for love feast, baptism, anointing, and the laying on of hands, and tell how they are practiced in your experience. Have you observed or experienced the holy kiss? Write down what changes you have observed in these ordinances over your lifetime.

Find, print out, or photocopy a copy of *The Brethren's Card*, either in a book or on the Internet at www.cob-net.org/bcard.htm.

Questions

1. Kettering suggests that Brethren ordinances have roots in Old Testament practice. Were you taught to consider the Old Testament as a source for these practices?

2. How does Kettering suggest the Brethren use the Old Testament as a means to interpret the New Testament? Name some texts from the writings of Alexander Mack and others that she cites. Which books does she identify as among the most important to Brethren?

3. Are there correlations between the Brethren ordinances and the Old Testament festival cycle? See Exodus 23:14-19; Leviticus 23; Numbers 9; Deuteronomy 16. If so, what are they and how do they influence the meaning and/or practice of Brethren ordinances?

4. Describe some of the practices of ritual cleanliness in Kettering's article. What are your "cleanliness" rituals? What is their relationship to actual cleanliness?

5. In his book *Another Way of Believing*, Brethren theologian Dale Brown talks about a Brethren woman who told him she'd secretly arranged for her infant to have infant baptism "just to be safe." Are there things you do "just to be safe" that may not be biblical? What fears are these things grounded in? What was the Brethren attitude toward infant baptism?

6. What is the connection, according to Kettering, between love feast and Passover? What elements of Passover do you find in your own congregational practices?

7. What is your memory of your first experience with feetwashing? Were there any difficulties? How do you explain feetwashing to new Brethren or non-Brethren, and what is their reaction?

8. Is it necessary for congregations to experience uniformity in communion practices? Does your church have bread and cup communion without love feast? If so, what was the reaction when it was first introduced? Have you experienced love feast and communion at more than one church? Outline the differences, if any.

9. Is the holy kiss practiced at love feast or at any other occasion in your church? What is the comfort level with it? Is there an equivalent practice to the kiss? How important is conforming with society when it conflicts with a practice such as the holy kiss?

10. Kettering writes of the connection Brethren made between anointing and the Old and New Testaments. What were those connections?

Bibliography

Introduction

Brueggemann, Walter. Foreword. *The Old Testament and the Significance of Jesus*. By Fredrick C. Holmgren. Grand Rapids: William B. Eerdmans, 1999. ix-xii.

Childs, Brevard S. "On Reclaiming the Bible for Christian Theology." *Reclaiming the Bible for the Church*. Ed. Carl E. Braaten and Robert W. Jenson. Grand Rapids: William B. Eerdmans, 1995. 1-17.

Holmgren, Fredrick C. *The Old Testament and the Significance of Jesus*. Grand Rapids: William B. Eerdmans, 1999.

McDonald, Lee Martin. *The Biblical Canon: Its Origin, Transmission, and Authority*. Peabody, MA: Hendrickson, 2007.

———. "Canon of the New Testament." *The New Interpreter's Dictionary of the Bible*. Volume 1. Nashville: Abingdon Press, 2006. 536-547.

1. Christians Reading the Old Testament

Alter, Robert. *The Art of Biblical Narrative*. New York: Basic Books, 1981.

Brueggemann, Walter. *Theology of the Old Testament*. Minneapolis: Augsburg Fortress, 1997.

Friedman, Richard Elliott. *Who Wrote the Bible?* New York: Summit Books, 1987.

Harnack, Adolph von. *Marcion: The Gospel of the Alien God*. Trans. John E. Steely and Lyle D. Bierma. Durham, NC: Labyrinth Press, 1924.

Josipovici, Gabriel. *The Book of God: A Response to the Bible*. New Haven: Yale University Press, 1988.

2. Conflict Transformation and the Jacob Saga

Genesis and Biblical Studies

Alter, Robert. *The Art of Biblical Narrative*. New York: Basic Books, 1981.

Brueggemann, Walter. *Finally Comes the Poet: Daring Speech for Proclamation*. Minneapolis: Augsburg Fortress, 1989.

———. *Genesis*. Interpretation. Atlanta: John Knox Press, 1982.

———. *The Prophetic Imagination*. Second ed. Minneapolis: Augsburg Fortress, 2001.

Divito, Robert. "Anthropology, O.T. Theological." *The New Interpreter's Dictionary of the Bible*. Volume 1. Nashville: Abingdon Press, 2006.

Fretheim, Terence. "The Book of Genesis." *The New Interpreter's Bible*. Volume 1. Nashville: Abingdon Press, 1994.

Hamilton, Victor. *The Book of Genesis 18–50*. New International Commentary on the Old Testament. Grand Rapids: William B. Eerdmans, 1995.

Jacobs, Mignon. *Gender, Power, and Persuasion: The Genesis Narratives and Contemporary Portraits*. Grand Rapids: Baker Academic, 2007.

Niditch, Susan. *Folklore and the Hebrew Bible*. Minneapolis: Fortress Press, 1993.

Roop, Eugene. *Genesis*. Believers Church Bible Commentaries. Scottdale, PA: Herald Press, 1987.

Steinberg, Naomi. *Kinship and Marriage in Genesis: A Household Economics Perspective*. Minneapolis: Augsburg Fortress, 1993.

Steinmetz, Devora. *From Father to Son: Kinship, Conflict and Continuity in Genesis*. Literary Currents in Biblical Interpretation. Louisville: Westminster John Knox, 1991.

Towner, Sibley. *Genesis.* Westminster Bible Companion. Louisville: Westminster John Knox, 2007.

Trible, Phyllis. *Hagar, Sarah and their Children: Jewish, Christian and Muslim Perspectives.* Louisville: Westminster John Knox, 2006.

Westermann, Claus. *Blessing in the Bible and the Life of the Church.* Trans. K. Crim. Overtures to Biblical Theology. Philadelphia: Fortress Press, 1978.

Wolff, Hans Walter. *Anthropology of the Old Testament.* Trans. M. Kohl. Philadelphia: Fortress Press, 1974.

Conflict Studies

Bowdine, Richard and Donna Crawford. *The Handbook of Conflict Resolution Education.* San Francisco: Jossey-Bass, 1998.

Borisoff, Deborah and David Victor. *Conflict Management: A Communication Skills Approach.* Second ed. Upper Saddle River, NJ: Allyn and Bacon, 1997.

Butchart, Robert and Barbara McEwan, eds. *Classroom Discipline in American Schools: Problems and Possibilities for Democratic Education.* New York: State University of New York, 1998.

Cloke, Kenneth, Joan Goldsmith and Warren Bennis. *Resolving Conflicts at Work: Eight Strategies for Everyone on the Job.* San Francisco: Jossey-Bass, 2005.

Corvette, Barbara A. Budjac. *Conflict Management: A Practical Guide to Developing Negotiation Strategies.* Upper Saddle River, NJ: Prentice Hall, 2006.

Deutsch, Morton and Peter Coleman, eds. *The Handbook of Conflict Resolution: Theory and Practice.* San Francisco: Jossey-Bass, 2006.

Gangel, Kenneth and Samuel Canine. *Communication and Conflict Management.* Eugene, OR: Wipf and Stock, 2002.

Kohn, Alfie. *Beyond Discipline: From Compliance to Community.* Alexandria, VA: Association for Supervision and Curriculum Development, 1996.

Kriesberg, Louis. *Constructive Conflicts: From Escalation to Resolution.* Second ed. New York: Rowman and Littlefield, 2003.

Lantieri, Linda and Janet Patti. *Waging Peace in our Schools.* Boston: Beacon Press, 1996.

Leas, Speed. "The Basics of Conflict Management in Congregations." *Conflict Management in Congregations.* Ed. David B. Lott. Herndon, VA: Alban Institute, 2001.

———. "Leadership and Conflict." *Creative Leadership Series.* Ed. L. Shaller. Nashville: Abingdon Press, 1982.

Lederach, John Paul. *Conflict Transformation Across Cultures.* Syracuse, NY: Syracuse University Press, 1995

———. "Into the Eye of a Storm." *A Handbook of International Peacebuilding.* San Francisco: Jossey-Bass, 2002.

———. "Journey from resolution to transformative building." *From the Ground Up: Mennonite Contributions to International Peacebuilding.* Ed. C. Sampson and J.P. Lederach. New York: Oxford University Press, 2000.

———. *The Little Book of Conflict Transformation.* The Little Books of Justice and Peacebuilding. Intercourse, PA: Good Books, 2003.

———. *The Moral Imagination: The Art and Soul of Building Peace.* New York: Oxford University Press, 2005.

Marzano, Robert J. *Classroom Management that Works.* Alexandria, VA: Association for Supervision and Curriculum Development, 2003.

McConnon, Shay and Margaret McConnon. *Conflict management in the Workplace: How to Manage Disagreements and Develop Trust and Understanding.* London: How to Books, 2008.

Montville, Joseph. "Justice and the Burdens of History." *Reconciliation, Justice and Coexistence: Theory and Practice.* Ed. Mohammed Abu-Nimer. New York: Lexington Books, 2001.

Schirch, Lisa. "Ritual Reconciliation: Transforming Identity/Reframing Conflict." *Reconciliation, Justice and Coexistence: Theory* and Practice. Ed. Mohammed Abu-Nimer. New York: Lexington Books, 2001.

3. Real Stuff: The Brethren Bible Part Too and the Heart of the Holiness Code

Augustine. *The City of God*. New York: Modern Library, 1950.

Bamburger, Bernard J. *Leviticus: A Modern Commentary*. New York: Union of American Hebrew Congregations, 1979.

Brown, Dale W. *Another Way of Believing: A Brethren Theology*. Elgin: Brethren Press, 2005.

Friedman, Richard Elliott. *Commentary on the Torah: with a New English Translation and the Hebrew Text*. New York: HarperCollins, 2001.

Funk, Benjamin, ed. *The Life and Labors of Elder John Kline, the Martyr Missionary: Collated from His Diary*. Elgin: Brethren Publishing House, 1900.

Hartley, John E. *Leviticus*. Word Biblical Commentary. Dallas: Word Books, 1992.

Kaiser, Jr., Walter C. "Leviticus." *The New Interpreter's Bible*. Volume 1. Nashville: Abingdon Press, 1994.

Levine, Baruch. *Leviticus*. The JPS Torah Commentary. Philadelphia: The Jewish Publication Society, 1989.

Milgrom, Jacob, *Leviticus 1–16: A New Translation with Introduction and Commentary*. The Anchor Bible. New York: Doubleday, 1991.

———. *Leviticus 17–22: A New Translation with Introduction and Commentary*. The Anchor Yale Bible. New Haven and London: Yale University Press, 2000.

Morse, Kenneth I., ed. *Preaching in a Tavern*. Elgin: Brethren Press, 1997.

Nead, Peter. *Theological Writings on Various Subjects; Or a Vindication of Primitive Christianity*. Dayton: New Edition, 1866. Reprinted by Dunker Springhaus Ministries, Youngstown, Ohio, 1997.

Sarna, Nahum. *Exodus*. The JPS Torah Commentary. Philadelphia: The Jewish Publication Society, 1991.

Tolkien, J. R. R. *The Fellowship of the Ring*. New York: Ballantine Books, 1965.

4. Will We Listen? Attending to the Shema in Christian Education

Achtemeier, Paul J., ed. *Harper's Bible Dictionary*. New York: Harper & Row, 1985.

Archer, Gleason L. and G. C. Chirichigno. *OT Quotations in the NT: Complete Survey*. Chicago: Moody Press, 1983.

Bell, Chip R. *Managers as Mentors: Building Partnerships for Learning*. San Francisco: Berrett-Koehler Publishers, 2002.

The Brethren Encyclopedia. Three Volumes. Philadelphia: The Brethren Encyclopedia, Inc., 1983.

Byars, Ronald P. "Deuteronomy 6:1-15." *Interpretation* 60 (2006): 194-196.

Cahill, Thomas. *The Gifts of the Jews: How a Tribe of Desert Nomads Changed the Way Everyone Thinks and Feels*. New York: Doubleday, 1998.

Cover, Joseph and Samuel Murray. *Annual Meetings of the Brethren*. Two Vols. in one, with three parts. Dayton: Christian Publishing Association, 1886.

Fox, Everett. *The Five Books of Moses*. New York: Shocken Books, 1995.

Gray, J. "Baal (Deity)." *The Interpreter's Dictionary of the Bible*. Volume 1. Nashville: Abingdon Press, 1962.

Hertz, J. H., ed. *The Pentateuch and Haftorahs*. London: Soncino Press, 1956.

Hirsch, Samson Raphael. *The Pentateuch: translated and explained*. Volume 6. Gateshead: Judaica Press, 1982.

Kugel, James L. *How to Read the Bible: A Guide to Scripture, Then and Now*. New York: Free Press, 2007.

Jacobs, A. J. *The Year of Living Biblically*. New York: Simon & Schuster, 2007.

Matthews, Victor H. and Don C. Benjamin. *Social World of Ancient Israel: 1250-587 BCE*. Peabody, MA: Hendrickson, 1993.

Meier, Levi. *Ancient Secrets: Using the Stories of the Bible to Improve Our Everyday Lives*. New York: Villard, 1996.

Michael, Oscar S. *The Sunday-School: in the development of the American Church*. Milwaukee: The Young Churchman Company, 1904.

The Mishnah. Trans. Herbert Danby. London: Oxford University Press, 1933.

Neusner, Jacob. *Torah from Our Sages: Pirke Avot*. Chappaqua, NY: Rossel Books, 1984.

Plaut, W. Gunther. *The Torah: A Modern Commentary*. New York: Union of American Hebrew Congregations, 1981.

Simon, Solomon and Morrison David Bial. *The Rabbis' Bible: Volume One: Torah*. New York: Behrman House, Inc., 1966.

Thompson, Thomas L. *The Mythic Past: Biblical Archeology and the Myth of Israel*. London: Basic Books, 1999.

von Rad, Gerhard. *Deuteronomy*. Philadelphia: Westminster Press, 1975.

5. Justice-Talk in the Tanakh (Old Testament)

Ahn, John. "A Generational Approach to Immigration." *Insights: The Faculty Journal of Austin Seminary* 124 (2009): 3-12.

Andersen, Francis I. and David Noel Freedman. *Amos*. Anchor Bible 24A. New York: Doubleday, 1989.

Benjamin, Don C. and Victor H. Matthews. *Social World of Ancient Israel*. Peabody: Hendrickson Publishers, 2005.

Brown, Dale. *Another Way of Believing: A Brethren Theology*. Elgin: Brethren Press, 2005.

Carroll R, M. Daniel. *Christians at the Border: Immigration, the Church and the Bible*. Grand Rapids: Baker Academic, 2008.

Leiter, David A. *Neglected Voices: Peace in the Old Testament*. Scott-dale, PA: Herald Press, 2007.

Mafico, Temba L. J. "Just, Justice." *Anchor Bible Dictionary*. Volume 3. New York: Doubleday, 1992: 1127-1129.

Ruiz, Jean-Pierre. "Abram and Sarai Cross the Border: Reading Genesis 12:10-20 with People on the Move." *Border Crossings: Cross Cultural Hermeneutics*. Ed. D. N. Premnath. Maryknoll: Orbis Books, 2007: 15-34.

Smith, Daniel. *Religion of the Landless: The Social Context of the Babylonian Exile*. New York: HarperCollins, 1989.

Spencer, John R. "Sojourner." *Anchor Bible Dictionary*. Volume 6. New York: Doubleday, 1992: 104.

6. Is There Peace in the Old Testament?

Anderson, Bernard with Steven Bishop. *Out of the Depths: The Psalms Speak for Us Today*. Third ed. Louisville: Westminster John Knox, 2000.

Brueggemann, Walter. "The Embarrassing Footnote." *Theology Today* 44 (1987): 5-14.

Carroll. Robert P. *Jeremiah: A Commentary*. The Old Testament Library. Philadelphia: Westminster Press, 1986.

Clements, R. E. *Jeremiah*. Interpretation: A Bible Commentary of Teaching and Preaching. Atlanta: John Knox Press, 1988.

Coats, George W. *Genesis: Forms of Old Testament Literature*. Grand Rapids: Eerdmans, 1983.

Collins, John J. "Isaiah." *Collegeville Bible Commentary*. Collegeville: Liturgical Press, 1992.

Hanson, Paul D. "War, Peace, and Justice in Early Israel." *Bible Review*. Fall. 1987: 32-45.

Hobbs, T. R. *2 Kings*. Word Biblical Commentary. Waco: Word Books, 1985.

Leiter, David A. *Neglected Voices: Peace in the Old Testament*. Scott-dale, PA: Herald Press, 2007

————. "Visions of Peace in Isaiah." *Inspired Speech: Prophecy in the Ancient Near East, Essays in Honor of Herbert B. Huffmon.* Journal for the Study of the Old Testament Supplement Series, 378. Ed. John Kaltner and Louis Stuhlman. New York: T & T Clark, 2004.

Neff, Robert W. "Paradigms of Peace in the Book of Genesis." *Brethren Life and Thought* 23 (1978): 41-44.

Nelson, Richard. *First and Second Kings.* Interpretation: A Biblical Commentary for Teaching and Preaching. Louisville: John Knox, 1987.

Strecker, Georg. "Die biblische Friedensbotschaft." *Kerygma und Dogma* 30 (1984): 131-46.

Wallis, Jim. *God's Politics: Why the Right Gets It Wrong and the Left Doesn't Get It.* San Francisco: HarperCollins, 2005.

Wenham, Gordon J. *Genesis 16–50.* Word Biblical Commentary. Dallas: Word Books, 1994.

7. Prophetic Rhetoric and Preaching

Bowman, Christopher. *Congregational Transition as Environment for Transformation.* Diss. San Francisco Theological Seminary, 1999.

Bowman, Robert C. "Bible Teachers At Bethany: Mentors and Models." *Brethren Life and Thought* 28 (1983): 49-56.

Brueggemann, Walter. "At the Mercy of Babylon: A Subversive Rereading of the Empire." *Presidential Voices: The Society of Biblical Literature in the Twentieth Century.* Ed. Harold W Attridge and James C Vanderkam. Atlanta: Society of Biblical Literature, 2006.

————. *The Creative Word: Canon as a Model for Biblical Education.* Philadelphia: Fortress Press, 1982.

————. *Deep Memory, Exuberant Hope: Contested Truth in a Post-Christian World.* Minneapolis: Augsburg Fortress, 2000.

————. "Life-Giving Speech Amid an Empire of Silence." *Michigan Law Review* 105 (2007): 1115-1132.

————. *The Prophetic Imagination*. Second ed. Minneapolis: Augsburg Fortress, 2001.

Coote, Robert B., and Mary P. Coote. *Power, Politics, and the Making of the Bible: An Introduction*. Minneapolis: Augsburg Fortress, 1990.

Fiorenza, Elisabeth Schüssler. "The Ethics of Interpretation: De-Centering Biblical Scholarship." *Journal of Biblical Literature* 107 (1988): 3-17.

Gardner, Richard B. "Brethren and the Bible." *Brethren Life and Thought* 28 (1983): 7-14.

Gray, Mark C. *Rhetoric and the Social Justice of Isaiah*. New York: T & T Clark Publishers, 2006.

Harris, John F. "God Gave U.S. 'What We Deserve,' Falwell Says." *Washington Post* 14 September 2001: C03.

Jost, Walter, and Michael J. Hyde. "Prologue." *Rhetoric and Hermeneutics in Our Time: A Reader*. Ed. Walter Jost and Michael J. Hyde. New Haven: Yale University Press, 1997.

Koch, Klaus. *The Prophets Volume 2: The Babylonian and Persian Periods*. Trans. Margaret Kohl. Philadelphia: Fortress Press, 1984.

Koptak, Paul E. "Rhetorical Criticism of the Bible: A Resource for Preaching." *The Covenant Quarterly* 54 (1996): 26-37.

Kugel, James L. *How to Read the Bible: A Guide to Scripture, Then and Now*. New York: Free Press, 2007.

Muilenburg, James A. "Form Criticism and Beyond." *Journal of Biblical Literature* 88 (1969): 1-18.

Neff, Robert W. "Taking Biblical Authority Seriously." *Brethren Life and Thought* 28 (1983): 15-20.

Neuman-Lee, Jeff. "The Map." *Brethren Life and Thought*, 53 (2008): 33-45.

Petersen, David L. "Introduction to Prophetic Literature." *The New Interpreter's Bible*. Volume 6. Nashville: Abingdon Press, 1994.

Ricoeur, Paul. *Interpretation Theory: Discourse and the Surplus of Meaning*. Fort Worth: Texas University Press, 1976.

———. "Rhetoric—Poetics—Hermeneutics." *Rhetoric and Hermeneutics in Our Time: A Reader*. Ed. Walter Jost and Michael J. Hyde. New Haven: Yale University Press, 1997: 60-72.

Trible, Phyllis. *God and the Rhetoric of Sexuality*. Philadelphia: Fortress Press, 1978.

Waltersdorff, Christy. "The Practice of Preaching." *Messenger* Oct. 2008: 12.

8. Jonah the Christian

Cary, Philip. *Jonah*. Grand Rapids: Brazos Press, 2008.

Charlesworth, James H. ed. *The Old Testament Pseudepigrapha*. Vol. 2. The Anchor Bible Reference Library. New York: Doubleday, 1985.

Currens, Dietrich. "Jona and Salomo." *Wort in der Zeit*. Ed. Wildred Haubeck und Michael Bachmann. Leiden: Brill, 1980: 86-94.

Duval, Yves-Marie. *Le livre de Jonas dans la littérature chrétienne grecque et latine; sources et influence du Commentaire sur Jonas de saint Jérôme*. Paris: Etudes Augustiniennes, 1973.

Edwards, Richard A. *The Sign of Jonah in the Theology of the Evangelists and Q*. Naperville, IL: Alec Allenson Inc., 1971.

Howton, John. "The Sign of Jonah." *Scottish Journal of Theology* 15 (1962): 288-394.

Lawrence, Marion. "Ships, Monsters and Jonah." *American Journal of Archaeology* 66 (1962): 289-296.

———. "Three Pagan Themes in Christian Art." *De Artibus Opuscula XL*. New York:1961.

Lloyd, Joan.E.Barclay. "The Prophet Jonah in Early Christian Art." *Sidic* 18 (1985): 17-19.

MacDonald, Dennis Ronald. *Christianizing Homer: The Odyssey, Plato, and the Acts of Andrew*. New York: Oxford University Press, 1994.

Mack, Burton L. *The Lost Gospel: The Book of Q & Christian Origins.* San Franciso: HarperCollins, 1993.

Michael, J.Hugh. "The Sign of Jonah." *Journal of Theological Studies* 21 (1920): 146-159.

Schneemelcher, Wilhelm, ed. *New Testament Apocrypha, Vol. 2: Writings Relating to the Apostles Apocalypses and Related Subjects.* Revised ed. Louisville: Westminster John Knox, 2003.

Seidelin, Paul. "Das Jonaszeichen." *Studia Theologica* 5 (1951): 119-131.

Simon, Marcel. *Hercule et le christianisme.* Paris: Les Belles Lettres, 1955: 11-53.

Snyder, Graydon F. *Ante Pacem: Archaeological Evidence of Church Life Before Constantine.* Revised ed. Macon, GA: Mercer University Press, 2003.

Speigl, Jakob. "Das Bildprogramm des Jonasmotivs in den Malerein der römischen Katakomben." *Römische Quartalschrift* 73 (1978): 1-15.

Stommel, Eduard. "Zum Problem der frühchristlichen Jonasdarstellungen." *Jahrbuch für Antike und Christentum* 1 (1958): 112-115.

Stoudaert, Benoit. "Jesus and Jonah." *Sidic* 18 (1985): 8-16.

Swetnam, James. "Some Signs of Jona." *Biblica* 68 (1987): 74-79.

Vögtle, Anton. "Der Spruch vom Jonaszeichen." *Synoptische Studien.* München: Karl Zink Verlag, 1953: 230-277.

9. Suffering in the Book of Job and Psalms: A Study of Our Devotional Response to Loss

Brueggemann, Walter. *The Psalms and the Life of Faith.* Ed. Patrick D. Miller. Minneapolis: Augsburg Fortress, 1995.

Gutiérrez, Gustavo. *On Job: God-Talk and the Suffering of the Innocent.* Maryknoll: Orbis Books, 1987.

Habel, Norman C. *The Book of Job: A Commentary.* Old Testament Library. Louisville: Westminster John Knox, 1985.

Miller, Patrick D. *Interpreting the Psalms*. Minneapolis: Augsburg Fortress, 1986.

Mowinckel, Sigmund. *The Psalms in Israel's Worship*. Vol. II. Nashville: Abingdon Press, 1962.

Pritchard, James B., ed. *Ancient Near Eastern Texts Relating to the Old Testament*. Third Edition with Supplement. Princeton: Princeton University Press, 1969.

Weems, Ann. *Psalms of Lament*. Louisville: Westminster John Knox, 1995.

Westermann, Claus. *Lamentations: Issues and Interpretation*. Trans. Charles Muenchow. Minneapolis: Fortress Press, 1994.

10. Love and Desire in the Song of Songs

Davis, Ellen F. *Proverbs, Ecclesiastes, and the Song of Songs*. Westminster Bible Companion. Louisville: Westminster John Knox, 2000.

———. "Wisdom, Desire, and Holy Love." *The Living Pulpit*. July–September 2000: 8-9.

Durnbaugh, Hedwig T. *The German Hymnody of the Brethren, 1720-1903*. Philadelphia: Brethen Encyclopedia, 1986.

Farley, Wendy. *The Wounding and Healing of Desire: Weaving Heaven and Earth*. Louisville: Westminster John Knox, 2005.

Garrett, Duane. *Song of Songs*. Word Biblical Commentary, 23B. Nashville: Thomas Nelson, 2004.

Gowan, Donald E., ed. *The Westminster Theological Wordbook of the Bible*. Louisville: Westminster John Knox, 2003.

Jenni, Ernst, and Claus Westermann, eds. *Theological Lexicon of the Old Testament*. Trans. Mark E. Biddle. Three Volumes. Peabody, MA: Hendrickson, 1997.

Keel, Othmar. *The Song of Songs: A Continental Commentary*. Trans. Frederick J. Gaiser. Minneapolis: Fortress Press, 1994.

Keller, Catherine. *On the Mystery: Discerning Divinity in Process*. Minneapolis: Fortress Press, 2008.

Linafelt, Tod. "The Arithmetic of Eros." *Interpretation* 59 (2005): 244-258.

McFague, Sallie. *Models of God: Theology for an Ecological, Nuclear Age*. Philadelphia: Fortress Press, 1987.

McGinn, Bernard. "Mysticism." In *The New Westminster Dictionary of Christian Spirituality*. Ed. Philip Sheldrake. Louisville: Westminster John Knox, 2005: 19-25.

Schweitzer, Carol L. Schnabl. "Song of Songs: A Metaphorical Vision for Pastoral Care." *Interpretation* 59 (2005): 278-289.

Trible, Phyllis. *God and the Rhetoric of Sexuality*. Philadelphia: Fortress, 1978.

Whedbee, J. William. *The Bible and the Comic Vision*. Cambridge, England: Cambridge University Press, 1998.

11. Daniel: Piety, Politics, and Perseverance

Bakhtin, Mikhail M. *Problems of Dostoevsky's Poetics*. Minneapolis: University of Minnesota, 1984.

Charlesworth, James H. *How Barisat Bellowed*. North Richland Hills: Bibal, 1998.

Chia, Philip P. "On Naming The Subject: Postcolonial Reading of Daniel." *Jian Dao* 7 (1997): 17-36.

Green, Barbara. *Mikhail Bakhtin and Biblical Scholarship: An Introduction*. Atlanta: Society of Biblical Literature, 2000.

Gruen, Erich S. *Heritage and Hellenism: The Reinvention of Jewish Tradition*. Berkeley: University of California Press, 1998.

McKinney, William, ed. *The Responsibility People: Eighteen Senior Leaders of Protestant Churches and National Ecumenical Agencies Reflect on Church Leadership*. Grand Rapids: Eerdmans, 1994.

Neff, Robert W. "The Bible, Devotion, and Authority." *Brethren Life and Thought* 43 (1998): 75-80.

———. "The Biblical Basis for Political Advocacy." *Brethren Life and Thought* 32 (1987): 201-207.

———. "Saga." *Saga, Legend, Tale, Novella, Fable: Narrative Forms in Old Testament Literature.* Ed. George W. Coats. JSOT Supplement Series 35. Sheffield: JSOT Press 1985: 17-32.

———. "Taking Biblical Authority Seriously." *Brethren Life and Thought* 28 (1983): 15-20.

Perdomo, E. Alan. "La protesta satirica en Daniel 7: Una lectura evangelica latinoamericana," *Vox scripturae* 6 (1996): 163-73.

Ramirez, Frank. *Cracking the Code: Making Sense of Daniel and Ezekiel for Today.* Good Ground Bible Studies. Elgin: Brethren Press, 2001.

Rovell, Darren. *First in Thirst: How Gatorade Turned the Science of Sweat into a Cultural Phenomenon.* New York: Amacom, 2006.

Scott, James C. *Domination and the Arts of Resistance: Hidden Transcripts.* New Haven: Yale University Press, 1990.

Smith-Christopher, Daniel. "Daniel." *The New Interpreter's Bible.* Volume 7. Nashville: Abingdon Press, 1996.

Valeta, David M. *Lions and Ovens and Visions: A Satirical Analysis of Daniel 1–6.* Sheffield: Sheffield Phoenix Press, 2008.

Wills, Lawrence M. *The Jewish Novel in the Ancient World.* Ithaca: Cornell University Press, 1995.

Wink, Walter. *Engaging the Powers: Discernment and Resistance in a World of Domination.* Minneapolis: Augsburg Fortress, 1992.

Wolters, Al. "Untying the King's Knots: Physiology and Word Play in Daniel 5." *Journal of Biblical Literature* 110 (1991): 117-22.

12. Prefiguring Fulfillment: Brethren Approaches to the Old Testament

Bashor, S. H. *The Gospel Hammer and the Highway Grader, or Rubbish Cleaned from the Way of Life.* Lanark, IL: Brethren at Work Steam Printing House, 1878.

Beissel, Conrad [Irenici Theodicäi]. *Zionitischen Stiffts I. Theil Oder eine Wolrichende Narde.* Ephrata: Drucks und Verlags der Brüderschaft, 1745.

Calvin, John. *Institutes of the Christian Religion.* Trans. John T. McNeill. The Library of Christian Classics. Volumes 20-21. Philadelphia: Westminster, 1960.

Eshelman, Matthew M. *Nonconformity to the World; or, A Vindication of True Vital Piety.* Dayton, OH: Christian Publishing Association, 1874.

Frantz, Michael. *Einfältige Lehr=Betrachtungen, und kurtzgefaßtes Glaubens=Bekäntniß.* Germantown, PA: Christoph Saur, 1770.

González, Justo L. "How the Bible Has Been Interpreted in the Christian Tradition." *The New Interpreter's Bible.* Volume 1. Nashville: Abingdon Press, 1994.

Holsinger, H. R. *Holsinger's History of the Tunkers and the Brethren Church.* Oakland, CA: the author, 1901.

Kurtz, D. W. *The Gospel of Jesus.* Elgin: Elgin Press, 1936

Leckrone, Quincy. *The Great Redemption.* North Manchester, IN: Bible Student Publishing Co., 1898.

Mack, Alexander, Jr. ["A Letter Concerning Feetwashing"]. *The Brethren in Colonial America.* Ed. and Trans. Donald F. Durnbaugh. Elgin: Brethren Press, 1967.

Mack, Alexander, Sr. *The Complete Writings of Alexander Mack.* Ed. William R. Eberly. Winona Lake, IN: BMH Books, 1991.

Major, Sarah Righter. "A Letter by Sarah Major." *The Brethren in the New Nation.* Ed. Roger E. Sappington. Elgin: Brethren Press, 1976, 228-31.

McCann, S. N. *The Lord Our Righteousness.* Second ed. Mount Morris, IL: Brethren Publishing House, 1897.

Moomaw, Benjamin F. *Discussion on Trine Immersion.* Singer's Glen, VA: Joseph Funk's Sons, 1867.

———. *The Divinity of Jesus Christ. The Truth Maintained.* Elgin: Brethren Publishing House, 1899.

Nead, Peter. *Primitive Christianity, or, a Vindication of the Word of God.* Staunton, VA: Kenton Harper, 1834.

———. *Theological Writings on Various Subjects; Or a Vindication of Primitive Christianity as Recorded in the Word of God.* Dayton, OH: for the author by E. F. Ells, 1850. Poland, OH: Dunker Reprints, 1985.

Rosenberger, I. J. *The Holy Spirit with Its Varied Functions.* Covington, OH: the author, [n.d.].

Stoffer, Dale R. *Background and Development of Brethren Doctrines 1650-1987.* Philadelphia: Brethren Encyclopedia, 1989.

Stoll, Jacob. *Geistliches Gewürtz-Gärtlein Heilsuchener Seelen.* Johannes Baumann, 1806.

13. Brethren Ordinances and Old Testament Practices

Bowman, Warren D. "Anointing for Healing." *Brethren Life and Thought* 4 (1959): 54-62.

Brown, Dale W. *Another Way of Believing: A Brethren Theology.* Elgin, Brethren Press, 2005.

———. "A Baptismal Theology with Implications for Evangelism, Conversion and Church Growth." *Brethren Life and Thought* 28 (1983): 151-160.

Bucher, L. Gene. "Brethren and the Old Testament." *Brethren Life and Thought* 28 (1983): 29-36.

Durnbaugh, Donald F. *Brethren in Colonial America.* Elgin: Brethren Press, 1967.

———. *European Origins of the Brethren.* Elgin: Brethren Press, 1958.

Eberly, William, ed. *The Complete Writings of Alexander Mack.* Winona Lake, IN: BMH Books, 1991.

Eshbach, Warren M. "Another Look at John 13:1-20." *Brethren Life and Thought* 14 (1969): 117-125.

Flora, Delbert B. "Ordinances." *The Brethren Encyclopedia*. Volume 2. Philadelphia, PA and Oak Brook, IL: Brethren Encyclopedia Inc., 1983: 976-80.

Gardner, Richard B. "Brethren and the Bible." *Brethren Life and Thought* 28 (1983): 7-14.

The Inglenook Cookbook. Elgin: Brethren Publishing House, 1906.

Lehman, James H. *The Old Brethren: People of Wisdom and Simplicity Speak to Our Time*. Revised ed. Elgin: Brethren Press, 2008.

Minutes of the Annual Meetings of the Church of the Brethren: Containing All Available Minutes from 1778-1909. Elgin: Brethren Publishing House, 1909.

Neff, Robert W. "Taking Biblical Authority Seriously." *Brethren Life and Thought* 28 (1983): 15-20.

Ramirez, Frank. "Lobster or Sop: Clement of Alexandria, the Love Feast, the Local and the Translocal Church." *Brethren Life and Thought* 43 (1998): 9-34.

Simmons, James W. "Baptism in the Early Church." *Brethren Life and Thought* 7 (1962): 36-46.

Slabaugh, Dennis L. "Annual Meeting." *The Brethren Encyclopedia*. Volume 1. Philadelphia, PA and Oak Brook, IL: Brethren Encyclopedia Inc., 1983: 33.

Stayer, Jonathan R. "An Interpretation of Some Ritual and Food Elements of the Brethren Love Feast." *Brethren Life and Thought* 30 (1985): 199-208.

Index of Scriptures

OLD TESTAMENT